GREAT
ANSWERS

TO TOUGH
INTERVIEW
QUESTIONS

10TH EDITION

GREAT ANSWERS

TO TOUGH INTERVIEW QUESTIONS

MARTIN JOHN YATE

KoganPage

First published in the United States as *Knock 'Em Dead* in 1985 by Bob Adams Inc
First published in Great Britain as *Great Answers to Tough Interview Questions* in 1986 by Kogan Page Limited
Tenth edition 2017

2nd Floor, 45 Gee Street	c/o Martin P Hill Consulting	4737/23 Ansari Road
London	122 W 27th St, 10th Floor	Daryaganj
EC1V 3RS	New York, NY 10001	New Delhi 110002
United Kingdom	USA	India

www.koganpage.com

ISBN   978 0 7494 8142 1
E-ISBN   978 0 7494 8143 8

British Library Cataloguing-in-Publication Data

A CIP record for this book is available from the British Library.

Typeset by Integra Software Services, Pondicherry
Print production managed by Jellyfish
Printed and bound by CPI Group (UK) Ltd, Croydon, CR0 4YY

CONTENTS

PART THREE Great Answers to Tough Interview Questions 129

PART FOUR Finishing Touches 243

ACKNOWLEDGEMENTS

Great Answers to Tough Interview Questions is now in its third decade of publication and has become a staple for job hunters around the world. My thanks to Peter Archer, the finest editor I have had in thirty years; Jane Hauptman for her accurate and conscientious copy-editing; Bethany Carland-Adams for her PR efforts; and Angela Yate for her consistent contributions to this book.

INTRODUCTION

You didn't come to this book because everything is going well in your professional life. You came because these are times of upheaval, crisis and change. Managing a successful career isn't easy, so I'm not going to waste your time pretending it is.

You are somewhere in the middle of a half-century-long working life, where, statistically speaking, you are likely to change jobs every four years (not always by choice), and have three or more distinct careers over that span.

Add an awareness that recessions causing widespread job loss rear their ugly heads every seven to ten years (I have worked in career management through five of them in the past 35 years), and you can see that smart career management strategies and a firm grasp of practical job search tactics are critical to your survival and happiness. *In the context of your whole working life, career management and job search skills are the most important skills you can ever develop, bar none.*

All the advice you've been given about careers – get an education, choose a career, settle down and do a good job; patience and loyalty to the company will be rewarded with job security and life success – have proved themselves false.

We live in a global economy where voracious political and corporate greed has turned your life into a disposable commodity to be used and discarded. It is time for a radical shift in your career management strategy. You need to move from helpless employee at the whim of financial currents beyond your control to enlightened professional who puts the pathway to personal success in its proper context.

What's this context? Those job changes coming round every four years or so add up to 12 or more over 50 years, with perhaps three of them involving the greater challenges involved with career change. *This means professional change is constant.* You need to recognize that your career is not a fixed thing that came as a gift with your degree. Instead, it's a critical aspect of your life, and it needs management. Face this and you can begin to change your situation, today and forever.

It's time for enlightened self-interest

Enlightened self-interest means placing your financial survival front and centre in your life. Think of yourself not as a person looking for a job, but as a company, a financial entity that must maintain a steady cash flow over half a century. Start to think of yourself as MeLtd, a company that must always plan and act in the best interests of its survival and you will perhaps learn to look at this job search and the management of your career in a new light.

As a company, MeLtd has products and services that are constantly under development. These are the bundle of skills that define the professional you and are positioned and sold to your targeted customer base: those employers who hire people like you.

The success of MeLtd depends on how well you run your company, which means that just like every successful company in the world, you must have ongoing initiatives for:

- **R&D:** Your identification and development of products and services that will appeal to your customers. This translates into skill building in response to market trends; it also relates to your development of job search, interview and career management skills.

- **Strategic planning:** The development of effective career management strategies that make you more visible and more desirable for the times when you must look for work, and strategies you pursue when employed to make your job more secure and to encourage professional growth with that company as you continue with strategies that build your credibility and visibility within your company and profession.

- **Marketing and PR:** The establishment of personal credibility for the services you deliver, and the positioning of these services so that your professional credibility becomes visible to an ever widening circle of potential customers.

- **Sales:** A state-of-the-art sales programme to sell your products and services, including CV, job search and interviewing tactics.

Now, this may or may not be your first job search, and it almost certainly won't be your last, but this can be the last one that you enter in confusion. This can be the last time you have no clear idea of your options or how best to pursue them.

In these pages you will learn how to understand the interview process, and transform those interviews into job offers. This book gives you a flexible, down-to-earth plan of attack to help you get out of a tough spot in your life and into a better place for the future.

The book is written in four interconnected parts. 'The Well-Stocked Briefcase' gets you ready for the fray. Here, you will learn to build a CV with broad appeal and use a customizing technique guaranteed to make your job application stand out as something special.

Once you are ready for action, 'Getting to Square One' will show you effective job-hunting techniques, and how to tap into thousands of opportunities that never reach the newspaper or your favourite website. You will learn simple and effective techniques for setting up multiple interviews, and how to steer yourself through the intimidating telephone screening process that companies increasingly use.

The job interview is a ritualistic dance in which the best partners whirl away with the glittering prizes. Learn the steps and you too can dance the dance. 'Great Answers to Tough Interview Questions' gives you a comprehensive understanding of why interviewers ask the questions they do, what is behind them and how to answer in a way that enhances your application. Your partner in the dance is the interviewer, who will lead with tough questions that contain subtleties hidden from the untrained ear. You will learn how to recognize these 'questions within questions'. You'll get hundreds of sneaky, mean, trick questions that interviewers love to throw at you. With each question, I will show you what the interviewer wants to find out, and explain how you should reply. After each explanation, I'll give you a sample answer and advice on how to customize it to your individual circumstances. The examples themselves come from real life (I've been at this for over 30 years) – they're all things that people like you have done to get themselves noticed. I'll show you how they packaged those responses, how they used their practical experience to turn a job interview into a job offer, and with this knowledge you will be cooler, calmer and more collected at your job interviews.

The final section, 'Finishing Touches', ensures that you will learn how to negotiate the best salary and benefits package for yourself once the offer is made, and even discover how to get a job offer after you have been turned down. Most importantly, the sum of all these techniques will give you tremendous self-confidence when you go to an interview: no more jitters, no more sweaty palms.

If you want to land a *good* new job, and get a better grip on the direction and trajectory of your career as you learn how to win over the interviewer *without lying*, then this book is for you. Now let's get to it!

PART ONE

THE WELL-STOCKED BRIEFCASE

This section will show you how to discover, define and package your skills, and put together a comprehensive plan of attack that uses all the most effective job search techniques.

Once upon a time, in a town plagued by bears, there lived a man. The man had always wanted to travel but had neither the right job nor the money to do so. If he could kill a bear, he thought, then he could travel to other places plagued with bears and make his living as a bear-slayer. Every day he sat on the porch and waited for a bear to come by. After many weeks of waiting, he thought he might go looking for bears. He didn't know much about them, except that they were out there.

Full of hope, he loaded his single-shot musket and headed for the forest. On reaching the edge of the forest, he raised the musket and fired into the dense undergrowth.

Do you think he hit a bear or, for that matter, anything else? Our hero went hunting unprepared and got what he deserved. The moral of the tale is this: when you go bear or job hunting, keep a grip on reality and don't go off half-cocked.

Out there in the forest of the professional world are countless opportunities. Even in times of severe economic downturn – and remember, they are cyclical and likely to occur every seven to ten years throughout your career – there are always jobs out there. Yes, they are harder to find; and yes, the competition is tougher, but someone is going to land those job offers. It can be you.

All companies are in business to make money, but things go wrong so they hire problem-solvers to fix things. This is an important life lesson. Think about your present job. You were hired to cope with certain problems within your area of expertise, to anticipate and prevent them from arising and, where they cannot be prevented, to solve them. Everyone in every profession and at every level, is paid to be a problem-solver. There are three lessons you should remember on this score:

- **Lesson 1:** Companies are in business to make money; they have loyalty only to the bottom line. They make money through sales and by being efficient and saving time. If they save time, they save money, so have more time to make more money. We call this productivity.

- **Lesson 2:** Companies and you are exactly alike. You both want to make as much money as possible in as short a time as possible. Think efficient systems and procedures, and multitasking (time management and organization). Think of focus and goal, not task and activity.

- **Lesson 3:** There are buyer's markets (advantage: employer) and there are seller's markets (advantage: employee). Job offers put you in a seller's market and give you the upper hand.

Lesson 1 tells you the three things every company is interested in. Lesson 2 teaches you to recognize that you really have the same goals as the company. Lesson 3 reminds you that anyone with any sense wants to be in a seller's market.

If you look for jobs one at a time, you put yourself in a buyer's market. If you implement my advice in this book, you will have multiple job offers (even in a tough economy) and put yourself in a seller's market, regardless of the economy climate.

This means making sure MeLtd is ready with a properly packaged product and an integrated sales process.
In this first part of the book you will:

- Learn to evaluate market needs and package your professional skills for those needs.

- Discover how to identify companies in your target location that could be in need of your services.

- Get connected to the most influential people in your profession so that you'll have personal introductions at many prospective companies.

- Implement an integrated job search plan of attack.

While I will cover each of these areas in sequence, I recommend that you mix and match the activities. In other words, when working on your CV starts to drive you nuts, switch to researching your target market or building your professional networks. An hour of one activity followed by an hour of another will keep your mind fresh and your programme balanced.

THE REALITIES OF JOB HUNTING

A job search isn't nanotechnology; you'll find a common-sense logic in everything I show you and wonder why you didn't see it before. You can get your job search moving onto a new trajectory this week, and reap the rewards for the rest of your career. You can do this.

Everyone feels unsure when they are looking for a job – you aren't the only one – but while there used to be a stigma about looking for a job, times have changed. Job change is an integral part of modern life. It comes around about every four years, making change and job search a constant factor for everyone.

Because everyone understands this, once you organize and follow the plan of attack, you will find many, many people are ready to give you a helping hand if they can.

We live and work in a time of immense change. When you were born, there still existed a world in which hard work, dedication, and sacrifice led to long-term job security and a steady, predictable climb up the ladder of success. The world you now work in is entirely different. Companies still expect hard work, dedication and sacrifice, but their only loyalty is to the profit imperative. You are expendable.

Different times require different strategies; you need a new mind-set for today's job search and for your long-term career success. The job security and professional growth our parents expected is a thing of the past. Here are the realities you're facing, expressed in numbers:

50–4–3–7–10

A **50**-year work life

Job change about every **4** years

3 or more distinct careers

Economic downturns every **7–10** years

Changing careers at the same time as you change jobs adds another level of complexity to the process because you are leaving behind many of the skills that usually help you land that new job.

How business works

Companies exist to make money, as quickly, efficiently and reliably as possible. They make money by selling a product or service, and they prosper by becoming better and more efficient at it. When a company saves time, it saves money, and then has more time to make more money; this is called productivity.

If a company can make money without employees, it will do so, because that means more money for the owners. Unfortunately for the owners, a company requires a complex machinery to deliver those products and services that bring in revenue. You can think of any and every job as a small but important cog in this complex money-making machine, and every cog has to be oiled and maintained; this costs money. If the company can redesign its machinery to do without that cog (automation) or can find a cheaper cog (outsourcing that job to Mumbai), of course it is going to do so.

There are two reasons jobs exist. First, as I've said, every job is a small but important cog in the organization's complex money-making machine; it exists to help the company make money. Second, the company hasn't been able to automate that job out of existence because in your area of technical expertise, problems arise.

Consequently, the company hires someone who has the *technical skills* to solve the problems that typically occur within an area of specific expertise. The company hopes to hire someone who knows the territory well enough to predict and prevent many of these problems from arising in the first place.

It doesn't matter what your job title is, you are always hired to be a problem solver with a specific area of expertise. Think about the nuts and bolts of any job you've held. At its heart, that job is chiefly concerned with the *anticipation, identification, prevention* and *solution of problems*. This enables the company to make money, as quickly, efficiently, and reliably as possible.

These aren't the only factors that are critical to your success and that all jobs have in common. In the next chapter, you'll learn about a specific set of *transferable skills* and *professional values* that all employers are anxious to find in candidates, whom they then hire and promote just as quickly as they can find them.

TRANSFERABLE SKILLS AND PROFESSIONAL VALUES

Understand what your customers want to buy.

There are certain keywords you see in almost every job posting that relate to skills: *communication, multitasking, teamwork, creativity, analytical thinking, leadership, determination, productivity, motivation* and a few more we'll discuss shortly. These words represent a secret language that few job hunters ever show they understand. The ones who do 'get it' are also the ones who get the job offers.

That is because, as discussed in the previous chapter, these keywords and phrases represent the skills that enable you to do your job well, whatever that job may be. They are known as *transferable skills* and *professional values* because no matter what the job, the profession or the elevation of that job, these skills and values make the difference between success and failure.

You thought, 'Pick up after myself? I guess I've got to develop a new way of doing things.' And so you started to observe and emulate the more successful professionals around you. You weren't born this way. You developed new skills and ways of conducting yourself, in effect creating a *professional persona* that enabled you to survive in the professional world.

There is a specific set of *transferable skills* and *professional values* that underlie survival and professional success: skills and values employers all over the world in every industry and profession are anxious to find in applicants from the entry level to the boardroom. Why this isn't taught in schools and in the university programmes that cost a small fortune is unfathomable, because these skills and values are the foundation of every successful career. They break down into these groups:

1 **The technical skills of your current profession**
   These are the technical competencies that give you the ability to do your job – those skills needed for a task and the know-how to use them productively and efficiently. These *technical skills* are mandatory if you want to land a job within your profession. *Technical skills*, while transferable, vary from profession to profession, so many of your current *technical skills* will only be transferable within your current profession.

2 **Transferable skills that apply in all professions**
   This set of skills underlies your ability to execute the *technical skills* of your job effectively, whatever that job might be. They are the foundation of all the professional success you will experience in this and any other career (including dream and entrepreneurial careers) that you may pursue over the years.

3 **Professional values**
   These are a set of beliefs that enable all professionals to make the many judgment calls required during the working day to ensure that the best interests of the department and the employer are always promoted. They complement the *transferable skills* and together form a firm foundation for a successful professional life.

A review of transferable skills and professional values

As you read through the following breakdown of each *transferable skill* and *professional value*, consider your own varying strengths and weaknesses. You may, for example, read about *communication*, and think, 'Yes, I can see how communication skills are important in all jobs and at all levels of the promotional ladder, and, hallelujah, I have good communication skills.' Take time to recall examples of your *communication skills* and the role they play in the success of your work.

You might also read about *multitasking skills* and realize that you need to improve in that area. Whenever you identify a *transferable skill* that needs work, you have found a *professional development project*: improving that skill. Your attention to those areas will repay you for the rest of your working life, no matter how you make a living.

Here are the *transferable skills and professional values* that will speed the conclusion of this job search and your long-term professional success. You'll find that you already have some of them to a greater or lesser degree, and if you are committed to making a success of your life, you'll commit to further development of all of them.

Transferable skills	Professional values
Technical	Motivation and energy
Critical thinking	Commitment and reliability
Communication	Determination
Multitasking	Pride and integrity
Teamwork	Productivity
Leadership	Systems and procedures
Creativity	

Transferable skills

There is a body of skills that transcends industries. These skills will not only enhance your employability in your current profession, but will make it easier should you ever change your career – something that the statistics say you will do three or more times over the span of your work life.

Employers are always on the lookout for employees who, in addition to the must-haves of the job, possess the *written communication skills* to create a PR piece or a training manual; who know how to structure and format a proposal; who are able to stand up and make presentations; or who know how to research, analyse, and assimilate hard-to-access data.

Some of the *transferable technical skills* sought across a wide spectrum of jobs include:

- Selling skills – even in non-sales jobs, the art of persuasive communication is always appreciated, because no matter what the job, you are always selling something to someone.

- Project management skills.

- Quality management skills.

- Lean management skills.

- Quantitative analysis skills.

- Theory development and conceptual thinking skills.

- Counselling and mentoring skills.

- Customer resource management (CRM) skills.

- Research skills.

- Social networking skills.

There are also *technology skills* that have application within all professions in our technology driven world. It is pretty much a given that you need to be computer literate to hold down any job today, as just about every job expects competency with Microsoft Word and e-mail. Similarly, proficiency in Excel and PowerPoint is becoming a skill it is risky not to possess.

Any employer is going to welcome a staff member who knows his way around spreadsheets and databases, or who can update a web page. Some of the *technology skills* that enhance employability on non-technological jobs include:

- Database management.

- Spreadsheet creation.

- Word processing.

- Building and designing presentations.

- E-mail and social media communication.

Eventually, more and more of these skills will become specific requirements for the jobs of the future. Until then, possession of these skills will add a special sauce to your application for any job.

All the *transferable skills* are interconnected – for example, good *verbal skills* require both *listening* and *analytical thinking skills* to process incoming information accurately. These enable you to present your outgoing verbal message persuasively to your audience so that it is understood and accepted. Develop effective skills in all seven of the subsets that together comprise the *transferable skills* and you'll gain enormous control over what you can achieve, how you are perceived and what happens in your life.

Technical

The *technical skills* of your job are the foundation of success within your current profession; without them you won't even land a job, much less keep it for long or win a promotion. They define *ability* to do the job, those essential skills necessary for the day-to-day execution of your duties. These *technical skills* vary from profession to profession and do not refer to anything technical as such or to technology.

However, it is a given that one of the *technical skills* essential to every job is technological competence. You must be proficient in all the technology and internet-based applications relevant to your work. Even when you are not working in a technology field, strong *technology skills* will enhance your stability and help your professional growth.

Some of your *technology skills* will only be relevant within your current profession, while others (Word, Excel and PowerPoint, to name the obvious) will be transferable across all industry and professional lines. Staying current with the essential *technical* and *technology skills* of your chosen career path is the keystone of your professional stability and growth.

When people are referred to as 'professionals', it means they possess the appropriate *technical* and *technology skills* necessary for success in their profession and have interwoven them with the other major *transferable skills*. Keeping up with the essential *technical* and *technology skills* of your chosen career path through ongoing professional education is going to be an integral part of your growth and stability. That's why the education section towards the end of your CV can be an important tool in developing your *professional brand*; it demonstrates your technical competence and your commitment, exemplified by your continuing pursuit of professional skills.

Technology constantly changes the nature of our jobs and the ways in which they are executed. As a result, if you want to stay employable, you need to stay current with the skills most prized in your professional world.

Communication

Without *communication*, you live in silence and isolation. With *communication*, you make things happen in your life.

As George Bernard Shaw said, 'The greatest problem in communication is the illusion that it has been accomplished.' Every professional job today requires *communication skills*; promotions and professional success are impossible without them. Good verbal *communication skills* enable you to process incoming information accurately and also to present outgoing information persuasively and appropriately so that it is understood and accepted.

But *communication* embraces much more than listening and speaking. When the professional world talks about *communication skills*, it is referring to four primary skills and four supportive skills. The primary *communication skills* are:

- **Verbal skills** – what you say and how you say it.

- **Listening skills** – listening to understand, rather than just waiting for your turn to talk.

- **Writing skills** – clear written communication, essential for success in any professional career. It creates a lasting impression of who you are.

- **Technological communication skills** – your ability to evaluate the protocols, strengths and weaknesses of alternative communication media, and then choose the medium appropriate to your audience and message.

The four supportive *communication skills* are subtler, but, nevertheless, they impact every interaction you have with others. They are:

- **Grooming and dress** – they tell others who you are and how you feel about yourself.

- **Social graces** – these are demonstrated by how you behave around others. If your table manners are sketchy, odds are you'll never sit at the CEO's table or represent your organization at the higher levels.

- **Body language** – this displays how you're feeling deep inside, a form of communication humankind learned before speech. For truly effective communication, what your mouth says must be in harmony with what your body says.

- **Emotional IQ** – your emotional self-awareness; your maturity in dealing with others in the full range of human interaction.

Develop effective *communication skills* in all these areas and you'll gain enormous control over what you can achieve, how you are perceived and what happens in your life.

Analytical thinking

Life and the world of work are full of opportunities, and every one of those opportunities is peppered with problems. With *analytical thinking skills*, you can turn those opportunities into achievement, earnings and fulfilment. This is the professional-world application of all those problem-solving skills you've been developing since school: a systematic approach to uncovering all the issues related to a particular challenge that will lead to its solution.

Analytical or problem-solving skills allow the successful professional to think through and clearly define a challenge and its desired solutions and then evaluate and implement the best solution for that challenge from all available options.

You examine the problem and ask the questions:

- What's the problem?

- Who is it a problem for?

- Why is it a problem?

- What is causing this problem?

- What are the options for a solution?

- What problems might a given solution create?

- What is the most suitable solution?

You look through the factors affecting each possible solution and decide which solutions to keep and which to disregard. You look at the solution as a whole and use your judgment as to whether to use it or not. Once you have decided on a course of action, you plan out the steps, the timing and the resources to make it happen:

- How long will it take to implement this solution?
- How much will it cost?
- What resources will I need?
- Can I get these resources?
- Will the solution really resolve the problem to everyone's benefit?
- Will this solution cause its own problems?

Einstein said that if he had one hour to save the world, he would spend 55 minutes defining the problem. Fifty per cent of the success of any project is in the preparation.

Multitasking (time management and organization)

This is one of the most desirable skills of the new era. According to numerous studies, however, the *multitasking* demands of modern professional life are causing massive frustration and meltdowns for professionals everywhere. The problem is not multitasking, the problem is the assumption that multitasking means being reactive to *all* incoming stimuli and therefore jumping from one task to another as the emergency of the moment dictates.

Few people understand that *multitasking* abilities are built on sound *time management* and *organizational skills*. Here are the basics.

Establish priorities

Multitasking is based on three things:

1 Being organized.
2 Establishing priorities.
3 Managing your time.

Plan, do, review cycle

At the end of every day, review what you've accomplished:

- What happened: am and pm?

- What went well? Do more of it.

- What went wrong? How do I fix it?

- What projects do I need to move forward tomorrow?

- Rank each project. A = Must be completed tomorrow. B = Good to be completed tomorrow. C = If there is spare time from A and B priorities.

- Make a prioritized to-do list.

- Stick to it.

Executing the plan, do, review cycle at the end of every day keeps you informed about what you have achieved, and lets you know that you have invested your time in the most important activities today and tomorrow.

Teamwork

If you become a successful leader one day, it will be due to the fact that you were a great *team player* first. The professional world revolves around the complex challenges of making money, and such challenges require teams of people to provide ongoing solutions. You need to work efficiently and respectfully with others who have totally different responsibilities, backgrounds, objectives and areas of expertise.

Teamwork asks that a commitment to the team and its success come first: you take on a task because it needs to be done, not because it makes you look good. The payback, of course, is that management always recognizes and appreciates a *team player*.

As a *team player*, you always:

- cooperate;

- make decisions based on team goals;

- keep team members informed;

- keep commitments;

- share credit, never share blame.

Teamwork skills are especially important if you intend to be a leader. It is only by being a *team player* that you will understand the subtleties of what makes a team pull together and function productively as a unit. If you intend to be a leader, learn to be a *team player*.

The complex transferable skills

Each of the *transferable skills* helps you become successful in whatever career you pursue because they help you do whatever you do well. At the same time, *transferable skills* rarely exist in a vacuum, each interacts with one or more of the others. For example, *communication skills* include listening skills, listening implies the goal of understanding, and understanding requires the use of your *analytical thinking skills*.

There are seven *transferable skills*, and the sixth and seventh, *creativity* and *leadership*, are called *complex transferable skills* because they only come into being when a fully integrated combination of the other *transferable skills* is brought into play.

Creativity

Your *creativity* comes from the frame of reference you have for your work, profession, and industry. This enables you to see the *patterns* that lie behind challenges, and so connect the dots and come up with solutions. Others might have missed those solutions because they didn't have that frame of reference that enabled them to step back and view the larger context.

There's a big difference between *creativity* and just having ideas. Ideas are like headaches: we all get them once in a while, and like headaches, they disappear as mysteriously as they arrived. *Creativity*, on the other hand, is the ability to develop those ideas with the strategic and tactical know-how that brings them to life. *Creativity* also demands that you harness other *transferable skills* to bring those ideas to life.

Creativity springs from your:

● *Analytical thinking skills*, applied within an area of *technical expertise* (which gives you a frame of reference for what works and what doesn't).

- *Multitasking skills*, which in combination with your *analytical thinking* and *technical skills* allow you to break your challenge down into specific steps and determine which approach is best.

- *Communication skills*, which allow you to explain your approach persuasively to your target audience.

- *Teamwork* and *leadership skills*, which enable you to enlist others and bring the idea to fruition.

Here are five rules for building *creativity skills*:

1 **Whatever you do in life, engage in it fully**
Commit to developing competence in everything you do, because the wider your frame of reference for the world around you, the higher octane fuel you have to propel your ideas to acceptance and reality.

2 **Learn something new every day**
Treat the pursuit of knowledge as a way of life. Absorb as much as you can about everything. Information exercises your brain and fills your mind with the ever-widening frame of reference that allows you to make creative connections where others won't see them.

3 **Catch ideas as they occur**
Note them in your smartphone or on a scrap of paper.

4 **Welcome restrictions in your world**
They encourage *creativity* – ask any successful writer, artist, musician or business leader. Restrictions in time, money or resources are all negative in their initial impact, but they become the realities under which you must operate. From a production point of view (and *creativity* is all about giving abstract ideas concrete form), restrictions make you think harder about the essentials of your task. When you can take complex ideas and reduce them to their elemental parts, you have a real understanding of that task. Similarly, restrictions increase the need for simplicity in design, function and expression, and simplicity leads to elegance.

5 **Don't spend your life glued to Facebook or TV**
You need to live life, not watch it go by. If you do watch television, try to learn something or motivate yourself with

science, history or biography programming. If you surf the internet, do it with purpose.

Building *creativity skills* enables you to bring your dreams to life, and the development of each of these interconnected *transferable skills* will help you do just that.

Leadership

'A leader has two important characteristics; first, he is going somewhere; second, he is able to persuade other people to go with him.' The man who said this, Maximilien Robespierre, was a principal figure in the French Revolution and literally changed the world. As you develop *teamwork skills*, notice how you are willing to follow true leaders, but not people who don't respect you and who don't have your best interests at heart. When others believe in your competence, and believe you have everyone's success as your goal, they will follow you. When your actions inspire others to think more, learn more, do more and become more, you are on your way to becoming a leader. This will ultimately be recognized and rewarded with promotion into and up the ranks of management.

Leadership is the most complex of all the *transferable skills* that you will develop to make a success of your professional work life. It is a combination and outgrowth of all the other *transferable skills*:

- Your job as a leader is to make your team function, so your *teamwork skills* give you the ability to pull your team together as a cohesive unit.

- Your *technical* expertise, *analytical thinking* and *creativity skills* help you to define the challenges your team faces and give you the wisdom to guide them towards solutions.

- Your *communication skills* enable your team to appreciate your directives and goals. There's nothing more demoralizing than a leader who can't clearly articulate why you're doing what you're doing.

- Your *creativity* comes from the wide frame of reference you have for your work and the profession and industry in which you work, enabling you to come up with solutions that others might not have seen.

- Your *multitasking* (time management and organization) *skills* enable you to create a practical blueprint for success, and they help your team to take ownership of the task and deliver the expected results on time.

Leadership is a combination and outgrowth of all the *transferable skills* plus the clear presence of all the *professional values* we are about to discuss. Leaders aren't born; they are self-made. And just like anything else, it takes hard work.

Professional values

Motivation and energy

Employers realize that a *motivated* professional will do a better job on every assignment. *Motivation* expresses itself in a commitment to the job and the profession, an eagerness to learn and grow professionally and a willingness to take the rough with the smooth in pursuit of meaningful goals.

Motivation is invariably expressed by the *energy* you demonstrate in your work. You always give that extra effort to get the job done and get it done right.

Commitment and reliability

This means dedication to your profession, and the empowerment that comes from knowing how your part contributes to the whole. The *committed* professional is willing to do whatever it takes to get a job done, whenever and for however long is necessary, even if that includes duties that might not appear in a job description and that might be perceived by less enlightened colleagues as beneath them.

Commitment is also a demonstration of enlightened self-interest. The more you are engaged with your career, the more likely you are to find opportunities for advancement. At the same time, this dedication will repay you with better job security and improved professional horizons.

Your *commitment* expresses itself in your *reliability*. Showing up is half the battle; the other half is your performance on the job. This requires following up your actions – not relying on anyone else to ensure the job is done and done well – and it also demonstrates your *reliability* as a *team player* committed to the greater good of the team.

Determination

Your *determination* indicates a resilient professional who doesn't get worn down or back off when a problem or situation gets tough. It's a value that marks you as someone who chooses to be part of the solution rather than standing idly by being part of the problem.

The *determined* professional has decided to make a difference with his presence every day, because it is the *right* thing to do.

The *determined* professional is willing to do whatever it takes to get a job done, even if that includes duties that might not appear in his or her job description.

Pride and integrity

If a job's worth doing, it's worth doing well. That's what *pride* in your work really means: attention to detail and a *commitment* to doing your very best. This, in turn, means paying attention to details and to time and cost constraints.

Integrity means taking responsibility for your actions, both good and bad, and it also means treating others, within and outside of the company, with respect at all times and in all situations. With *pride* in yourself as a professional with *integrity*, your actions will always be in the ethical best interests of the company, and your decisions will never be based on whim or personal preference.

Productivity and economy

Always work towards enhanced *productivity* through efficiencies of time, resources, money and effort. Most problems have two solutions, and the expensive one isn't always the best.

Remember the word 'frugal'? It doesn't mean miserliness. It means making the most of what you've got, using everything with the greatest efficiency. Companies that know how to be frugal with their resources will prosper in good times and bad, and if you know how to be frugal, you'll do the same. Ideas of efficiency and *economy* engage the *creative* mind in ways that others would not consider.

Systems and procedures

This is a natural consequence of all the other *transferable skills* and *professional values*. Your *commitment* to your profession in all these ways gives you an appreciation of the need for systems and procedures and their implementation only after careful thought. You understand and always follow the chain of command. You don't implement your own 'improved' procedures or encourage others to do so. If ways of doing things don't make sense or are interfering with economy and productivity, you work through the system to get them changed.

How transferable skills and professional values affect your job search

Development of *transferable skills* and *professional values* will be repaid with job offers, better job security and improved professional horizons. When you are seen to embody these *transferable skills* and *professional values* in your work and in the ways you interact with the people of your professional world, you will become known and respected as a consummate professional, and this can dramatically affect your application.

That you have these admirable traits is one thing; that I know you have them, well, that's another matter. You need to:

- Develop these skills and values.

- Make them a living dimension of your professional brand.

- Understand how each enables you to do every aspect of your job just that little bit better.

- Display them subtly in your CV and other written communications.

- Promote them appropriately in your meetings with employers as the underlying skills that enable you to do your work well.

Examples of your application of these skills or the impact of these values on your work can be used in your CV, cover letters and as illustrative answers to questions in interviews. But most important, when these skills become a part of you, they will bring greater success to everything you do.

THE PRODUCTIVE CV

How to build a killer CV and fix one that isn't working

Your CV is the most financially important document you will ever own. When it works, the doors of opportunity open for you. When it doesn't work, you don't either, so this is a job that deserves your full attention. Your CV opens the doors of opportunity for interviews, prepares you for the questions interviewers will ask and acts as a powerful ambassador at decision time.

A good CV is not simply a recitation of all the things you have done in your work life. In fact if your CV is just that, it is likely to sit unread in countless CV databases.

The growth of technology in the workplace has had a major influence on how CVs have evolved. In the not-so-distant past, someone would have viewed your CV almost as soon as it was received. Today, CVs no longer go straight to a manager's desk, they are more likely to go onto a CV database. Some of those databases contain over 50 million CVs. So you can see that for a human being to review your CV, it needs to be discoverable in an ocean of other CVs by an employer typing in search terms, just like you do on the internet.

The discoverable CV

When employers search CV databases, they always do so with a specific job description in mind. This is important because job postings invariably reflect the exact wording of the job descriptions they come from. This means you can identify the words and phrases your target companies use when they are looking for someone like you.

Here's how the process works. You or I want to hire an accountant, so, first, we define the job title by typing 'accountant' into the dialogue box and specifying a location. Next, we click on the keyword options that describe the skills of that job. We can also add words that do not appear in the supplied-keyword choices.

The software scours the database and builds a list of all the CVs that contain *any* of those keywords. It then weights the list. Those CVs with the most frequent *and* greatest number of keywords come to the top of the list. Mentioning keywords in a Professional Skills/ Core Competencies section at the top of your CV, and then repeating them within the contex of the jobs in which they are used, will increase your ranking in database searches.

This is the *first* keyword test your CV *must* pass. Because employers very rarely go beyond the top 20 CVs in a database search, not enough relevant keywords in your CV means that no human will view it.

The *second* keyword test your CV *must* pass comes when your CV gets in front of human eyes. The first scan takes no more than six seconds according to a recent study. No relevant keywords/ phrases means no second read.

The next read is a little more careful. The reviewers are checking *the CV reflects the skills and competencies required for the job they are trying to fill.* Recruiters or HR people typically create a 'long list' of up to six candidates. Here it may land in front of the manager who actually has the authority to hire you, but who hates to read CVs and just wants to hire someone and get back to work.

A CV that tries to cram in everything you have done without any real focus is doomed to fail any and all of these hurdles, and failure means no interviews and no job offers.

In a world without job security, you need to learn how to build a CV that works.

Get inside the employer's head

The first lessons in the business world are invariably 'The customer is always right, listen to the customer', and 'Learn the customer's needs and sell to those needs'. So, before writing your CV, you are going to get inside the employer's head and examine what he or she looks for when hiring. What I am going to show you will deliver:

- a template for the story your CV must tell to be successful;
- an objective tool against which to evaluate your CV's performance;
- an understanding of where the focus will be at interviews;
- a good idea of the questions that will be heading your way and why;
- relevant examples with which to illustrate your answers;
- a behavioural profile for getting hired and for professional success throughout your career.

Start with simple common sense

Your CV will always be more effective if it begins with a clear focus on, and understanding of, a specific target job. With this focus you can look back into your work history for those experiences that make you suitable. This will enable you to tailor a killer CV.

How do you do this? The answer is what I call the Target Job Deconstruction (TJD) process.

Step 1: Decide on a specific target job

Focus on a specific and realistic target job, one in which you can succeed based on the skills you possess. Some people think you change jobs in order to get a promotion, but this is largely incorrect, especially in a tight job market. *People get hired based on their credentials, not their potential.* Most people don't get a promotion when they change jobs, because that would mean coming onboard as an unknown quantity in a job they've never done. Most professionals accept a position similar to the one they have now, but which offers opportunity for growth. So of all the jobs you can do – and we can all do more than one – decide on the one that will be the easiest for you to sell and the easiest for the employer to buy. This will be:

- a job you can do and that you can justify on paper;
- a job you can convince skilled interviewers that you can do;
- a job in which you can succeed.

The ability to do 70 per cent or more of the job will usually put you in the running for selection. You'll be able to deliver the job's requirements and have room for professional growth, making such a target job a good choice. Less than this and you may need to reconsider your target job, but don't throw out an opportunity because one line in the job description mentions a skill you lack.

If you have more than five years of experience, there are probably a couple of jobs you can do. More than 15 years of experience and there could be half a dozen jobs in which you can succeed. Carefully evaluate and rank these jobs based on their availability, remuneration, fulfilment and their potential for growth. This way you will target a 'primary job' based on practicality and common sense.

This does not mean you cannot pursue other jobs for which you have the desire and qualifications.

However, be sensible, create your primary CV with a single 'primary target' job in mind, and make that job one you can nail!

Targeted CVs for different jobs

The one-size-fits-all CV covering all the skills you possess for all the jobs you can do doesn't work any more. You have to have a CV focused on a single target job. This means that you have to tailor individual CVs for each of the different jobs you want to pursue. Fortunately, this isn't nearly as hard as it sounds.

Once you have a *prime* CV tailored to the most logical target for your next job, you can quite easily customize it for any of those other jobs you are interested in. Usually there is considerable overlap in the deliverables of the different jobs for which we are qualified, so you can take that primary CV, make a copy, retitle it and make the necessary changes to give it a specific focus. You won't have to start from scratch, and you'll have customized CVs for every opportunity.

Step 2: Collect job ads

Collect a half-dozen job ads for your chosen primary target job.

From the collected job descriptions we will define exactly the way all employers think about, prioritize and express their needs when they think about someone like you. The result will be a template that describes your target job *the way employers themselves think about, prioritize and describe it.*

Step 3: Look at your job from the other side of the desk

Understand exactly how employers *think about, prioritize and describe the deliverables of your job*:

1 Start a new Word document, and name it 'Prime TJD' or something similar.

2 Under the subhead 'Target Job Titles', cut and paste all the variations on the job title you are pursuing from your collection of job postings.

3 Under a subhead 'Experience/responsibilities/deliverables' review your collection of job postings and find one requirement that is common to all six postings. Copy and paste it into your document. (You may want to place a '6' alongside it to remind yourself that it is common to all six postings.)

 Underneath it list any different or additional keywords used to describe this same requirement.

 For this step you may find it easier to work with the printed copies, since your kitchen worktop is bigger than your computer screen.

 Repeat this for any other requirements common to all six job descriptions, placing the number 6 alongside each one.

4 Repeat this process with requirements that are common to five of the six job postings, then four of the six postings... and so on down the line.

At the end of this first part of the TJD process you will be able to read the document and say to yourself, *'When employers are looking for _____, these are the job titles they use; this is the order in which these needs are prioritized; these are the skills, experiences, deliverables and professional behaviours they look for; and these are the words with which they describe them.'*

As you read, the story your CV needs to tell will be laid out before you.

Step 4: Identify what's missing

Add to your TJD any skills and experience you believe are relevant to this job. This is important, because job descriptions, helpful as they are, don't always tell the whole story. They can be maddeningly vague because the company hasn't paid close enough attention to the hard skills of the job. If you know a specific skill is mandatory for this job, feel free to add it to your list.

Step 5: Problem solving

At their most elemental level, all jobs are the same – they focus on problem identification, avoidance and solution. This is what we all get paid for, no matter what we do for a living. Go back to your TJD and start with the first requirement. Note the problems you identify, solve and/or prevent in the course of a normal workday as you deliver this requirement for the job. Then list specific examples, big and small, when you've successfully done this. Quantify your results when possible.

Repeat this with each of the TJD's other requirements, identifying the problems inherent in that particular responsibility. Some examples may appear in your CV as significant professional achievements, while others will provide you with the ammunition to answer all those interview questions that begin, 'Tell me about a time when...'

Step 6: Achievements

Make a list of your greatest professional achievements from each of the jobs you have held, quantifying the results where you can, to demonstrate the value of your work. Add to this list examples of team achievements to which you contributed.

Once you have made this list, come up with a couple of examples of projects that went wrong and couldn't be fixed. You need these to illustrate your answers to questions that might be asked about projects that went wrong. Ideally, you want examples that are in the past, less than catastrophic and where other people were involved, so you weren't solely responsible. In every example you must be able to illustrate what you learned from the experience.

Interviewers are fond of asking you questions about the following:

- Things that didn't work out well (but did in the end).
- Things that didn't work out well ever, and what you learned.

- Unpopular decisions you have had to make.

- How you developed new processes (because existing ones didn't work or weren't efficient).

- How you improved something that was already working well.

- How you fixed something that was broken.

Being ready with appropriate answers for tough questions in these areas takes some thought. Now is a good time to think about examples to use.

Come back to these examples when you are preparing for an interview. This may seem like a lot of work, but the better prepared you are, the more job offers you will land and the better the companies you will land those job offers with.

Step 7: Profile for success

Interviewers always have an image of the person they want to hire. This is not about height, weight or hair colour; it's a composite behavioural profile of the best people they've known in the job. It's what hiring managers want to find and will hire when they see. Have you ever thought about the behavioural profile that defines success in your area of expertise and then measured yourself against it? Doing so can help you define the professional you want to be and the persona you want to show to the professional world. Not understanding how your behaviour can help or hinder your success usually means that you are unwittingly sabotaging future potential. Work your way through each of the responsibilities itemized in your TJD one by one, profiling the *best* person you ever saw doing that aspect of the job and what made her stand out. Describe how she went about the work, skills, hard and soft, interaction with others, general attitude and demeanour and anything else that sticks in your mind, and you'll get something like: *Carole Jenkins, superior communication skills, always asking questions and listening, a fine analytical mind, great professional appearance and a nice person to work with; she'd do anything for anyone.* Do this for each one of the job's deliverables and you will have a detailed profile of the person all employers want to hire and everyone wants as a colleague: *You will have a profile that will help you land job offers and, just as important, a behavioural profile for professional success.*

Step 8: Transferable skills and professional values

The final step of the TJD is to review each of the skills/responsibilities/deliverables of the job to identify which of the transferable skills and professional values covered in Chapter 2 help you execute your responsibilities in each of the target job's requirements.

Once you complete your TJD, you will have a clear idea of the way employers think about, prioritize, and express their needs for this job. You'll know what they'll ask about at interviews and, beyond the hard skills, exactly the type of person they will hire. Yes, it will take time and it would be easy to skip it, but this is your career and this is your life: make the choice that is right for your long-term success and happiness.

The immediate result will be to give you a template for the story your CV has to tell and an objective tool with which to evaluate your work. And when you apply what you learn from the TJD exercise to your professional life, it will increase your job security and open professional doors for you.

Promotions, ongoing employability and career strategy

While this section is primarily focused on creating a CV to get you a new job, these same tactics can be applied to pursuing a promotion and maintaining your desirability as an employee in the event of the unforeseen occurring.

In fact, the TJD process we discussed should play a twice-yearly role in your ongoing career strategy, both for maintaining employability and for pursuing professional growth.

Maintain employability

To keep yourself employable, you must stay in tune with the new skills that employers are seeking when they hire people like you.

Twice a year, collect half a dozen job postings for the job you have now and the job you would likely pursue in the event of unexpected redundancy. Review these job postings for the skills employers are seeking. You should consider adding any skill you do not have to your professional skill development programme. If the skill is relevant to your work, employers will often support you in acquiring it.

Pursue professional growth

You can also use the TJD approach to climbing the ladder of professional success. Many people mistakenly assume that promotions come with time, hard work and loyalty. Promotions do indeed take time and hard work, but are based more on the presence of the necessary skills.

It is common sense to identify the skills and experience needed to take that next step up the ladder, then set about acquiring them.

CV building

Once you have a clearly defined target job, you can look back into your work history to pull out the information that will help you build a CV that reflects your ability to do this job.

Problem (and opportunity) identification and solution

All jobs revolve around problem identification and solution.

Develop examples of problem identification and opportunity initiatives, both small and large, for every job you have held. The more you come up with the better, because they will add weight and reality to your CV and show that you think with employers' needs in mind. To help you bring out the information you can apply the PSRV process (you might know this as STAR – same process, different acronym):

- Identify a **Problem**.

- Envisage your **Solution**, including strategy and tactics.

- Take note of the **Result** of your actions.

- Understand the **Value** of this to the company (usually in earnings or productivity enhancements).

Now describe four typical or notable problems with which you have been involved and analyse each in terms of PSRV.

Putting it all together

Now you need to take what you have gathered and package it in a new CV that focuses on your target job.

Check your CV against these six CV rules:

Rule 1: Always have a target job title

Place a target job title at the top of your CV, immediately after your contact information. This will help your visibility in database searches and will give human eyes an immediate focus. Use the most common job title as your target job title because different employers use different titles for the same job, and you want to use a title specific enough to put you in the running. One way you can make a job title 'specifically vague' is to add the term 'specialist' (Computer Specialist, Administration Specialist) or the term 'management' (Operations Management, Financial Management).

Rule 2: Always have a performance profile or career summary

Following your Target Job Title give a summary of your capabilities as they relate to the demands of the target job. Your intention is to highlight your ability to do the target job. Refer back to your TJD exercise and rewrite the major priorities as your performance profile. This will help your CV's database visibility and will create immediate resonance when read by the recruiter. Always note any bilingual skills here since we live in a global economy. If you are starting your career and have no relevant experience, start your

---

EXAMPLE

Performance Profile

Strategic communications professional with nine years' experience developing effective, high-impact and cost-efficient media outreach plans for consumer, business and policy audiences in media, entertainment and technology practice areas. Experienced in managing corporate and crisis communications. Goal- and deadline-orientated with five years' experience managing internal and external communications team members. Adept at working with multiple teams and stakeholders.

objective with 'The opportunity to' and then, referring back to your TJD exercise, rewrite the target job's major priorities as your job objective.

Rule 3: Always have a core competencies section
Depending on your skills, you may even consider a separate Technology Competencies section. This helps database visibility because it guarantees you are using the words employers use. You can repeat many of them again in the body of your CV in the context of each job, further increasing your visibility. For the human eyes that see your CV, each word or phrase acts as a topic for the interview and increases the odds of that interview happening.

You can also use keywords in these sections that won't fit in the body of your CV; this will result in better database performance. Here's an example of a Core Competencies section followed by a Technology Competencies section.

EXAMPLE

Core Competencies
Strategic Planning – Full-Cycle Project Management – Technical & Application Standards – IT Governance Process – Technical Vision & Leadership – Architecture Roadmaps – Technical Specifications & Project Design Best Practices – Teambuilding & Leadership – Standards & Process Development

Technology Competencies
Hardware: Sun Servers; HP-UX; AIX; p-Series; Windows Server
Operating Systems: Sun Solaris; AIX; HP-UX; Linux; z/OS; OS/400
Languages: C / C++; COBOL; Visual Basic; Java; Unix; Korn Shell Scripting; Perl; Assembler; SQL*Plus; RPG
Databases: Oracle; DB2; SQL Server; Microsoft Access; Informix Visio; HP Service
Applications: MQSeries; Tuxedo; CICS; Microsoft Project, Word, Excel, Outlook, PowerPoint, Sharepoint and Visio; HP Service Desk; Provision; Telelogic Doors; Change
Synergy: Rational System Architect; Rational System Developer; Visual Studio; CA Clarity; LiveLink Other Cobit 4.1

Rule 4: Never put salary on a CV

It does not belong there. If salary information is requested, put it in your covering letter and don't tie yourself to a specific figure; give a range. For details on developing a realistic salary range, see Chapter 21, 'Negotiating the offer'.

Rule 5: Keep your CV focused

The standard length for a CV used to be never more than two pages. However, as jobs have become more complex, they require more explanation. The length of your CV is less important than its relevance to the target job. If the first page of your CV is tightly focused and contains a target job title, performance profile, core competencies and perhaps a career highlight section, you will have the reader's attention. If the first page makes the right argument, the rest of your CV will be read carefully. However, you should still make every effort to maintain focus and an 'if in doubt, cut it out' editing approach.

Rule 6: Emphasize your achievements

Make your achievements, problem-solving skills and professional profile the focus of your CV.

Below, you will see a CV template. This is to show you all the component parts an ideal CV might contain to maximize its effectiveness.

CV template

Name
Address
Telephone and mobile phone
E-mail address

Professional Target Job Title
This helps database visibility and gives focus to human eyes about what they will be reading.

Performance Profile / Career Summary
No more than five lines of unbroken text can be followed by a second similar paragraph or short list of bullet points. Your intention is to portray your ability to do the target job. What goes in here? Take the most common requirements from your TJD exercise Step 3 and rewrite as your performance profile. This will help your CV's database visibility and will create immediate resonance with the recruiter. Always note bilingual skills, since we live in a global economy.

Core Competencies
Specific and detailed. This is a bulleted list of keywords that you identified in Step 3 of the TJD. It can be as long as you like. This list gives the reader an immediate focus ('Oh, she can talk about this and this') and each word can be repeated in the context of the job where it applied.

Technical Competencies
An optional category, depending on your needs.

Professional Experience
Company name and location.
Job title and employment dates.
(Repeat this format as many times as necessary.)

Education
This may come at the front of the CV if these credentials are critical, especially relevant to the TJD or highlight your greatest strength.

Licences / Professional Accreditations
This may come at the front of the CV if these credentials are critical, especially relevant to the TJD or highlight your greatest strength.

Ongoing Professional Education
Professional Organization / Affiliations.
Publications / Patents / Languages.

Extracurricular Interests
If they relate to the job.

References Available on Request
Employers *assume* that your references are available. Only end your CV with this if there is no better use of the space. Never list references on your CV.

An excellent final test for your revamped CV is to first reread your TJD and then read your CV. If it clearly echoes your TJD, then you are likely to have a productive CV. If it doesn't, you'll readily be able to tell where your content needs fine-tuning.

Sample CV

Jane Swift, 9 Any Street, Anywhere AA00 0AA 01234 567890 janeswift@isp.co.uk

SUMMARY: Ten years of increasing responsibility in the employment
services industry.
Concentration in the high-technology markets.

EXPERIENCE: ABC Systems International, 2008–Present
Management Consulting Firm
Personnel Manager

Responsible for recruiting and managing staff of five. Set up office and organized the recruitment, selection, and hiring of consultants. Recruited all levels of MIS staff from financial to manufacturing markets.

Additional responsibilities:

- Coordinated with outside advertising agencies.
- Developed PR with industry periodicals – placement with over 20 magazines and newsletters.
- Developed effective referral programs – referrals increased 32 per cent.

EXPERIENCE: Technical Aid Corporation 1996–2008
National Consulting Firm. MICRO/TEMPS Division

Division Manager 2001–2008
Area Manager 1998–2001
Branch Manager 1996–1998

As Division Manager, opened additional South West office. Staffed and trained all offices with appropriate personnel. Created and implemented all divisional operational policies responsible for P&L. Sales increased to £5 million, from £0 in 1990.

Additional responsibilities:

- Achieved and maintained 30 per cent annual growth over seven-year period.
- Maintained sales staff turnover at 14 per cent.

As Area Manager, opened additional offices, hiring staff, setting up office policies, and training sales and recruiting personnel.

Additional responsibilities:

- Supervised offices in two regions.
- Developed business relationships with accounts – 75 per cent of clients were regular customers.
- Client base increased 28 per cent per year.
- Generated over £100,000 worth of free trade-journal publicity.

As Branch Manager, hired to establish the new MICRO/TEMPS operation. Recruited and managed consultants. Hired internal staff. Sold service to clients.

EDUCATION: Reading University
BA Business Studies 1995.

Your covering letter

Even when the majority of CVs end up in CV banks, there is still a need for covering letters:

1 When you identify managers by name (advice on how to do this coming up) you can avoid the CV banks altogether and at these times a covering letter is a very effective marketing tool.

2 Many CV banks and company websites have a place where you can upload or paste a covering letter along with your CV, and employers look more favourably on candidates who take the extra step.

In a professional world where communication skills are a must for any job, your covering letter introduces you, puts your CV in context and demonstrates your writing skills. From your first contact with an employer to the day you start that new job there are a number of opportunities to use letters/e-mails to improve your chances that we will be looking at.

The Executive Briefing

I developed this type of covering letter many years ago, and it continues to get rave reviews from users.

An executive briefing enables you to link your skills to employers' needs and is especially helpful to recruiters, hiring managers, HR professionals or administrative assistants, who may not understand all the requirements of a specific job. It is a powerful focusing tool that allows you to update and customize a CV for a specific job with lightning speed. The executive briefing is beautiful in its simplicity. It is a covering letter on your standard letterhead/e-mail with the company's requirements for the job listed on the left side and your skills – matching point-by-point the company's needs – on the right. It looks like the example overleaf.

An executive briefing sent with a CV provides a comprehensive, easy-to-read synopsis that details exactly how you can help with current needs. Using the executive briefing as a covering letter for your CV will greatly increase the chance that your query will be picked out of the pile and hand-carried to the appropriate manager.

The use of an executive briefing is obviously not appropriate when the requirements of the job are unavailable.

EXAMPLE Executive Briefing

From: A1coordpro@abc.net
Subject: Assessment Coordinator
Date: 28 February 2014 11:18:39 PM
To: jobs@abc.com

Dear HR Staff,

Your advertisement on the *Times* website on 27 February 2017 for an Assessment Coordinator seems to match my background and experience perfectly. As the International Brand Coordinator for KZT, I coordinated meetings, prepared presentations and materials, organized a major off-site conference and supervised an assistant. I believe that I am an excellent candidate for this position, as I have illustrated below:

YOUR REQUIREMENTS	*MY QUALIFICATIONS*
Highly motivated, diplomatic	Successfully managed project teams involving different flexible, quality-driven professional business units. The defined end results were achieved for every project.
Exceptional organizational skills and attention to detail	Planned the development and launch of the KZT Heritage Edition. My former manager enjoyed leaving the details and organization to me. I also have project management training.
University degree and six years of experience	BA from Exeter University (2004). 6+ years' relevant business experience in productive, professional environments.
Computer literacy	Extensive knowledge of Windows and Mac applications.

I'm interested in this position because it fits well with my new career focus in the human resources field. Currently, I am enrolled on an adult career planning and development certificate programme and working at Harrison Ltd.

My CV, pasted below and also attached in MS Word, will provide more information about my strengths and career achievements. If after reviewing my CV you believe that there is a match, please call me. Thank you for your consideration.

Yours sincerely,
Jane Swift

NETWORKING AND THE SUCCESSFUL JOB SEARCH

An effective job search strategy demands an understanding of how companies recruit people, and requires you to integrate networking tactics into every aspect of your plan of attack.

When networking strategies are integrated into your job search, they can quadruple your odds of netting an interview.

How companies recruit employees

At most companies, staffing is planned up to 12 months in advance, so the interviews you go to this year were probably planned and budgeted for last year. Once recruitment budgets are approved, they can be swung into action at any time, but most often they open at the start of the calendar year and are staggered throughout. This means that the early part of every year usually has plenty of opportunities, so if you read this in November you should be especially diligent about working on your job hunt right through Christmas! That does not mean you can't find jobs at other times of the year; there are always jobs available if you know how to find them.

The cost of employing and training personnel runs into thousands and sometimes tens of thousands of pounds, so the entire recruitment process is entirely cost/productivity conscious. The people involved – the manager and human resources – all want the same thing: good, fast recruitment done as cheaply as possible. Understanding how and why things are done, and in what sequence, will help you focus your efforts on the tactics that consistently result in job interviews.

How recruitment affects networking

Put yourself on the other side of the desk for a moment. If possible, you want to recruit from within the company, because it is the cheapest way, you are dealing with known quantities and it is motivating for everyone to see internal promotion. Many positions are filled this way. Knowing this can give you a head start; whenever you hear about internal promotions and transfers at your own, or other companies it means another opening will be created downstream.

Who do you know?

When a manager can't recruit internally, he or she will ask, 'Who do we know, and who do my people know?'

The recruitment team will review all the CVs in the company's database and those of promising candidates who have been interviewed in the past for similar positions – one of the many reasons why follow-up is important. The manager will also create an internal job posting and will consider people known to the recruitment team through their involvement in the professional community. This will include professional associations and online social networks. Developing a networking presence will help you become visible to recruiters and increase your chances of hearing about jobs.

These are the first steps of any recruitment campaign because they are fast, cheap, and because employees 'known to us', are seen to be better choices, thought to get up to speed more quickly and stay with the company longer. They account for around a third of all recruitments made externally. This is why networking is such an effective job search tactic and why you have to ask yourself these questions:

1 How do I get to know, and be known by, my peers?

2 How do I become more visible in my professional community?

Recruitment advertising

The next step – more expensive and time-consuming – is to look outside the company completely. The first choice is often the internet. As cost now becomes a serious consideration, it won't surprise you to learn that the vast majority of internet appointments come directly through the company's own website.

This is especially so in depressed economic times, when companies will often decide that they don't need to advertise with the big job banks because plenty of smart, well-qualified people will find their way to them.

When they do advertise the recruiter's preference for speciality job sites makes sense: he or she can expect more consistently suitable CVs and fewer time wasters.

The balance of recruitment, about 30 per cent, comes from job fairs, temporary appointments becoming permanent, and headhunters.

So we can now put together a job-hunting plan that reflects these realities.

The hidden job market

On a radio talk show I listened to a caller's problem. She said, 'I'm in the academic field and I've been unemployed for two years, and I don't know what to do.' I asked her how many possible employers there were, and she said about 3,000. I said, 'Next caller, please.' The world owes no one a living. You have to go out and find that next job.

Anyone struggling in a job hunt 10 years ago was probably relying exclusively on the situations vacant ads in the newspapers. That same person struggling today is probably relying on its modern equivalent: internet job boards. This is not to say that these approaches are invalid. On the contrary, each is a valuable resource, just as long as you know how to use it to best advantage and integrate it into a comprehensive plan.

Job hunters who go beyond scanning the job ads and posting a CV on the job sites all too often then fall back on applications to the large, well-known companies. They forget that 90 per cent of the growth in commerce is among small companies with fewer than 500 employees.

Not only that, the majority of the growth is from small companies who are also young, the first 3–10 years of a company often being a period of strong employee growth.

You need to organize a comprehensive job-hunting strategy that will give you maximum penetration of your target area, and the ability to keep track of all the opportunities and potential employers you unearth.

You'll remember that about one-third of appointments come from internet resources and cross-media advertising. I'll help you get the most out of posting CVs on online job sites; how to find and use tools that lead you directly to employers in your profession and target location; and how to double, triple and even quadruple your chances of getting an interview.

Another one-third of appointments tend to come from employers' personal networks and prior contacts. I'll outline effective networking techniques using your personal networks, and ways for getting connected to your professional community through involvement with professional associations, college placement offices and alumni associations.

The balance of appointments – the remaining third – come from job fairs, third-party employment suppliers including temporary employment companies, employment agencies and headhunters, and what is quaintly referred to as 'smokestacking' – that is, keeping an eye out for potential employers as you go about town on your daily business.

Networking

A typical career spans half a century, and in that time you can reasonably expect the good, the bad and the downright ugly to occur in your professional life. It's during the rough times that you need people, and networking, with its focus on talking to friends and colleagues, offers a great job search technique that also eases the feelings of rejection everyone suffers at these times.

But for most of us it doesn't work as effectively as it should because our networks lack depth and relevance. It is a tremendously valuable career survival tool, and not one to be treated with disrespect. An approach along the lines of, 'Hey Harry, how are you? We haven't spoken for 10 years but do you know where I can get a job?' is likely to fail. Networking is a process of building relationships over time, and your networks' effectiveness will reflect the effort you put into their development.

Getting personal referrals for job openings demands that you get connected to both your professional community and to the other networks available in your target area.

You should think in terms of *networks*, rather than a single *network*. We all have a number of networks available to us, any of which may produce that all-important job offer. Here are the typical networks we can all tap into.

Professional networks

- Other job hunters. Professionals seeking a position in the same profession or industry can be valuable resources; they don't have to be looking for the same type of position.

- Managers, past and present. They can be useful to you throughout your job hunt.

- Colleagues. This includes professional colleagues, past and present.

- Other professionals in your field. Professional associations are a good place to start in order to find these contacts.

- College alumni. Educational institution networks are a valuable job search resource.

- Company alumni associations. Companies increasingly see the value in maintaining contact with ex-employees.

Community networks

- Family and relatives. This includes your spouse's family and relatives.

- Friends. This includes neighbours and casual acquaintances, and those you know through your personal interest.

- Service industry acquaintances. This includes your banker, solicitor, insurance agent, doctor, dentist, hairdresser and the like.

- Social and civic associations, including business groups, sports clubs, etc.

- Hobbies. This includes everything from the golf club to chess club, and any activity you enjoy that involves a loosely knit group of similar people.

Networking approaches

You will have networks of people you can approach now and networks you will have to build. Their effectiveness will depend on the scope of your networks and their relevance to your life. Whatever the network you have choices about making contact and nurturing those relationships:

- By letter, telephone, e-mail, online chat or message posting.

- In person. Conventions, association meetings, class reunions, fundraisers, continuing-education classes, community groups and events.

In practice, the professional who integrates intelligent networking into his or her professional life will use all of these approaches. Networking is much more than a series of single events, it is a *process* of building relationships. Your networks become more effective with the effort you put into their development.

In the following section, you'll learn how to build and nurture networks in both your professional and personal life.

Professional associations

Joining and being active in a professional association is the best long-term vehicle for increasing your professional visibility to future employers. In fact, if you have heard disgruntled job hunters mutter, 'It's not what you know, it's who you know', it probably means they are not members of a professional association, and they don't understand networking.

Associations have meetings in most major towns and cities, plus regional and national get-togethers every year. Of immediate interest are the local meetings. When you join, you get to know and be known by the most committed and best-connected people at all levels of your profession. Your membership will help you stay attuned to what is going on in your profession. These associations also offer training programmes that make you a more knowledgeable and therefore a more desirable employee.

Your membership also becomes a link to colleagues, most of whom will gladly talk to you, based on your mutual connectivity through the association. The professional association is a new 'old boy/old girl' network for the modern world.

If you fit the profile of a special interest or minority group you will find professional associations that cater to another dimension of the professional you. If you can find a niche association that fits, join it as well, as it represents another even more finely tuned network.

You'll get the most benefit if you attend the meetings, because this is where you will meet fellow professionals. But don't just attend the meetings; volunteer to get involved. Associations always need someone to set out chairs or hand out paperwork and name-tags. The task itself doesn't matter, your visible willingness to be an active participant does and will get you on first-name terms with people you would probably never otherwise meet.

The association directory, which comes with your membership package, provides you with a superb networking resource for verbal contact and e-mail networking. You can feel comfortable calling any other member on the phone and introducing yourself: 'Hi, Brenda Massie? My name is Martin Yate. We haven't spoken before, but we are both members of the ABC Association. I need some advice; can you spare a minute?'

Your mutual membership will guarantee you a few moments of anyone's time. Your association contacts will also feel more comfortable about referring you to others in their own networks.

You can also use your association membership directory to generate personal introductions for jobs you have heard about elsewhere. Rather than apply cold, return to your membership directory and find people who work for that company. A judicious call or two will frequently get you a personal referral and some inside information on the opening. Once you have an interview arranged, these same contacts can help you prepare for the interview with insider knowledge about the company, the department and the hiring manager.

Professional associations all have newsletters. Many have a jobs section on the website or linked to the newsletter, where companies advertise because of the qualified applicants who respond. Consequently, you will see recruitment ads that often don't appear anywhere else.

Active association membership puts you on the radar of all the best-qualified and connected professionals in your area. You can also list it at the end of your CV under a *Professional Affiliations* heading. This is guaranteed to get a second glance, as it signifies professional awareness.

Social networks

For corporate recruiters and headhunters, social networking sites are honey pots, offering millions of qualified candidates. For you, social networks provide a reliable pathway to millions of jobs through the people connected to them. Social networking competency is a must for any effective job search plan of attack. It allows you to reach out to friends, colleagues and specific categories of as-yet-unknown professional colleagues who might have the perfect lead or introduction.

The better connected you are to your profession, the greater your odds of locating opportunities in the hidden job market. The connections you make can lead to referrals and introductions to employers, and in many instances you'll be able to bypass the CV banks (always a good thing). You can search a social networking site's database by job title, company name, location or any keywords of your choice. The database will pull up the profiles of people who match your requirements and allow you to initiate contact directly, through your common membership in groups or through the chain of people who connect you.

For example, a soldier who was coming out of the army sought my help in her search for a new civilian career. First, to find other individuals with a similar background, I plugged the word *army* into the premier professional online networking site LinkedIn. The result was more than 4,000 profiles of people who shared her military experience. We then tried a search using the phrase *information technology* (reflecting her desired career change) and got 39,000 profiles. While both these potential networks would have relevance to her job search, it got even better when we combined the keywords, *information technology* and *army*. This pulled up 908 profiles of people who shared her life experience and who had, in about half of these results, already made the same transition into her desired profession.

This shows how fast social networking is growing and how important it can be in building productive relationships with a wide range of people, all of whom can be helpful to your job search.

Networking and confidential job search

When you are employed and engaged in a confidential job search, a properly constructed social media profile will make you *discoverable*. If you are changing from one profession to another, you can use social networking sites to build a network of people who do the target job in your chosen profession and, whenever possible, people who have made a similar transition – and who can therefore offer you useful advice on making that transition yourself.

Which social networks are right for you?

You'll find networking sites that cater to an almost limitless array of special interests. There are thousands of these social networks, and the list is growing every day (see Wikipedia entries for a complete list of sites). For the most effective network-integrated job search, consider having presence on the top four: LinkedIn, Facebook, Twitter and Google+.

This is not the place to go into great detail about setting up and using social media profiles, but do bear in mind that you are creating a professional impression and displaying your employability to its best advantage.

Social networking sites have become catnip for corporate recruitment and headhunters, and this should shape the information you make available about yourself. For the professional in a job search this will start with simply cutting and pasting your CV into your official profile. You make yourself visible without an 'I'm for sale' sign, which is useful when you are employed and looking for a new position.

If you don't use your CV word for word as your profile take care that the same keywords appear. Just as you will search for others on the site using keywords, members who are hiring managers, HR people or headhunters will be searching for you through the site's search engine using keywords.

Many sites allow you to identify topics that you would like to discuss with others. For example: advice and information on hiring people, looking for job or business opportunities, and partnering opportunities in your area of expertise. The more areas of interest you check, the more options other people will have to contact you. You also have a choice of whether or not to allow direct contact.

Check for digital dirt

If you grew up with social networking, there are probably details of your wilder times available online for the world to see. You need to do searches for yourself to discover exactly what is out there about you, and when you find something that is inappropriate for your professional image, go back and clean up your digital dirt.

I just returned from an appearance at a major convention for college career services and corporate campus recruiters. It was noted at the conference that upward of 80 per cent of recruiters are using publicly available online data about short-list candidates as a screening tool; 25 per cent said they would reject a candidate based on this information. This means we all have to police the image we have online.

Social networks are local and global

Online networking can get you useful introductions to people throughout the country and the world – people who might know of jobs at their own companies or who can introduce you to people at companies that have openings.

The internet is global, so all sites have a worldwide reach. Facebook, for example, stretches around the Earth and is consequently a major destination for recruiters. Professionally focused sites can claim members in hundreds of countries. In a global economy, people with language skills have a special edge, so sites that encourage bilingual professionals can help you promote those language skills with any global company searching for multicultural awareness in its employees.

Most social networking sites also offer an array of tools for your professional networking activities:

- Job postings from employers and headhunters.
- Reminders of when to follow up with a call or e-mail to nurture your relationships.
- Message boards and forums for common-interest groups, such as women in business and profession-specific groups for job hunters.
- Links to job boards.
- Offline social events to meet and mingle in person.

Alumni associations

Almost every school, college and university has an alumni association, and being a member of your alma mater's association can have a pivotal role in your professional life, if handled correctly. Going to the meetings, networking online, and occasionally volunteering for some task are all activities that will ease you into collegial relationships with men and women on every rung of the corporate ladder – people who are in a position to boost your career.

The membership directory puts you in touch with the other graduates from your alma mater, and people hire people with whom they share something in common. Alumni associations all have newsletters, and many include information about job openings. Some even have semi-formalized job-hunting networks where alumni are encouraged to pass on their company's employment needs. As a member of an alumni association, you can also continue an informal relationship with the school's director of career services, so even when your school days are in the misty past, don't forget these people and the valuable resource they represent.

If you are graduating, take advantage of this resource, but remember that the college placement office is not there to hold your hand or provide you with job offers. Career services staff are horrendously overworked and they work hard merely to keep pace with the Herculean task of providing assistance to the student body.

Take the time to make yourself known here, and stress your willingness to listen to good advice. If you are then seen to act on it you will have earned respect and will garner extra attention and guidance. Treat your entire interaction with career services the same way you would the interview process. Make a real effort with your appearance and professional demeanour and, of course, you'll find that courtesy will go a long way.

Company associations

Companies increasingly see the value of maintaining contact with ex-employees through online corporate associations, as a source of future recruitment and of leads for future recruitment.

Your former managers as a networking resource

As a rule, we are confident that our former managers will speak well of us, so why not use that goodwill throughout your job hunt?

At the very start you should identify as many potential contacts as possible. The more options, the better your likelihood of coming up with excellent connections. With some experience under your belt you might be pursuing different job titles, and consequently different contacts might be appropriate. Of course, when employed, avoid using current managers and colleagues if you know this is going to cause problems.

The process is simplicity itself, starting with an introduction: 'Bob, this is _____. We worked together at XYZ between 2003 and 2008. How's it going?' Catch up on gossip, then broach the subject of your call.

'John, I wanted to ask your advice.' (Everyone loves to be asked for an expert opinion.) 'We had some cutbacks at Fly-By-Night Finance, as you probably heard', or 'The last five years at Bank of Crooks and Criminals International have been great, and the _____ project we are just winding down has been a fascinating job. Nevertheless, I have decided that this would be a perfect time for a strategic career move to capitalize on my experience.'

Then, 'John, I realize how important references can be and I was wondering if you would have any reservations about my using you as a reference?' At this point of the job search, references, though important, are an added bonus. Your real agenda is to use these contacts for your professional network.

The response will usually be positive, so you can then move to the next step.

'Thanks, John, I hoped you would say that. Let me update you about what I have been doing recently and tell you about the type of job I'm after.' Give a capsule description of what you've done since you worked together and what you are looking for. Also ask your contacts if they will keep an ear to the ground for you, and if they would mind giving you advice as situations arise during your job hunt. You'll also want to show courtesy by following your call with a thank-you letter.

With the scene set in this manner, you can network with each of these potential references every month or two, and you will have developed another small but very finely tuned networking resource for your job hunt.

Personal networks

There are a wide variety of personal and community-based networks available to you, depending on your interests and willingness to become an active member of your local community.

Your personal networking efforts break into two categories: those people you already know personally, and those you can meet through involvement in your community. With the first you can be direct, while the second group requires a little more time and diplomacy. You might contact some of these networks by phone or e-mail, and some will combine both personal interaction and telephone or e-mail communication, but on the whole most of your personal networking will be done, well, personally.

Family and friends

The good news is that the people who know you best, your family and friends, will really try to help you, but unlike the contacts you make in your professional networks, they probably don't have a full grasp of what you do for a living. Many job hunters make the mistake of confusing the members of this network by giving too much information about their professional life. With the right guidance, though your immediate circle will cast a wide net and come up with leads for you, even if they have nothing to do with the professional world.

Here are the steps to help your loved ones help you:

1 Think carefully about what you do for a living and put it in
a one- or two-sentence description that even Aunt Aggie can
grasp: 'I am a computer programmer; I write the instructions
that help computers run.'

2 Think carefully about the job you want, the kind of
company you will work for and the kind of people you
need to talk to; condense it into a one- or two-sentence
explanation: 'I'm looking for a job with another computer
company. It would be great if you or your friends know
anyone I could talk to who works with computers.'

3 Give them the information you need to get in touch with
these people: 'I am looking for the names and telephone
numbers of anyone in these areas. I'm not looking for
someone to hire me; I'm looking for people in my field with
whom I can network.'

This process of breaking your networking needs into three or four
simple statements gives the people you know socially something
they can easily remember and something they can really work with.

Civic, social, volunteer and special-interest networking groups

It is good to be involved in your local community. Your involvement will reward you with a richer personal life, as well as a wide
array of networking opportunities.

At the same time, you can't possibly join all the groups your
community has to offer, so you will have to make some decisions
about what is practical. Most people have time for no more than
three ongoing social activities. These might comprise:

● A community volunteer group – volunteer communities help
us achieve a sense of meaning and balance in our lives, and
such groups are especially helpful in the emotionally
troubled times of job and career change. They get you
involved with others who wish to make a difference.

● A hobby or special-interest group – this could be a chess
club, a women's/men's group or a dance class. It doesn't
matter as long as the activity is one that energizes you.
The people you meet will all share a common bond based
on your special interests.

- Business, professional and civic groups – all communities have networks of professionals: Rotarians, Chamber of Commerce, women in business, etc. These community-based associations have a professionally oriented membership, but they aren't focused on one profession; they straddle the line between your professional and community-based networking activities.

In all these groups your need for job leads must take a back seat to becoming involved as a productive member. Soon enough you'll learn what people do for a living, just as they'll learn about you. As opportunities arise you can talk about your job-hunting needs; we'll talk about how to manage these conversations shortly. You can find out about these groups in your local newspapers, at the library or by using your internet browser.

Gathering leads and referrals from networking conversations

You never know whom you are going to meet at the hairdresser, or gym. For your networking in any of these situations to be effective, you need a 'networking mindset'.

A 'networking mindset' means you are always prepared to show an interest in others, and to speak to them in a friendly way, so you won't let opportunities for expanding your networks slip by. With a 'networking mindset', you will be surprised at the range of useful people you meet. Even when those people know nothing about your profession, they have the potential to know someone who can be useful to your job hunt.

There are one or two unique considerations about networking in person.

In-person networking

Always carry business cards. If your company doesn't supply you with cards, get some made at your own expense. When you attend social and professional events, keep those business cards handy.

You will need an introduction for yourself, and while it's tough to do, you have to make the effort to reach out to others. 'Hello, I'd like to introduce myself. My name is Mark Germino. I'm in accounting/just started playing tennis; how about you?' Always try to end with a question that encourages your contact to introduce and talk about him- or herself; it doesn't really matter what the question is. Once there has been a conversational exchange, you can begin to move forward with your networking agenda. (We'll go into a whole series of networking questions shortly.)

Try to keep your initial networking conversations to under five minutes. You can end them gracefully with an offer of your business card and should recognize that a request for yours is a signal for you both to move on. If someone you meet isn't carrying a card, ask him or her to write their name and contact information on the back of one of yours; always try to get both a telephone number and an e-mail address.

Whenever you meet someone in person, send an e-mail to thank him or her for any helpful information you may have gathered from the conversation. It also serves to keep you on that person's radar.

The secrets of successful networking conversations

Here are some ideas for the content of your networking conversations. Show interest in your contacts as human beings, then – and only then – move on with your agenda.

The conversation happens in four stages, none of which should be rushed.

Introduction

Recall the last memorable interaction you had with that person or mention someone you both know. Ask what is happening in that person's personal and professional life. Listen to what is said and respond appropriately.

State your situation

Prepare a statement that states your situation succinctly: 'I just got laid off because of the recession', or 'We have a baby on the way, and XYZ is a company where there just isn't the room for me to grow professionally', or 'My job just got sent to Mumbai, India, so it's time for me to make a move'.

Information gathering

When common professional ground exists, you can politely cut to the chase. You could begin, 'Brenda, I have been an accountant with Anderson for the last four years. I work in the small business area, and I'm considering making a change.' Rather than rambling, in less than 10 seconds you have courteously provided a focus.

Rather than describing your ideal job in detail, it is more productive to talk in terms of what you do day-to-day, or even just tell the contact you are looking for a new opportunity.

If you handle yourself in a pleasant and professional manner, most people will try to be helpful.

Ask for assistance

You can ask for general guidance about your tactics: 'If you were in my situation, Charlie, what would you do?' You can ask if he or she has heard about local companies recruiting. These are all good questions, and they typically comprise the content of 99 per cent of all networking calls, but you can achieve more with the right sequence of questions.

Great networking questions

This sequence of networking questions will lead you to jobs in the hidden job market. These are exactly the question sequences asked by the headhunting and employment services industry when prospecting for job openings.

They follow a logical sequence – but that order might not suit your needs. Decide what question you would ask if you had time for only one, then if you had time for only two, and so on. The result will be a prioritized set of questions. Avoid ones like 'How's business these days?' Each should be specific. When you're satisfied with your list, have a copy on your desktop, another by your phone (never at work) and a third that can go in your wallet or handbag.

General questions

You can ask if there are openings in the department or at the company and whom you should speak to about them. Don't ask, 'Can you or your company hire me?' You can ask:

- 'What needs does your company have at present?'
- 'Who in the company might need someone with my qualifications?'
- 'Is the company/department planning any expansion or new projects that might create an opening?'
- 'When do you anticipate a change in company manpower needs?'
- 'Does your company have any other divisions or subsidiaries? Where are they?'
- 'I'd appreciate any e-mail addresses or telephone numbers of headhunters you hear from.'

Profession-specific questions

You might wish to add some profession-specific questions. For instance, people in information technology might find questions about the operating systems, communication protocols, programs and languages a company uses to be useful. After receiving an answer add a focused follow-up question: 'Thanks, Gail. Who else do you know who uses these configurations?' This would lead you to other companies likely to have similar needs.

Even when an offer of an introduction is made – 'Let me speak to Charlene Howarth for you' (rather than being told to make direct contact yourself: 'Call Charlene on extension 912') – don't rely on your contact to get you into that company. Execute your own plan of attack, seeking other introductions within the company from your networking resources and making direct application by telephone or by e-mail and a traditional posted CV.

Leads at other companies

When you are sure that no openings exist within a particular department or company, move on to gathering leads in other companies: 'Do you know of anyone at other [banks] in town I might speak to?'

or 'Whom do you know in the business community who might have a need for someone like me?'

If your contact can't think of a person, ask about other companies: 'Which companies have you heard about that are recruiting now?' or 'If you were going to make a move, which companies would you look at?' or 'Which are the most rapidly growing companies in the area?'

Whenever you are offered a lead, say, 'That's a great idea. I never thought of IBM.' Your encouragement is positive reinforcement. Then after a suitable pause, ask for another company name, as in, 'I really appreciate your help, Sam. I never thought of IBM... Who else comes to mind?' When people see that their advice is appreciated, they will often come up with more helpful information. When you have gathered two or three company names, you can backtrack with a request for contact names at each of the companies: 'Do you know of anyone I could speak to at _____?'

You can also ask for leads at companies you plan to call, or even ones you have already called: 'Jack, I was planning to contact _____ Ltd. Would you happen to know anyone there?'

If you are changing or considering a career change, your priorities might be different. In this case you can explain that you are considering a particular profession for a new career direction and ask what it is like working in the profession; what your contact likes least and most about the work; what education, experience and professional behaviours help people succeed in the profession; who fails and why; and how one gets into and moves ahead in the profession.

When you get a referral

When you get leads, be sure to thank your benefactor and ask to use his or her name as an introduction. 'Thank you, Bill. I didn't know XYZ was building a facility in town, and I appreciate getting Holly Barnes's name. May I use your name as an introduction?'

The answer will invariably be yes, but asking demonstrates professionalism. It is also quite acceptable to add afterwards, 'That's very helpful, Bill. Does anyone else come to mind?'

When you get permission to use your contact's name, use it in an introduction: 'Jane, my name is _____. I'm a friend of Bill Smith, who suggested I call, so before I go any further, Bill has asked me to say hello.' This is a bridge-building phrase and usually leads to a brief exchange about your mutual contact before you go into your information-gathering agenda.

When you do get help, say thank you. If you do it verbally, it's a nice touch to follow it up with a note. The impression you make might get you another lead. It never hurts to include a copy of your CV with the thank-you letter.

When your networking call comes to its natural conclusion, say thanks, offer to return the favour and leave the door open for future calls: 'Jack, thanks so much for your help. I do appreciate it. At times like this you realize how important your colleagues are, so I'd like to give you my telephone number and e-mail so that one day I might return the favour. Let's stay in touch. May I call you again sometime?'

Other statements that you could use at the end of your conversation include:

- 'I'll let you know how it works out with Holly Barnes.'

- 'May I get in touch in a couple of months to see if the situation has changed?'

- When talking to a management contact in your profession, you might suggest, 'Would it be worth me e-mailing a copy of my CV for your personal management database?'

Stay in touch with your contacts, whether they were able to help you or not. Let them know when you get a job, and try to stay in contact at least once a year. A career is a long time, and it might be next week or a decade from now when a group of managers (including one from your personal network) are talking about filling a new position, and the first thing they'll ask is, 'Who do we know?' That someone is more likely to be you when you are connected to your profession and your local community.

NETWORK-INTEGRATED JOB SEARCH TACTICS

In a competitive job market, you cannot rely exclusively on networking, or any other single job-search approach. You need to use a number of different job-search strategies and integrate networking into each of them.

All the job-search tools and approaches that I discuss in this section of the book – job banks, CV banks, headhunters and direct research – have proved to be effective. No single one is a guaranteed silver bullet, and any of them could deliver the ideal opportunity for you. Your plan of attack should embrace as many of these approaches as is practical in your situation. Intelligently pursuing all useful approaches will generate job leads. Then use your networks for leads about and introductions to the recruitment managers.

It's a digital world

Corporate recruitment has moved online, so your job search must respond to these recruitment preferences.

With tens of thousands of job sites and CV banks out there, you could spend eternity trawling from one to the next. The danger is that this feels like productive work, and because it involves zero rejection it can be highly addictive. An internet-based job search can seem magical because the media tells you it is magical, but *job banks and CV banks are not magical*. The internet increases your ability to gather and disseminate information, but you need to understand, control and use this power, not be controlled by it.

The importance of your e-mail address and subject line

In a competitive job search, the little things can make a big difference, and the way you introduce yourself is one of them. The majority of job search communications are e-mail based, so your e-mail address and subject line are the first things employers see. They offer a perfect opportunity to define your professional offering and can become powerful marketing tools that your competitors overlook.

As one of the first things any recruiter or potential employer sees, you want the impression it creates to be professional. This might be a good time to restrict addresses like *BinkyPoo@yahoo.co.uk* and *BigBoy@hotmail.co.uk* to non-professional activities where they won't detract from your professional reputation.

You have unlimited access to different e-mail addresses, so take advantage of this and add an e-mail account devoted exclusively to your job search and career management affairs.

Your e-mail address is a primary brand identifier

E-mail addresses act as headlines to tell the reader who is calling, so you need a professional e-mail address for your professional affairs. Create an e-mail address that reflects your professional identity; for example, *SystemAnalyst@hotmail.co.uk* or *TopAccountant@yahoo.co.uk*. In addition to identifying the sender, a profession-focused e-mail also offers some idea of what the communication is about.

Using a professional e-mail address serves you in another way: it succinctly introduces the *professional you* and, because it refers to a job rather than your name, it has the added benefit of helping to protect your identity.

Subject lines are for teasing

In any written communication, a headline acts to grab your attention and draw you into the story, offering an enticing taste of what's to come. To recruiters and hiring managers buried in junk mail, the right subject line can make the difference between your e-mail getting read or deleted.

If you are responding to a job posting, the job title and job posting number are necessary, and you can combine the required factual information with a brief marketing pitch about your credentials:

Financial Analyst #MB450 – CPA/MBA/8 yrs' exp

Posting 2314 – Oxford grad is interested

Job #6745 – Top sales professional here

Or if there is no job posting:

IT Manager – 7 yrs' IT Consulting

Benefits Consultant – Insurance and Corporate

Referral from Tony Banks – Product Manager

Subject line as condensed CV

Your incoming e-mail typically reveals anywhere between 35 and 60 characters of the subject line, so you have enough space to include more selling points in your subject line. To be safe, try to get the 'must haves' of your headline in the first 35 characters; in this example, an HR management job that required specific credentials:

Your next Reg HR Manager – EEOC, FLSA

However, once opened, an e-mail can sometimes show up to 150 characters in the subject line. You can make this space work for you as an abbreviated CV by showcasing the highlights of your CV. This example uses 130 characters (including spaces):

Your next Reg HR Manager – EEOC, FLSA, ADA, OSHA.
10 yrs' arbitration, campus, executive recruitment, selection,
compensation, T&D

No one likes to read CVs, but in a competitive job search, the little things your competitors never learned, like an informative e-mail address and enlightening subject line, can make a big difference. They won't get you hired, but they just might get your e-mail and the attached CV read with serious attention.

Job sites and CV banks

There are so many thousands of job sites, you could never hope to visit them all. Start by identifying which sites are relevant to your search.

1   Does the site have jobs that are suitable for you? If it doesn't, you can move on to the next site. If it does, you will want to keep an eye on the site for relevant jobs as they come in. This means you will want to register with the site and receive a job alert e-mail when new jobs matching your criteria get posted to the site.

2   When you are asked to define the jobs that interest you, set your sights wide. You may get too many responses initially, but can gradually narrow the parameters. It is better to plough through a little junk than miss a great opportunity.

3   If this is a good site for you, other sites it is linked to might also be useful; check the partners/links pages. These aren't always obvious, so, if not, look for a site map and in those little links that always crowd the very bottom of the page.

4   Because companies hire more people from smaller niche sites, you must check the specialty sites.

5   Before you file any job postings, go through them carefully looking for keywords that describe skills you have that are not depicted as such in your existing CV. List these on a desktop document and use this document to update your CV and to refresh it in the CV banks.

6   Make a folder for each relevant site you visit, and as postings come in store them in the appropriate folder. You'll quickly see which sites are most productive.

7 When you are asked to create a profile – and this is usually part of setting up your account on a site – you essentially copy and paste your CV as this represents your most carefully considered packaging of the professional you.

Most job sites are free, it's the employers who are paying to post their job openings and search the CV bank. The job sites work with employers to develop ever more efficient screening tools. Setting up your account and filling out a profile is part of this process.

CV banks

If suitable jobs are posted on the job site, it probably means that recruiters are also visiting its CV bank. In that case you may well want to upload your CV. Some considerations to bear in mind:

1 Use the same considerations and values for filling out dialogue boxes as you would on any job site registration.

2 CV banks have purge dates, mostly so that the recruiters who pay for access can be assured that they are not looking at stale CVs. The purge usually happens every 90 days, and you will want to bear the dates in mind so that you can refresh your CV before then.

3 Of course, recruiters also have the ability to restrict their searches by the date a CV was uploaded, so for example they might be able to restrict a search to CVs uploaded in the last 10 days. This is important when a particular site has job postings suitable for you, because it also means that recruiters will be cruising its CV bank for candidates.

4 To maintain the highest visibility on a site like this, go in once a week and update your CV with new keywords you have identified in other job postings. Make any change to your CV and the database search engine will recognize it as a new document.

5 When there are no new words you can achieve the same effect quite simply: log into your account, open up your CV, replace a couple of words with a string of Xs and log out.

Take a couple of deep breaths, log in again, and replace the Xs with the original words and log out again; to all intents and purposes you now have a brand-new document.

Finding more hidden jobs

Companies all use their websites as recruitment vehicles and usually have their vacancies posted there. Even if they do not appear to have an opening for someone like you, upload your CV anyway. You don't really know what is going on at that company, and at the very least you will be in their database and therefore on their radar when a need arises.

If a company is looking for anyone at all remotely connected with your area of professional expertise, they could also be looking for someone like you. Upload your CV and research the company to approach the appropriate managers directly.

You can also use company names in database searches on the social networking sites to find contacts for leads and introductions at these target companies. Everything in a successful job search is geared towards getting into conversation with people who could make the decision to hire you.

After visiting a company website, add the link to the appropriate folder in your database. When you visit job-sites, identify all the profession-specific employers, then visit each of those employer websites and add them to a potential employers' folder; your hit list of potential employers will grow exponentially.

Finding names for the direct approach

Responding to job postings is a big part of most job searches, but you can increase your chances of getting interviews from job postings by making direct approaches to the people in a position to hire you.

Whenever you see a suitable job, respond to the posting in the requested way. Also flag all contact information for the company, website and mailing address. As you discover the names and titles of managers you can approach them directly in three different ways:

- E-mail your CV directly to that manager with a personalized covering letter, at least doubling your chances of a hit.

- Send a CV and personalized covering letter to that manager, at least tripling your chances of a hit.

- Make a follow-up telephone call to that manager first thing in the morning, at lunchtime or at 5 pm, at least quadrupling your chances of a hit.

The more frequently you get into conversation with managers who have the authority to hire you, the faster you will land that new position because you have the attention of the actual decision maker to make a direct and personal pitch.

Your target for the direct approach is always someone who can hire you although any management title offers opportunity for referral. For example, while HR people won't have the authority to hire you, the pivotal nature of their work makes them aware of all areas within a company that could use your skills.

Getting the scoop on target companies

If you want to do a little research on the company to tweak your CV, personalize your covering letter, or to prepare for an interview, you can do this from your computer, too. Google News Search will search for press stories about the company, and in the process produce names of people within the company. An employer's own website is also a major source of information.

When you gather information about a company, create a company folder and paste the knowledge in; it will provide useful background information for interviews and show that you have done your homework. This is flattering to the interviewer: he or she sees it as demonstrating effort and enthusiasm, both of which can end up as being deciding factors in a tightly run job race.

Newspapers and magazines

Almost all recruitment has now moved to the internet, as have newspapers, so their role in your job search is not as it was in years gone by. However, there are still uses for a local or national newspaper in your job search campaign.

1 Companies that rely on the local community for both customers and employees still use the newspaper as a major recruitment vehicle.

2 The business news stories can tell you about company success stories, contracts signed, products and services introduced, and companies coming to town. They keep you informed and mention movers and shakers by name. Reminding that person of the article ('I saw you quoted in the *Argus* last week...') is flattering and will get you a few minutes of that person's time to make a pitch, get an interview or get some leads.

3 Industry overviews and market development pieces can tip you off to subtle shifts in your local professional marketplace.

There are still some great job leads in newspapers and magazines, and the fact that most people aren't using them as a job search resource is a good enough reason to at least check them out. A good place to start online is onlinenewspapers.com, which helps you identify and link to newspapers all over the world.

Employment agencies

There are essentially four categories: state employment agencies, private employment agencies and executive headhunters, temporary help organizations and career counsellors.

Jobcentres

These will make efforts to line you up with appropriate jobs and will send CVs on your behalf to interested employers who have jobs listed with them. It is not mandatory for employers to list jobs with these agencies, but more and more are taking advantage of these free services. Once the bastion of minimum-wage jobs, the choice is getting wider, so it's a resource not to be ignored.

If you are moving to another part of the country your local Jobcentre can see what jobs might be available there. The most effective way to use the service, though, is to visit your local office and ask for an introduction to the office in your destination area.

Private employment agencies

When working with an employment agency, choose your agent with care and attention. The calibre of the agency you choose could well affect the calibre of the company you ultimately join. Further, if you choose prudently, he or she can become a lifetime counsellor who can guide you step by step up the ladder of success.

There are different types of employment services:

- Permanent employment agencies where you pay the fee.

- Permanent agencies where the employer pays the fee.

- Contingency and retained search firms.

So what type of company is best for you?

Let's dispel one or two myths. A retained executive search firm is not necessarily any better or more professional than a contingency search firm, which in turn is not necessarily better or more professional than a regular employment agency. Your goal is to get representation by an exemplary outfit. Make the choice carefully, and having made the choice, stick with it and listen to the advice you are given.

Check on the date of the firm's establishment. If the company has been in town since you were in nappies, the chances are good that they are reputable.

A company's involvement in professional associations is always a good sign and involvement in independent or franchise networks can also be a powerful plus. These networks also have extensive training programmes that help to ensure a high-calibre consultant. Franchise offices can be especially helpful if you are looking to change jobs and move across the country (or further).

Experienced recruitment consultants can also be relied upon to have superior knowledge of the legalities and ethics of the recruitment process, along with the expertise and tricks of the trade that only come from years of hands-on experience. All of this can be put to work on your behalf.

Finally, don't get intimidated. Confirm who is paying the fee before you start. Remember you are not obliged to sign anything, and neither are you obliged to guarantee to an agency that you will remain in any employment for any specific length of time.

Executive recruitment

These people rarely deal with salary levels under £50,000 per year. All the advice I have given you about employment agencies applies here. They are going to be more interested in getting your CV for their database than in seeing you right then and there, unless you match a specific job they are trying to fill for a client. They are far more interested in the employed than in the unemployed, because an employed person is a more desirable commodity.

Executive recruiters are there to serve the client, not to find you a job. They neither want nor expect you to rely on them for employment counselling, unless they specifically request that you do – in which case you should listen closely.

Working with a headhunter

Mutually beneficial relationships can be developed with headhunters, after all, their livelihood depends on who they know. But do be circumspect.

Ascertain network and association membership and how this might help in your job search. Determine who pays the fee and whether any contracts will need to be exchanged. Define titles and the employment levels they represent, along with geographical areas. Know what you want, or ask for assistance in defining your parameters. This will include title, style of company, salary expectations, benefits and location.

Keep the recruiter informed about any and all changes in your status, such as salary increases, promotions, redundancies or other offers of employment.

Don't consider yourself an employment expert. You get a job for yourself every three or four years. These people do it for a living every day of every week. Ask for their objective input and seek their advice in developing interviewing strategies with their clients.

Temporary employment agencies

These provide employment services to companies in all industries and at most professional levels, from unskilled and semi-skilled to administration, finance, technical, sales and marketing professionals, doctors, lawyers and even interim executives.

Temporary employment services can be a useful resource if you are unemployed. You can get temporary assignments, maintain continuity of employment and skills, and perhaps enhance your marketability in the process.

If you are changing careers or returning to work after an absence, temporary assignments can help get new or rusty skills up to speed and provide you with a current work history in your field.

Working with a temp company can also get you exposure to employers in the community who, if you shine, could ask you to join the staff full time. This 'temp-to-perm' hiring approach is becoming increasingly popular with companies, as it allows them to try before they buy. You will also develop another group of networking contacts.

Here is some advice for working successfully with a temporary employment agency:

- Investigate the turnover of the temporary staff. If other temporaries have stayed with the company long term, chances are that company does a good job and has good clients.

- Select a handful of firms that work in your field; this will increase the odds of suitable assignments appearing quickly.

- Define the titles and the employment levels they represent, along with geographical areas they cover.

- Do not overstate your job duties, accomplishments or education.

- Find out first what the agency expects of you in the relationship, then explain what you expect. Reach commitments you both can live with, and stick to them.

- Judge the assignments not solely on the pay (although that can be important) but also on the long-term benefits that will accrue to your job search and career.

- Keep the agency informed about any and all changes in your status, such as offers of employment or acquisition of new skills.

- Resolve key issues ahead of time. Should an employer want to take you on full time, will that employer have to pay a set amount, or will you just stay on as a temporary for a specific period and then go on the employer's payroll?

Career counsellors

Career counsellors charge for their services. For this you get assistance in your career realignment or job search skill development. What you don't get is a guarantee of employment.

If you consider this route, speak to a number of counsellors and check multiple references for all of them.

When it comes to headhunters and career counsellors, good people come from many backgrounds. My personal choice for someone who can give you the best possible advice is the person who has both corporate HR experience *and* employment agency or retained search experience.

Job fairs

Job fairs (sometimes called career days) are occasions where companies get together to attract large numbers of potential employees to a one-day-only event.

Job fairs aren't regular events, so they won't be taking much of your time, but you should become an active participant when they do occur. They are always advertised in the local newspapers and frequently on local radio. Job fairs sometimes charge a small entrance fee, in return for which you get direct access to and time with all the employers and formal presentations by company representatives and local employment experts.

When you attend job fairs, go prepared with:

- Proper business attire. You may be meeting your new boss, and you don't want the first impression to be less than professional.

- Business cards. (If employed, remember to request the courtesy of confidentiality in calls to the workplace.)

- CVs – as many as there are exhibitors, times two. You'll need one to leave at the stand and an additional copy for anyone you have a meaningful conversation with.

- Notepad and pen, preferably in a folder.

It's easy to walk into a job fair and be drawn to just the biggest and most attractive stands, sponsored by the largest and most established companies. But remember that 90 per cent of jobs are generated by small companies of fewer than 500 employees. Go with specific objectives in mind:

- Talk to someone at every stand. You can walk up and ask questions about the company activities, and who they are looking for, before you talk about yourself. This allows you to present yourself in the most relevant light.

- Collect business cards from everyone you speak to so that you can follow up with a letter and a call when they are not so harried. Very few people actually get offered a post at job fairs; for most companies the exercise is one of collecting CVs so that meaningful meetings can take place in the ensuing weeks. But be 'on' at all times, because serious interviews do sometimes occur on the spot. If you have a background and CV that makes you a good match for a specific opportunity, then make a pitch, get the person's business card and fix a date for a follow-up call. If on the other hand there's a job you can do, but your CV needs some adaptation, you'll need a different approach. By all means talk to the company representative, but don't hand over a CV that will detract from your application (you can come up with a harmless pretext, such as having run out of copies). Instead get the contact's business card and promise to follow up with a CV, which you can then custom-fit to the opportunity.

- Collect company brochures and other materials.

- Arrange times and dates to follow up with as many employers as possible. 'Ms Jones, I realize you are very busy today, and I would like to speak to you further. Your company sounds very exciting. I should like to set up a time when we could meet to talk further or perhaps set a time to call you in the next few days.'

In addition to the exhibit hall, there are likely to be formal group presentations by employers. As all speakers love to get feedback, move in when the crush of presenter groupies has died down; you'll get more time and closer attention. You will also have additional knowledge of the company and the chance to spend a few minutes customizing the emphasis of your skills to meet the stated needs and interests of the employer in question.

On leaving each stand, and at the end of the day, go through your notes while everything is still fresh in your mind. Review each company and what possibilities it may hold for you. See what you might glean about industry needs, marketplace shifts and long-term staffing requirements. Make notes and determine that everyone you spoke to will receive an e-mail and a follow-up call within the next week.

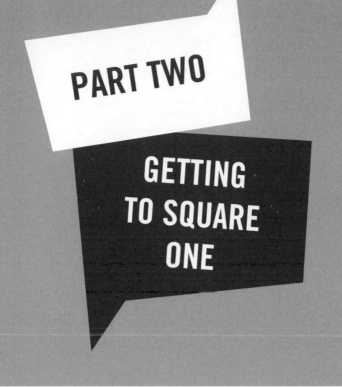

PART TWO

GETTING TO SQUARE ONE

You have to get the word out and make contact with employers to land job interviews, and you make the most contacts in the shortest time when you do it simultaneously with e-mail, mail and by picking up the telephone.

MAKING CONTACT

Every activity in your job search should focus on getting into conversations with the people who can hire you. The frequency of these conversations will determine the length of your job search.

E-mails and letters

How many e-mails should you send out every week is a difficult question to answer. You want to establish communication with every possible employer because this will create the maximum opportunity for you. Two contacts a week is the behaviour of the long-term unemployed.

On the other hand, mass e-mailing 700 companies with one CV isn't the answer either because you can't identify the right people to approach, personalize your pitches, or follow them up. Your campaign needs a strategy. Maintain a balance between the *number* of letters you send out on a weekly basis and the *types of people to whom they are sent*. The key is to organize and balance your job search activities so that you send as many CVs as possible directly to people by name in a volume that will allow you to make follow-up calls. Start out with modest goals. Try to send between two and ten e-mails per day addressed to someone by name and spread across each of the following areas:

- in response to internet job postings;
- to contacts in any of your professional networks;
- to contacts in any of your personal networks;
- to those you identify within target companies;
- to headhunters;
- to miscellaneous contacts.

Do you need to create and use more than one letter? Almost certainly, because you will be approaching different types of people for different reasons. However, there is no need to craft every written communication entirely from scratch. The key is to do each variation once and to do it right, then save copies of your letters and CVs to use as templates. This way you'll be ready regardless of when opportunity comes knocking on your door.

Multiple submissions

You will find it valuable to make a number of contacts within a company, especially the larger ones, to ensure all the important players know of your existence. Let's say you are a young engineer who wants to work for Last Chance Electronics. It is possible to post or e-mail covering letters and accompanying CVs to any, or all, of the following people, each ideally addressed to someone by name, so they have less likelihood of being lost: the managing director, the head of engineering, the chief engineer, the engineering manager, the head of human resources, the technical recruitment manager and the technical recruiter. You wouldn't necessarily send all these communications out at once but rather spread them out over a period of time.

Keep a log of your mail and e-mail contacts so you know when to follow up with a phone call, usually between three and seven working days later. Exclude Monday mornings from this count, as everyone is either in meetings or getting up to speed for the week.

You can comfortably resend mail to everyone on your list every couple of months if necessary. Most recipients won't register that they heard from you two months ago, and of those who do, most won't take offence. Any who do are people who have no need for your professional skill set and whom you are therefore unlikely to run into anytime soon.

An organized campaign will proceed on two fronts:

- **Front one:** A carefully targeted approach to a select group of companies. You will continue to add to this list as you unearth fresh opportunities in your day-to-day research. You may choose to hold back from contacting these special employers until comfortable with your developing job search skills – no point getting into a conversation with a dream employer until you know now to handle that conversation.

- **Front two:** A carpet-bombing approach to every possible employer in your target area.

In both these approaches you respond to job postings and upload your CV to their database in the standard way. Then, as your direct research and networking identifies specific individuals within these companies, begin e-mailing one or two contacts within the company. Repeat the mailings to other contacts when your initial follow-up calls result in referrals or dead ends. Remember, just because Harry in engineering says there are no openings in the company, that doesn't make it true. Any one of the additional contacts you make could well be the person *who knows the person* who is anxious to meet you.

Once your campaign is in motion and you begin to achieve interviews from your calls, your emphasis will change. You'll spend time preparing for interviews and following them up afterwards.

This is the point at which most job hunts stall. We get so excited about the interview that we convince ourselves 'this will be the offer' and job search activities slow to a halt. Here's an unsettling fact of life: the offer that can't fail usually does fail and you are left with no interview activity. You have to keep that job search pump primed with ongoing activity to generate interviews and to keep your morale up, too.

The more contacts you make through e-mail and regular mail, the more follow-up calls you can make to arrange interviews.

The more interviews you get, the more proficient you will become at them. The better you get at interviewing, the more offers you will get – and the *more* offers you get, the more choices you will have when making your decision.

Direct-marketing calls

At the same time you are e-mailing and posting CVs, pick up the phone and call people. This is the single most effective way of generating job interviews but many people are terrified of picking up the phone to call strangers.

So, I'm going to show you how to build simple, sophisticated and productive presentations, and how to navigate conversations, recognizing and responding to the 'buy signals' that denote interest, and how to overcome objections. The result will be job interviews and live leads for additional opportunities.

If you have a single goal when you pick up the phone – get an interview – you have only one chance of success, but many more for failure. If you have multiple goals for your call, you have multiple chances of success. When headhunters make calls, for example, they typically have these five basic goals in mind:

- I will arrange an interview date and time.

- If my contact is busy, I will arrange another time to talk.

- I will develop leads about promising job openings elsewhere in this and other companies.

- I will leave the door open to talk to this person again in the future.

- I will send a CV for subsequent follow-up.

Keep these goals in mind every time you talk to someone during your job hunt, because every conversation has the potential to turn into an interview or lead you towards one that will generate first a telephone interview then a face-to-face meeting.

You might worry about calling people directly because you are concerned that they will be annoyed at the intrusion. This is a misconception; the first job of any manager is to get work done through others, so every intelligent manager is always on the lookout for talent. If that isn't enough to allay your fears, keep in mind that the person on the other end of the line has more than likely been in your position and is sensitive to your situation. If you can be concise and professional, you'll find that the great majority of people you contact will try to be helpful.

Paint a word picture

The secret is being succinct. With a presentation that comes in at well under a minute, you can't be accused of wasting anybody's time. Your aim is to paint a representation of your skills with the widest appeal while keeping it brief out of courtesy and to avoid giving information that might rule you out.

You should never make these calls without taking the time to construct a written presentation. Doing so makes you capture the essence of the 'professional you'. Read your presentation word for word the first few times until you have the meat of it by heart and it sounds conversational and relaxed, then keep it to hand as a safety net.

Step 1

Give the employer a snapshot of who you are and what you do. The intention is to give that person a reason to stay on the phone. You may sometimes have an introduction from a colleague, in which case you will build a bridge with that: 'Miss Shepburn? Good morning, my name is Martin Yate and Greg Spencer suggested I called you...'

Or you may have got the name and contact information from, for example, a professional association directory, in which case you will use that as a bridge: 'Miss Shepburn? My name is Martin Yate. We haven't spoken before, but as we are both members of XYZ association, I hoped you might give me a couple of minutes of your time for some advice...'

Using your CV and TJD for guidance, outline your most desirable skills and illustrate with a couple of achievements, if appropriate. Say enough about yourself to whet the listener's appetite and ignite a desire to know more. For example, you might initially describe yourself as experienced, rather than identifying a specific number of years in your field. This encourages the listener to qualify your statement with a question: 'How much experience do you have?'

Step 2

This is where you colour in your word picture. Pull out a couple of key features from your CV and follow your introductory sentence with a small selection. Keep them brief and to the point, without embellishments. 'As a salesperson in my company, I increased sales in my territory by 15 per cent to over 1 million per annum. In the last six months, I won three major accounts from our competitors.'

Step 3

You have introduced yourself professionally and succinctly. Now get to the reason for your call and move the conversation forward: 'The reason I'm calling is that I'm looking for a new challenge and as I know a little about your company, I felt we might have some areas of common interest. Are these the sort of skills and accomplishments you look for in your salespeople?'

The entire presentation can be spoken aloud in well under a minute and finishes with a question that encourages a positive response. At this point the right question is not 'Can you employ me?' You're just looking for agreement about the desirability of your skills which opens up the possibility of a conversation.

Once you have made your presentation, there is likely to be a silence on the other end of the line. Be patient, as the employer may need a few seconds to digest your words. When they do respond, it will either be with a question, denoting interest or with an objection.

Questions and buy signals

When the silence is broken by a question, you breathe a sigh of relief because any question denotes interest: 'Do you have a degree?' 'Have you done this kind of work?' 'Have you done that kind of work?'

Conversation is a two-way street. Just as the employer's questions show interest in you, your questions show your interest in the work done at the company. By asking questions – usually tagged on to the end of one of your answers – you advance the conversation. Also, such questions help you find out what particular skills and qualities are important to the employer. This will increase your

knowledge and help you customize your answers. If you leave all
the interrogation to the employer, it will place you on the defensive,
and at the end of the talk you will be as ignorant of the real parameters of the job as you were at the start.

Joan Jones: 'Good morning, Mr Grant. My name is Joan Jones.
I am an office equipment salesperson with experience of selling
to large organizations, institutions and small business. As a
salesperson in my company, I increased sales in my territory
15 per cent, to over £1 million. In the last six months, I won
three major accounts from my competitors.

'The reason I'm calling, Mr Grant, is that I'm looking for
a new challenge, and as I know and respect your company,
I felt we might have areas for discussion. Are these the types
of skills and accomplishments you look for in your staff?'

[*Pause*]

Mr Grant: 'Yes, they are. What type of equipment have you been
selling?' [*Buy signal!*]

Joan Jones: 'A comprehensive range from furniture to office
machines and supplies; I sell according to my customers' needs.
I have been noticing a considerable interest in _____ recently.
Has that been your experience?'

Grant: 'Yes, it is, actually.' [*Useful information for you.*]
'Do you have a degree?' [*Buy signal!*]

Joan Jones: 'Yes, I do.' [*Just enough information to keep the
company representative chasing you.*] 'I understand your
company prefers salespeople with a degree to deal with its more
sophisticated clients.' [*Your research is paying off.*]

Grant: 'Our customer base is very sophisticated, and they expect
a certain professionalism and competence from us.' [*An inkling
of the kind of person the company wants to hire.*] 'How much
experience do you have?' [*Buy signal!*]

Joan Jones: 'Well, I've worked in both operations and sales, so
I understand both the sales and fulfilment process.' [*General but
thorough.*] 'How many years' experience are you looking for?'
[*Turning it around, but furthering the conversation.*]

Grant: 'Ideally, four or five for the position I have in mind.' [*More
good information.*] 'How many do you have?' [*Buy signal!*]

Joan Jones: 'I have two with this company, and one and a half before that, so that would meet your needs, wouldn't you agree?' [*How can Mr Grant say 'No' to Ms Jones?*]

Grant: 'What's your territory?' [*Buy signal!*]

Joan Jones: 'I cover the North West region. Mr Grant, it sounds as if we might have something to talk about.' [*Remember, your first goal is the face-to-face interview.*] 'I am planning to take personal time off next Thursday or Friday. Can we meet then?' [*Make Mr Grant decide which day he can see you, rather than whether he will see you at all.*] 'Which would be best for you?'

Grant: 'How about Friday morning? Can you bring a CV?'

Your questions show interest, carry the conversation forward and teach you more about the company's needs. By the end of the conversation you have an interview arranged, along with several key issues you should note down while they are fresh in your mind. You can then do further research into these areas of interest prior to the interview:

- The company sees growth in a particular area, so be sure you research what is going on in this area.

- They want both professional and personal sophistication.

- They ideally want four or five years' experience.

- They are interested in your contacts.

Let's look at the building blocks again before moving on to getting live leads from dead ends:

Step 1: Give the employer a succinct verbal snapshot of who you are and what you bring to the table (your performance profile).

Step 2: Finish your introduction off with an example of professional achievements.

Step 3: Move the conversation forward by explaining the reason for your call and finishing with a question that elicits a positive response.

At this point, the employer will respond with a question or an objection. If it's a question, it shows that the listener is interested. The following questions are among the buy signals that often come up.

'How much experience do you have?'

Too much or too little experience could easily rule you out. Be careful how you answer this question and try to gain time. It is a vague question, and you have a right to ask for qualifications. Employers typically define jobs by years' experience. At the same time there is a major move away from simple chronological experience, towards a more important concern about what you can deliver on the job. Managers and HR people are now more open to thinking in terms of 'performance requirements' and 'competencies' than ever before.

Here are a couple of ways to handle it:

> 'I have X years' experience, but if you could give me a brief outline of the performance requirements, I can give you a more accurate answer.'

> 'I have X years' experience, but they aren't necessarily typical. If you'd give me a few details of the performance requirements I'd be able to give you a more accurate answer.'

With more information you might be able to answer: 'I am comfortable with all aspects of the sales process, and have considerable experience of business-to-business sales including public instiutions and start-up companies.'

The employer's response, while gaining you time, tells you what it takes to do the job and therefore what aspects of your experience are most relevant. Take mental notes as the employer talks – you can even write them down, if you have time. Then give an appropriate response.

You can move the conversation forward by asking a follow-up question of your own. For example: 'The areas of expertise you require sound like a match to my experience, and it sounds as if you have some exciting projects at hand. What projects would I be involved with in the first few months?'

'Do you have a degree?'

If your degree matches the stated needs for the position, by all means go ahead and state it. If not, qualify your answer and point the way forward. For example: 'My education was cut short by the necessity of earning a living at an early age. However, I am currently enrolled in classes to complete my qualifications.'

'How much are you earning/do you want?'

This is a direct question looking for a direct answer, yet it is a knockout question. Earning either too little or too much could ruin your chances before you're given the opportunity to shine in person. There are a number of options that could serve you better than a direct answer. First, you must understand that questions about money at this point in the conversation are being used to screen you in or screen you out. The answers you give now should be geared towards getting you in the door and into a face-to-face meeting. Handling the serious salary negotiations attached to a job offer are covered in Chapter 21, 'Negotiating the offer', but for now, your main options are as follows:

- **Direct answer:** if you know the salary range for the position and there is a fit, give a straightforward answer.

- **Indirect answer:** 'Around 30 or 35 thousand.'

- **Put yourself above the money:** 'I'm looking for an opportunity that will give me the chance to make a difference with my efforts. If I am the right person for the job, I'm sure you'll make me a fair offer. By the way, what is the salary range for this position?'

- **Give a range:** come up with two figures – a fair offer considering your experience, and a great offer considering your experience: 'Hopefully between £X and £Y. What's most important is the opportunity to make a difference. If I am the right person for the job, I'm sure you'll make me a fair offer. By the way, what is the salary range for this position?'

When you give a salary range rather than a single figure, you have more flexibility and have a greater chance of 'clicking with' the employer's approved range for the position.

When you are pressed a second time for an exact figure, be as honest and forthright as circumstances permit. If you have the skills for the job and you are concerned that your current low salary will eliminate you before you have the chance to show your worth, you might add, 'I realize this is well below industry norms, but it does not reflect my expertise or experience in any way. It demonstrates the need for me to make a strategic career move, to where I can be compensated competitively based on my skills.'

If your current earnings are higher than the approved range, you could say, 'Mr Smith, my current employers feel I am well worth the money I earn due to my skills, dedication and honesty. Were we to meet, I'm sure I could demonstrate my value and my ability to contribute to your department. A meeting would provide an opportunity to make that evaluation, wouldn't it?'

How to deal with objections

By no means will every presentation you make be met with a few simple questions and then an invitation to an interview. Sometimes the silence will be broken by the employer with an objection. This usually comes in the form of a statement, not a question: 'Send me a CV', or 'I don't have time to see you', or 'You are earning too much', or 'You'll have to talk to Personnel', or 'I don't need anyone like you right now.'

These seem like brush-off lines, but they can sometimes be turned into interviews, and when that isn't possible they can almost always be turned into leads elsewhere.

Notice that all the following suggested response models end with a question, one that helps you learn more about the reason for the objection, perhaps to overcome it, and lead the conversation towards a meeting.

In dealing with objections, nothing is gained by confrontation, while much is gained by appreciation of the other's viewpoint. Consequently, most objections you hear are best handled by first demonstrating your understanding of the other's viewpoint. Start your responses with phrases like 'I understand', or 'I can appreciate your position', or 'I see your point' or 'Of course'. Follow up with statements like 'However...', or 'Also consider...', or a similar line that allows the opportunity for rebuttal and to gather further information.

It's not necessary to memorize these responses verbatim, only to understand the underlying concept and then put together a response in words that is sympathetic to your character and style of speech.

Objection: 'Why don't you send me a CV?'

The employer may be genuinely interested in seeing your CV as a first step in the interview cycle, or it may be a polite way of getting you off the phone. You should identify the real reason without causing antagonism, and at the same time open up the conversation. A good reply would be, 'Of course, Mr Grant. Would you give me your exact title and address? Thank you. So that I can be sure that my qualifications fit your needs, what skills are you looking for in this position?' or 'What specific job title should I refer to when I send it?'

Notice the steps:

- agreement with the prospective employer;
- a demonstration of understanding;
- a question to further the conversation (in this instance to confirm that an opening actually exists).

Answering in this fashion will open up the conversation.

Mr Grant will relay the aspects of the job that are important to him, and you can use the additional information to move the conversation forward again or to draw attention to your skills in:

- your executive briefing or covering letter;
- a customized CV;
- your face-to-face meeting.

Following Mr Grant's response, you can recap the match between his company's needs and your skills:

'Assuming my CV matches your needs, as I think we are both confident that it will, could we pencil in a date and time for an interview next week? I am available next Thursday and Friday; which would you prefer?'

A pencilled-in date and time for an interview very rarely gets cancelled because it isn't actually 'pencilled in' in this electronic age so is immediately allocated a time-slot in the schedule.

Objection: 'I don't have time to see you.'

If the employer is too busy to see you, it indicates that he or she has work pressures, and by recognizing that, you can show yourself as the one to alleviate some of those pressures through your problem-solving skills. You should avoid confrontation, however; it is important that you demonstrate empathy for the person with whom you are speaking. Agree, empathize and ask a question that moves the conversation forward:

> *'I understand how busy you must be; it sounds like a competent, dedicated and efficient professional [whatever your title is] could be of some assistance. Perhaps I could call you back at a better time to discuss how I might make a contribution to easing the pressure at peak times. When are you least busy, in the morning or afternoon?'*

The company representative will either make time to talk now or will arrange a better time for the two of you to talk further.

You could also try, 'Since you are so busy, what is the best time of day for you? First thing in the morning, or is the afternoon a quieter time?' Or you could suggest, 'If you would like to see my CV, you could study my background at your leisure. What's your e-mail address? Thanks, what would be a good time of day to call to follow this up?'

Objection: 'You are earning too much.'

Don't give up immediately; follow the process through: 'Oh, I'm sorry to hear that – what is the range for that position?' Depending on the degree of salary discrepancy you can reiterate your interest. You can also refer to Chapter 21, 'Negotiating the offer', where you will find further advice on dealing with this issue.

If the job really doesn't pay enough, and there will be openings for which you are earning too much, you've come (as they say) 'close, but no cigar!'

Objection: 'We only promote from within.'

Your response could be, 'I realize that, Mr Grant. Your development of employees is a major reason I want to get in! I am bright, conscientious and motivated. When you do hire from outside, and it must happen on occasion, what do you look for?' or 'How might I be considered for such opportunities?'

The response finishes with a question designed to carry the conversation forward and to give you a new opportunity to sell yourself. Notice that the response logically assumes that the company does hire from the outside, as all companies obviously do, even though Mr Grant has said otherwise.

Objection: 'You'll have to talk to human resources.'

In this case, you reply, 'Of course, Mr Grant. Whom should I speak to in HR, and what specific position should I mention?'

You cover a good deal of ground with that response. You establish whether there is a job there or whether you are being fobbed off to HR to waste their time and your own. You move the conversation forward again while modifying it to your advantage. Develop a specific job-related question to ask while the employer is answering the first question. It can open a fruitful line for you to pursue. If you receive a non-specific reply, probe a little deeper. A simple phrase like, 'That's interesting. Please tell me more' or 'Why's that?' will usually do the trick.

Or you can ask, 'When I speak to HR, will it be about a specific job you have, or is it to see whether I might fill a position elsewhere in the company?'

Armed with the resulting information, you can talk to HR about your conversation with Mr Grant. Remember to get the name of a specific person in HR with whom to speak, and to quote this prior contact by name in any e-mail or verbal contact:

> 'Good morning, Ms Johnson. Cary Grant, over in marketing, suggested we should speak to arrange an interview for the open Sales Associate position.'

This way you show HR that you are not a time waster, because you have already spoken to the person for whom the requisition is open. Don't look at the HR department as a roadblock. It may contain a host of opportunities for you. In many companies different departments could use your talents, and HR is probably the only department that knows all the openings. With larger companies you might be able to arrange interviews for three or four different positions!

Objection: 'I really wanted someone with a degree.'

You should have learned the proper response to 'Do you have a degree?' But in case you were abducted by aliens a few pages ago, you could respond by saying, 'Mr Smith, I appreciate your viewpoint.

It was necessary that I start earning a living early in life. If we meet, I am certain you would recognize the value of my additional practical experience.' If you have been smart enough to enrol in a course to pursue that always-important qualification, you should add, 'I am currently enrolled on courses to complete my degree, which should demonstrate my professional commitment, and perhaps that makes a difference?' In a world of ongoing education it usually will.

You might then ask what the company policy is for support and encouragement of employees continuing their education. Your response will end with, 'If we were to meet, I am certain you would recognize the value of my practical experience, in addition to my ongoing professional commitment. I am going to be in your area at the end of next week, and I know you will find taking the time to meet well spent. Is there a day and time that would be best for you?'

Objection: 'I don't need anyone like you now.'

Short of suggesting that the employer fires someone to make room for you (which, incidentally, has been done successfully on a few occasions), the chances of getting an interview with this company are slim. With the right question, however, your contact will give you a personal introduction to someone else who could use your talents.

You can ask, 'When do you anticipate new needs in your area?' or 'May I send you my CV and keep in touch for when the situation changes?' or 'Who else in the company might need someone with my background and skills?' or 'Can you think of anyone at other companies who might have a need for someone with my background?'

Live leads from dead ends

By no means will every employer you call have a job opening that fits your skills, but you can still turn calls that don't result in interviews into successes. If there isn't a need for someone like you right now you can ask:

- 'When do you anticipate new needs in your area?'
- 'May I send you my CV and keep in touch for when the situation changes?'

- 'Who else in the company might need someone with my background and skills?'

- 'What other companies might need someone with my background?'

- If the response is positive: 'Thanks, I appreciate the help. Do you know who I should speak to?'

- If the response to *that* is positive: 'May I mention your name?'

- Mentioning a company you plan to call: 'Do you know anyone I could speak to at _____?'

If you ask just this sequence of questions you will get leads and introductions, and this enables you to open that next call with: 'Hello, Mr Jones? My name is Martin Yate, Charles Harris gave me your name and said to say hello...'

By adding these questions and others in the same vein you will achieve a measure of success from the call, leaving you energized and with a feeling of achievement after every conversation.

Here are six categories of questions that can lead to job openings, interviews and offers. Read through them and then develop specific questions you can ask in each area:

1 Leads in the department.

2 Leads in the company.

3 Leads in other divisions of the company.

4 Leads to other companies.

5 Contacts in other companies.

6 Open door to keep in touch.

Remember: networking and marketing are continuous activities.

Voicemail

Voicemail is on the increase. Rather than treating it as a dead end, turn it into a useful means of getting through to your target contact.

When you have an introduction, you can use it to navigate voicemail systems and to leave as a teaser on your voicemail message:

'Good morning, my name is William Powell. Ms Loy suggested I give you a call. She thought we might have something to talk about. I'll try you later.'

Don't leave long messages; be brief and get on with your job search and make another call. In cases where you don't get a response and need to call back again, do so, but if the person doesn't pick up and you get routed to the voicemail again, hang up and move on to your next call. If you leave countless voicemail messages, it will make you look needy.

Dealing with abject terror

The adrenaline rush you experience when picking up the phone to make the first of these calls is something we associate with fear, and is normal for anyone engaged in a critical performance activity. It is a very natural reaction, but because you:

- know the product you are selling inside out;
- know (from your TJD exercises) exactly what you are going to say and how you are going to say it; and
- know it will have the greatest relevance and therefore interest to the listener,

you will be able to harness the adrenaline rush and channel it into peak performance.

Stacking the odds in your favour

These job search commandments will see you successfully through the job change and career transition process:

- Start conversations. Make every effort to get into conversations with decision makers with hiring authority and sooner or later you will get that job offer. To get into those critical conversations isn't easy; it might take you hundreds of contacts, but if you make the commitment every day of your job search, you will succeed.

- Work at getting a new job. Work at least 40 hours per week at it. Divide your time between contacting potential employers and generating new leads; the internet, networking and all the other job search tools will generate plenty of leads for you.

- Research the companies you contact. In a tightly run job race, the candidate who is most knowledgeable about the employer has a distinct advantage; again, the internet can be of immense help.

- Follow up the CVs you send out with phone calls. Resubmit your CV to identified openings after six or seven weeks. Change the format of your CV and resubmit yet again.

- Stay in telephone contact with your job leads on a regular basis to maintain awareness. If you find yourself needing to call existing contacts more than every couple of months, you should be putting more emphasis on building your networks and doing direct research.

- Develop examples of your professional profile that make you special – and rehearse building these examples into your interview responses.

- Send follow-up notes with relevant news cuttings, and so on to those in your networks; it's a light-touch way to help people keep you in mind.

- Work on your self-image. Use this time to get physically fit. The more you do today, the better you will feel about yourself.

- Maintain a professional demeanour during the working week (clothing, posture, personal hygiene).

- Use regular business hours for making contacts. Use the early morning, lunchtime, after 5 pm and Saturday for doing the ongoing research and writing projects to maintain momentum.

- We all have two specific skills: our professional/technical skills – say, computer programming; and our industry skills – banking, for example. Professional/technical skills can be transferable to other industries; and industry skills can open other opportunities in your industry. For example, that programmer, given decent communication skills, could become a technical trainer for programmers and/or technophobes.

- Don't feel guilty about taking time off from your job search. Just do it conscientiously. If you regularly spend Saturday morning in the library doing research, you can take Wednesday afternoon off to go to the cinema once in a while.

- Never stop the research and job-hunting process until you have a written job offer in hand and you have accepted that job in writing with an agreed-upon start date; even then, continue with any ongoing interviews.

- Remember: it's all up to you. There are many excuses not to make calls or send CVs. There are many excuses to get up later or knock off earlier. There are many excuses to back off because this one's in the bag. But there are no real *reasons*. There are no jobs out there for those who won't look, while there are plenty of opportunities for those who work at it.

The more you do today, the better you will feel about yourself.

Using a contact tracker

Keep records of your contacts. They will benefit not only this job search but also those in the future.

As you get your job hunt up to speed, the number of baited hooks you have in the water will grow dramatically. The CVs you send out will require follow-up calls, and the networking and research calls you make to potential employers will create the need to send out CVs, which in return will generate more follow-up calls.

Without tracking mechanisms in place this can quickly get out of hand.

You can create a contact tracker on a spreadsheet program, with columns for company name, telephone number, contact name, e-mail address; the date you sent a CV, and the date you should follow up with a call (or vice versa); and room for comments on the substance of conversations.

Follow-up: the key ingredient

An IT manager of my acquaintance once advertised for a programmer analyst. By Wednesday of the following week he had over 100 responses. Ten days later he was still ploughing through them when he received a follow-up call (the only one he received) from one of the respondents. The job hunter was in the office that afternoon, returned the following morning and was hired before lunchtime.

The moral of this story? The candidate's CV was languishing in the database, waiting to be discovered. The follow-up phone call got it discovered. The IT manager wanted to get on with his work, and the job hunter in question made it possible by putting himself on the employer's radar. Follow-up calls do work.

Stay the course

Make phone calls to initiate contact, and you'll get requests for CVs and requests to come for an interview. Make follow-up calls on mailed and e-mailed CVs and you will generate further interviews.

No one is ever hired without passing through one or a series of formal interviews, and that is where this book is headed next: how to turn interviews into job offers.

THE TELEPHONE INTERVIEW

Interviewers use the telephone to weed out applicants. Your goal is a face-to-face meeting, and here are the methods you must use to get it.

Some aspects of job hunting are not clear-cut. For instance, a telephone interview for a job might be arranged for a certain date and time, so you have plenty of time to prepare for it. Then again, a networking call can turn into a presentation in a flash when you realize that the person on the other end of the phone line is in a position to hire you. Likewise, when that presentation progresses past the initial 'buy signs' and objections, it can suddenly become a telephone interview. These things happen, but as you understand the steps to take in order to move each of these situations forward, you must be sensitive to the possibility that while telephone interviews can be scheduled in advance, they are just as likely to occur on the fly.

Employers use the telephone as a time management tool; it is easier to screen out candidates via the telephone than in person. Your goal is a face-to-face meeting, so all you must do is convince the employer that he or she will not be wasting time meeting you in person. Here are the techniques you should use to turn the telephone conversation into a face-to-face meeting.

Be ready for calls and telephone interviews

Your first substantive contact with a potential employer will often be by telephone.

It happens in one of three ways:

- You are making a marketing or networking call and the person you are calling goes into a screening process because you have aroused interest.

- An employer calls unexpectedly as a result of a CV you have sent.

- You have arranged a specific time for a telephone interview.

The odds are good that you will experience plenty of telephone interviews during your job search. Whichever activities generate a telephone interview, you must think and act clearly to turn the opportunity into the real thing – a face-to-face meeting. How you perform will determine whether you move ahead or bite the dust.

A few words about telephone services: call waiting might be nice to have for social use, but responding to its demands during a job hunt will only annoy the person you have on the line at the time. If you have call waiting, disconnect it or ignore it. More and more telephone companies are also offering additional lines with distinctive rings for your basic service at no extra charge. With this facility you can have a permanent job search/career management line, and keep a constant eye on the job market without compromising day-to-day home life.

Perhaps the most important consideration about telephone interviews is that the employer has only his ears with which to judge you. If the call comes unexpectedly, and screaming kids or barking dogs surround you, stay calm, sound positive, friendly and collected: 'Thank you for calling, Mr Wooster. Would you wait a moment while I close the door?' You can then easily take a minute to calm yourself, bring up the company website on your screen and get your paperwork organized without causing offence. If you need to move to another phone, say so; otherwise, put the caller on hold, take a few controlled, deep breaths to slow down your pounding heart, put a smile on your face (it improves the timbre of your voice) and pick up the phone again. Now you are in control of yourself and the situation.

If you are heading out of the door for an interview or some other emergency makes this a bad time for an unexpected call, say so straight away and rearrange: 'I'm heading out of the door for an appointment, Ms Bassett. Can we arrange a time when I will call you back?' Beware of overfamiliarity: you should always refer to the interviewer by his or her surname until invited to do otherwise.

Allow the person calling to guide the conversation and to ask most of the questions, but keep up your end of the conversation. This is especially important when the interviewer does not give you the openings you need to sell yourself. Always have a few intelligent questions prepared to save the situation. The following questions will give you an excellent idea of why the position is open, and exactly the kind of skilled professional the company will eventually hire:

- 'What are the major responsibilities of this job?'
- 'What will be the first project(s) I tackle?'
- 'What are the biggest challenges the department faces this year and what will be my role as a team member in tackling them?'
- 'Which projects will I be most involved with during the first six months?'
- 'Who succeeds in this job and why?'
- 'Who fails in this job and why?'

When you get a clear understanding of an employer's needs with questions like these, you can seize the opportunity to sell yourself appropriately: 'Would it be useful if I described my experience in the area of office management?' or 'Then my experience in word processing should be a great help to you' or 'I recently completed an accounting project just like that. Would it be relevant to discuss it?'

When you identify an employer's imminent challenges and demonstrate how your skills can lessen the load, you portray yourself as a properly focused employee with a problem-solving mentality and immediately move closer to a face-to-face interview. Everyone hires a problem-solver.

You can also keep up your end of the conversation by giving verbal signals that you are engaged with it; you do this with occasional short interjections that don't interrupt the employer's flow but let him know you are paying attention. Comments like 'uh-huh', 'that's interesting', 'yes', 'great' and 'I see' are verbal equivalents of the body language techniques you'll use to show interest during a face-to-face meeting.

Always speak directly into the telephone, with the mouthpiece about one inch from your mouth. Numbered among the mystical properties of telephone technology is its excellence at picking up and amplifying background noise. This is exceeded only by its power to transmit the sounds of food and gum being chewed, or smoke being inhaled and exhaled. Smokers take note: non-smokers naturally discriminate; they will assume that even if you don't actually light up at the interview, you'll have been chain-smoking beforehand and will carry the smell with you as long as you are around. They probably won't even give you a chance to get through the door once they hear you puffing away over the phone.

You should take notes when possible; they will be invaluable if the employer is interrupted. You can jot down the topic under discussion, then when he or she gets back on the line, you helpfully recap: 'We were just discussing...' This will be appreciated and show that you are organized and paying attention; your notes will also help you prepare for the face-to-face meeting.

The employer may talk about the company, and from your research or the website on your screen, you may also know something about them. A little flattery goes a long way: admire a company's achievements, when you can, and by inference you admire the interviewer. Likewise, if any areas of common interest arise, comment on them, and agree with the interviewer when reasonably possible – people usually hire people like themselves.

On the 200 telephone interviews a year that I average, I've found that standing for the interview calms the adrenaline a little, helps my breathing, and allows me to sound confident and relaxed. It might work for you too, so give it a try.

How to handle Skype interviews

Skype is the fastest, cheapest telecommunications service available, and it has the best voice quality. If you don't have a Skype account, set one up now, because the odds of someone wanting to interview over Skype increases daily.

The call can be a simple telephone call or it can be a video call. Recruiters usually want to do video, and this affects how you should dress when attending virtual job fairs.

As I write this, I've just returned from my morning bike ride. I wanted to get the words flowing immediately, so I haven't shaved yet and I'm wearing shorts and a T-shirt and generally look like I slept in a hedge. This doesn't affect my subject-matter expertise, but I certainly don't look like a career expert. It is fine for me to dress like that when I'm sitting alone typing on my Mac, but if I thought there was a possibility of a Skype interview in my day, I would dress and prepare my environment for it.

Skype video interviews

With a Skype video meeting, you simply download the software, open the icon on your desktop and call a number. You can also enable the video option as needed. If video is at all likely, you need to dress at least semi-professionally.

Your Skype set

If you are on video, it will be a head-and-shoulders close-up with the area behind you framing the shot. Think about where you will be doing the interview and what will be behind you; a plain blank wall is usually the best option.

Your Skype performance

When you talk to someone on Skype, you tend to look at the person onscreen and not the camera lens on top of your laptop or tablet. This is a mistake. From the other end of the line you are seen to be looking down and can appear to be avoiding eye contact – not the impression you want to create.

The camera lens is usually at the top centre of your laptop/tablet. This means the simple solution is to put your laptop on a pile of books so that the lens on your device is at about eye level and looking straight at your face. Train yourself to look into the lens, not at the interviewer's onscreen image. Imagine that the lens represents the interviewer's eyes. Look straight into it and smile as you talk, just as you would in normal conversation. What the interviewer will experience is a warm and confident candidate who isn't afraid to make eye contact. This may take some practice, but job searches are going to increasingly use Skype for screening interviews, so it's worth taking the time to get this right.

No matter how much practice you get, you'll still be drawn to look at the onscreen image of the interviewer, but at the very least be sure that you look into the lens of your machine when you:

- say hello;
- are being asked a question;
- ask a question;
- are making a critical point;
- are finishing an answer;
- make your closing statement about wanting the job;
- say goodbye.

You won't do this successfully without practice, so I strongly urge doing a few Skype video calls with friends to get a feeling for how you and others typically come across, and to practise looking into the lens rather than at your interviewer's image.

Answering questions

Beware of giving yes/no answers, as they give no real information about your abilities and do nothing to advance your agenda. At the same time, don't waffle; your answers need to be concise. Understanding someone over the telephone can sometimes be a challenge, so if you didn't hear or didn't understand a question, ask the speaker to repeat it. If you need time to think about your answer, say so: 'Let me think about that for a moment...'

Whenever possible, you should give real-world examples to illustrate your points: 'That's interesting. I was involved in an audit like that a couple months ago and it presented some interesting challenges.'

There are some 200 questions you are likely to be asked during an interview, which we'll cover in detail over the coming pages.

Meanwhile there are a handful of questions often asked during telephone interviews, in addition to the ones that come after you make a presentation. Let's look at them in light of your probable lack of information about the company and the job.

'What are you looking for?' With so little real knowledge about the company at this point, you need to be careful about specificity. Don't say, 'I want to move into marketing', unless you know such opportunity exists. Otherwise keep your answer general and focus on: (a) improving yourself professionally; and (b) becoming a productive member of a respected team.

'What are your strengths?' If you know about specific skill requirements, emphasize them; if not, stick to a brief outline of your key technical skills along with a selection of your transferable skills and the professional values that support them.

'What is your greatest weakness?' Don't throw the opportunity away before you even get in the door and have a real understanding of the job. We all face two professional challenges: keeping up with the pace of technological change; and meeting the ever-increasing demands for improved productivity. Mention a brand-new technology/skill you have just developed, and say you have been working on it and try to keep abreast of the latest approaches in all aspects of your profession.

'I don't think you'll be suitable because you lack ____ skill.' If the statement is true, acknowledge it, then follow with an example of a similar skill you picked up quickly and apply with consummate skill: 'Yes, I understand. When I joined my current company I knew nothing about ____, but I studied on my own and with the help of a mentor within the department I was up to speed in a matter of weeks. Given my proven ability to learn quickly and my willingness to invest my own time, would you consider talking to me in more detail about this topic when we meet face-to-face?' With this type of response you are putting a positive spin on your shortcoming, which gives you a good shot at overcoming the objection. If you are successful in arranging a face-to-face interview, you'll now have time to bone up on the subject and identify a sensible self-development programme before you meet the employer.

Under no circumstances, though, should you ask about salary, benefits or holidays; that comes much later. Your single objective at this point is to meet face-to-face; money is not an issue. If the interviewer asks direct questions about how much you currently earn, you can't get around it, so be honest. On the other hand, if you are asked how much you want, answer truthfully that at this point you don't know enough about the company or the job to answer that question.

The telephone interview has come to an end when you are asked whether you have any questions – perhaps, 'What would you like to know about us?' This is a wind-down question, so it is a good opening to get some specific questions of your own answered that can advance your candidacy:

- 'What are the most immediate challenges of the job?'

- 'What are the most important projects of the first six months?'

- 'What skills and behaviours are most important to success on the job?'

- 'Why do some people succeed and others fail doing this work?'

By discovering answers to these questions now, you will have time before the face-to-face meeting to package your skills according to the needs at hand and to create an appropriate executive briefing for distribution with your CV to the different interviewers you meet.

If you have not already asked or been invited to meet the interviewer, now is the time to take the initiative.

'It sounds like a very interesting opportunity, Ms Bassett, and a situation where I could definitely make a contribution. The most pressing question I have now is when can we get together?' When an invitation for an interview is extended, there are practical matters that you need to clarify with a handful of simple questions that address the when (date and time), and where (don't assume the interview will be at a place that you associate with the company). You will also want to inquire about the interview procedure:

- 'How many interviews typically occur before a decision is made?'

- 'Who else will be part of the selection process, and what are their roles within the department or company?'

- 'What is the time frame for filling this position and how many other people are being considered?'

Follow with a casual inquiry as to what direction the meeting will take. You might ask, 'Would you tell me some of the critical areas you will discuss on Thursday?' The knowledge gained will help you to package and present yourself, and it will allow you time to bone up on any weak or rusty areas. This is also a good time to establish how long the meeting is expected to last, which will give you some idea of how to pace yourself.

Once the details are confirmed, finish with this request: 'If I need any additional information before the interview, may I come back to you?' The interviewer will naturally agree. No matter how many questions you get answered in the initial conversation, there will always be something you forgot. This allows you to call again to satisfy any curiosity – it will also enable you to increase rapport. Don't take too much advantage of it, though: one well-placed phone call that contains two or three considered questions will be appreciated; four or five phone calls will not.

In closing your conversation, take care to ascertain the correct spelling and pronunciation of the interviewer's name. This shows your concern for the small but important things in life – and it will be noticed, particularly when the interviewer receives your follow-up thank-you note.

It is difficult to evaluate an opportunity properly over the telephone, so even if the job doesn't sound right, go to the interview; it will give you practice, and the job may look better when you have more facts. You might even discover a more suitable opening elsewhere within the organization.

8

DRESSING FOR INTERVIEW SUCCESS

Dress like a professional and you are likely to be treated as one, and that's a good head start before saying a word.

The moment we set eyes on someone, our minds make evaluations and judgements with lightning speed.

What you see is what you get!

Potential employers also make the same lightning-speed evaluations when you first meet at the beginning of a job interview. It's a fair estimate that nine out of 10 of today's employers will reject an unsuitably dressed applicant without a second thought.

The initial respect you receive at the interview is in direct proportion to the image you project. The correct professional appearance won't get you the job offer, but it will lend everything you say that much more credence and weight.

Employers rarely make overt statements about acceptable dress codes to their employees, much less to interviewees; more often there is an unspoken dictum that those who wish to climb the professional career ladder will dress appropriately and those who don't, won't.

There are some areas of employment where on-the-job dress (as opposed to interview dress) is somewhat less conservative than in the mainstream – fashion, entertainment and advertising are three examples. In these and a few other fields, there is a good deal of leeway with regard to personal expression in workplace attire, but for most of us, our jobs and our employers require a certain minimal level of professionalism in our dress. Interviewees must exceed these standards. That is not to say that you must dress like the Chairman of the Board (although that probably won't hurt), but you should be aware that dressing for the Friday night party (or even 'dress down Friday') on the day of your interview is not in your best professional interests. For the interview, it is generally accepted that you should dress one or two levels up from the job you are applying for, while remaining consistent with the type of occupation it is within.

Your interviewing advantage

Your appearance tells people how you feel about yourself as an applicant, as well as how you feel about the interviewer(s), the company and the process of interviewing itself. By dressing professionally, you tell people that you understand the niceties of corporate life and send a subtle 'reinforcing' message that you can, for example, be relied on to deal one-to-one with members of a company's prized client base.

How you dress sends signals about:

- How seriously you take the occasion, and, by extension, how much respect you feel for your interviewers and all others whom you meet at the interviews.

- How well you understand the confidence a look of traditional professionalism gives clients, customers, peers and superiors.

Yet no matter how important these concerns might be, they pale in comparison to the impact a sharp appearance can have on your own sense of self. When you know you have taken care of your appearance and that you look the best you can, you feel pride and confidence: your posture is better, you smile more and you feel more 'in control' of your destiny. In turn, others will respond positively to the image of professionalism and self-confidence that you present. Portraying the correct image at an interview will give you a real edge over your competition. You can expect what you say to be strongly influenced in the mind of your interviewer by the way you present yourself. Appearances count.

The look

The safest look for both men and women at interviews is traditional and conservative. Look at investing in a well-fitting, well-made suit as your first step to a successful new career. Up until recent years, this was fairly easy for men, as their professional fashions tended not to change much from year to year. These days, men's fashions are experiencing a metamorphosis, with high-fashion designers offering affordable lines of updated, yet professionally acceptable looks. However, a man can always interview with confidence and poise in his three-year-old good-quality suit, provided that it isn't worn to a shine.

For women, the matter is a little more complicated. Appropriate female attire for the interview should ideally reflect the current fashion if the applicant is to be taken seriously. Moreover, in selecting her current professional look the female applicant must walk a fine line, combining elements of both conformity (to show she belongs) and panache (to show a measure of individuality and style).

The key for both sexes is to dress for the position you want, not the one you have. This means that the upwardly mobile professional might need to invest in the clothes that project the desired image. The employee who dresses like one of the corporate walking wounded is unlikely to move upwards. Positions of responsibility are awarded to those who demonstrate that they are able to shoulder the burden. Looking capable will inspire others with the confidence to give you the most visible challenges.

The correct appearance alone probably won't get you a job offer, but it will go a long way towards winning attention and respect. When you know you look right, you can stop worrying about the impression your clothes are making and concentrate on communicating your message.

Every interview and every interviewer is different; because of this, it isn't possible to set down rigid guidelines for exactly what to wear in each situation. There is, however, broadly based counsel that will help you make the right decision for your interview.

As we have seen, much of what we believe about others is based on our perception of their appearance, and this chapter will help you ensure that you are perceived as practical, well-mannered, competent, ethical and professional.

General guidelines

The right look varies from industry to industry. The university professor can sport tweed jackets with elbow patches on the job, but is, nevertheless, likely to wear a suit to an interview. The advertising executive may wear wild ties as a badge of creativity (that is what he is being paid for), but he, too, is likely to dress more conservatively for an interview. In all instances, our clothes are sending a message about our image, and the image we want to convey is one of reliability, trustworthiness and attention to detail.

Most of us are far more adept at recognizing the dress mistakes of others than at spotting our own sartorial failings. When we do look for a second opinion, we often make the mistake of asking only a loved one. It's not that spouses, lovers and parents lack taste; these people are, however, more in tune with our positive qualities than the rest of the world and so, frequently, they do not recognize how essential it is to reflect those qualities in our dress. Better candidates for evaluation of your interview attire are trusted friends who have proved their objectivity in such matters or even a colleague at work.

Whenever possible, find out the dress code of the company you are visiting. For example, if you are an engineer applying for a job at a high-tech company, a blue three-piece suit might be overpowering. It is perfectly acceptable to ask someone in HR about the dress code (written or informal) of the company. You may even want to make an anonymous visit to get a sense of the corporate style of the company. In the above example, you might be perfectly comfortable showing up *for work* in a jacket or blazer; nevertheless, you are advised to wear a suit for at least the first interview.

You may simply decide to change your look somewhat after learning that there is a more informal atmosphere with regard to dress at the firm you visit. If you are told that everyone works in shirt-sleeves and that there is never a tie in sight, a prudent and completely acceptable approach is to opt for your less formal suit, rather than dark blues, greys or pinstripes.

9

BODY LANGUAGE

**Learn to control negative body movements
and encourage positive ones. Discover the seven
guidelines for good body language during your interview.**

As human beings we rely to a remarkable degree on our ability to gather information visually. This really is not all that surprising, because while speech is a comparatively recent development, humans have been sending and receiving non-verbal signals since the dawn of the species.

In fact, the language of the body is the first means of communication we develop after birth. We master the spoken word later in life, and in so doing we forget the importance of non-verbal cues – but the signals are still sent and received (usually at a subconscious level).

It is common to hear people say of the body language they use, 'Take me or leave me as I am.' This is all very well if you have no concern for what others think of you. For those seeking professional employment, however, it is important to recognize that your body is constantly sending messages, and to make every effort to understand and control the information stream. If your mouth says, 'Employ me', but your body says, 'I'm not being truthful', you are likely to leave the interviewer confused. 'Well', he or she will think, 'the right answers all came out, but there was something about that candidate that just rubbed me up the wrong way.' Such misgivings are generally sufficient to keep a candidate from making the shortlist. The interviewer may or may not be aware of what causes the concern, but the messages will be sent and your cause will suffer.

Of course, interviewers can be expected to listen carefully to what you say, too. When your body language complements your verbal statements, your message will gain a great deal of impact, but when your body language *contradicts* what you say, the interviewer will be sceptical. In short, learning to use positive body signals and control negative ones during an interview can have a significant impact on your job hunt and on the new job.

Under the microscope

The challenge for the interviewer is to determine, using every means at his or her disposal, what kind of an employee you would make. Your task as a candidate is to provide the clues most likely to prompt a decision to hire you.

Let's begin at the beginning. When you are invited in to an interview, you are probably safe in assuming that your interviewer believes you meet certain minimum standards and could conceivably be hired.

In this context, the adage that actions speak louder than words appears to be something you should take quite literally. Studies done at the University of Chicago found that over 50 per cent of all effective communication relies on body language. Since you can expect interviewers to respond to the body language you employ at the interview, it is up to you to decide what messages you want them to receive.

There are also studies that suggest the impression you create in the first few minutes of the interview is the most lasting. Since the interviewer is doing most of the talking in the first few minutes of the interview, you have very little control over the impression you create with your words – you can't say much of anything! It is up to your body to do the job for you.

The greeting

For a good handshake:

1 Your hands should be clean and adequately manicured.

2 Your hands should be free of perspiration.

It is best to allow the interviewer to initiate the handshake. If, through nerves, you find yourself initiating the handshake, don't pull back, as you will appear indecisive. Instead, make the best of it, smile confidently and make good eye contact.

Your handshake should signal cooperation and friendliness. Match the pressure extended by the interviewer – never exceed it. A typical professional handshake lasts for between two and five seconds, just two or three reasonably firm up and down pumps accompanied by a smile. The parting handshake may last a little longer; smile and lean forward very slightly as you shake hands before departing.

Certain professional and cultural differences should also be considered as well. Many doctors, artists and others who do delicate work with their hands can and do give less enthusiastic handshakes than other people. If you work in media you'll notice that quite frequently on-air personalities don't want to shake hands at all; it's the easiest way to catch a cold and they depend on their voices and appearance more than most. Similarly, the English handshake is considerably less firm than the American, while the German variety is typically firm.

Use only one hand and always shake vertically. Do not extend your hand parallel to the floor with the palm up, as this conveys submissiveness. By the same token, you may be seen as too aggressive if you extend your hand outward with the palm facing down.

While a confident and positive handshake helps break the ice and gets the interview moving in the right direction, proper use of the hands throughout the rest of the interview will help convey an above-board, 'nothing-to-hide' message.

Watch out for hands and fingers that take on a life of their own, fidgeting with themselves or other objects such as pens, paper, your tie or your hair. Pen tapping is interpreted as the action of an impatient person; this is an example of an otherwise trivial habit that can take on immense significance in an interview situation. Rarely will an interviewer ask you to stop doing something annoying; instead, he or she will simply make a mental note that you are an annoying person, and congratulate themself for picking this up before making the mistake of employing you.

Other negative hand messages include:

- Clasping your hands behind your head: you'll expose perspiration marks, and you run the risk of appearing smug, superior, bored and possibly withdrawn.

- Showing insecurity by constantly adjusting your tie: when interviewing with a woman, this gesture might be interpreted as displaying something beyond a businesslike interest in the interviewer.

- Slouching in your chair, with hands in pockets or thumbs in belt: this posture can brand you as insolent and aggressive (just recall any teenage boy). When this error is made in the presence of an interviewer of the opposite sex, it can carry sexually aggressive overtones as well.

- Pulling your collar away from your neck: this may seem like an innocent enough reaction to the heat of the day, but the interviewer might assume that you are tense and/or masking an untruth. The same goes for scratching your neck during, before or after your response to a question.

- Moving your hands towards a personal feature that you perceive as deficient: this is a common unconscious reaction to stress. A man with thinning hair, for example, may thoughtlessly put his hand to his forehead when pondering how to respond to the query, 'Why aren't you earning more at your age?' This habit may be extremely difficult for you to detect in the first place, much less reverse, but make the effort. Such protective movements are likely to be perceived – if only on a subliminal level – as acknowledgements of low self-esteem.

- Picking at invisible bits of fluff on one's suit: this gesture looks exactly like what it is, a nervous tic. Keep your focus on the interviewer. If you do have some bit of lint somewhere on your clothing, the best advice is usually to ignore it until you can remove it discreetly.

By contrast, employing the hands in a positive way can further your cause:

- Subtly exposing your palms now and then as you speak can help demonstrate that you are open, friendly and have nothing to hide. You can see this technique used to great effect by politicians and television talk show hosts.

- It can, very occasionally, be beneficial to 'steeple' your fingers for a few seconds as you consider a question or when you first start to talk. Unless you hold the gesture for long periods of time, it will be perceived as a neutral demonstration of your thoughtfulness. Of course, if you overuse this or hold the position for too long, you may be taken as condescending. Steepling also gives you something constructive to do with your hands; it offers a change from holding your pad and pen.

Taking your seat

Some thirty inches from my nose
The frontier of my person goes.
Beware of rudely crossing it,
I have no gun, but I can spit.

W H Auden

Encroaching on another's 'personal space' is a bad idea in any business situation, but it is particularly dangerous in an interview. The 30 inch (75 cm) standard is a good one to follow: it is the distance that allows you to extend your hand comfortably for a handshake. Maintain this distance throughout the interview, and be particularly watchful of personal-space intrusions when you first meet, greet and take a seat.

A person's office is an extension of sorts of his or her personal space; this is why it is not only polite but also sound business sense to wait until the interviewer offers you a seat.

It is not uncommon to meet an interviewer in a conference room or other supposedly 'neutral' site. Again, wait for the interviewer to motion you to a spot, or, if you feel uncomfortable doing this, tactfully ask the interviewer to take the initiative: 'Where would you like me to sit?'

The type of chair you sit in can affect the signals you send with your body during an interview. If you have a choice, go with an upright chair with arms. Deep armchairs can restrict your ability to send certain positive signals, and encourage the likelihood of slumping. They're best suited for watching television, not for projecting the image of a competent professional.

Always sit with your bottom well back in the chair and your back straight. Slouching, of course, is out, but a slight forward-leaning posture will show interest and friendliness towards the interviewer. Keep your hands on the sides of the chair; if there are no arms on the chair, keep your hands in your lap or on your pad of paper.

Crossed legs, in all their many forms, send a mixture of signals; most of them are negative:

- Crossing one ankle over the other knee can show a certain stubborn and recalcitrant outlook (as well as the bottom of your shoe, which is not always a pretty sight). The negative signal is intensified when you grasp the horizontally crossed leg or – worst of all – cross your arms across your chest.

- Some body language experts feel crossed ankles indicate that the person doing the crossing is withholding information. Of course, since the majority of interviews take place across a desk, crossed ankles will often be virtually unnoticeable. This body signal is probably the most permissible body-language faux pas; if you must allow yourself one body language vice, this is the one to choose.

- When sitting in armchairs or on sofas, crossing the legs may be necessary to create some stability. In this instance, the signals you send by crossing your legs will be neutral, as long as your crossed legs point towards, rather than away from, the interviewer.

Facial signals

Once you take your seat, and the conversation begins, the interviewer's attention will be focused on your face.

Our language is full of phrases testifying to the powerful influence of facial expressions. When you say that someone is shifty-eyed, is tight-lipped, has a furrowed brow, flashes bedroom eyes, stares into space or grins like a Cheshire cat, you are speaking in a kind of shorthand and using a set of stereotypes that enables us to make judgements – consciously or unconsciously – about that person.

Tight smiles and tension in the facial muscles often demonstrate an inability to handle stress; little eye contact can communicate a desire to hide something; pursed lips are often associated with a secretive nature; and frowning, looking sideways, or peering over one's glasses can send signals of haughtiness and arrogance. Hardly the stuff of which winning interviews are made!

The eyes

Looking at someone means showing interest in that person, and showing interest is a giant step forward in making the right impression. Remember: we are all our own favourite subject!

Looking away from the interviewer for long periods while he or she is talking, closing your eyes while being addressed and repeatedly shifting focus from the subject to some other point are all likely to leave the wrong impression.

There is a difference between looking and staring at someone. Rather than looking at the speaker straight on at all times, create a mental triangle incorporating both eyes and the mouth; your eyes will follow a natural, continuous path along the three points. Maintain this approach for roughly three-quarters of the time; you can break your gaze to look at the interviewer's hands as points are emphasized or to refer to your notebook. This is the way we maintain eye contact in non-stressful situations, and it will allow you to appear attentive, sincere and committed.

Be wary of breaking eye contact too abruptly and of shifting your focus in ways that will disrupt the atmosphere of professionalism. Examining the interviewer below the head and shoulders, for instance, is a sign of overfamiliarity. This is especially important when being interviewed by someone of the opposite sex.

The eyebrows send messages as well. Under stress, one's brows may wrinkle; this sends a negative signal about your ability to handle challenges in the business world. The best thing to do is take a deep breath and collect yourself. Most of the tension that people feel at interviews has to do with anxiety about how to respond to what the interviewer will ask.

The head

Nodding your head slowly shows interest, validates the comments of your interviewer and subtly encourages him or her to continue. Tilting the head slightly, when combined with eye contact and a natural smile, demonstrates friendliness and approachability. The tilt should be momentary and not exaggerated, almost like a bob of the head to one side. (Do not overuse this technique unless you are applying for a job in a parrot shop!) Rapidly nodding your head can leave the impression that you are impatient and eager to add something to the conversation – if only the interviewer would let you.

The mouth

One guiding principle of good body language is to turn upward rather than downward. Look at two boxers after a fight: the victor's arms are raised high, his back is straight and his shoulders are square. His smiling face is thrust upward and outward, and you see happiness, openness, warmth and confidence. The loser, on the other hand, is slumped forward, brows knit and eyes downcast, and the signals you receive are those of anger, frustration, belligerence and defeat.

Your smile is one of the most powerful positive body signals in your arsenal and it exemplifies the up-is-best principle. Offer an unforced, confident smile as frequently as opportunity and circumstances dictate; *avoid* grinning idiotically, as this indicates that you may not be quite right in the head.

You should be aware that the mouth also provides a seemingly limitless supply of opportunities to convey weakness. This may be done by touching the mouth frequently; 'faking' a cough when confronted with a difficult question; or gnawing on one's lips absentmindedly. Employing any of these 'insincerity signs' when you are asked about, say, why you lost your last job, might instil or confirm suspicions about your honesty or openness.

Glasses

People who wear glasses sometimes leave them off when going on an interview in an attempt to project a more favourable image. There are difficulties with this approach. Long-sighted people who don't wear their glasses will (unwittingly) seem to stare long and hard at the people they converse with, and this is a negative signal. Also, pulling out glasses for reading and peering over the top of your glasses – even if you have been handed something to read and subsequently asked a question – carries professorial connotations that can be interpreted as critical. If you wear glasses for reading, you should remove them when conversing, replacing them only when appropriate.

Wearing dark glasses to an interview will paint you as secretive, cold and devious. Even if your prescription glasses are tinted, the effect will be the same. You might consider untinted glasses for your interview, or contact lenses. At the same time, glasses on a younger-looking person can add an air of seriousness and might be considered a plus.

Body signal barricades

Folding or crossing your arms, or holding things in front of the body, sends negative messages to the interviewer: 'I know you're there, but you can't come in. I'm nervous and closed for business.'

It is bad enough to feel this way, but worse to express it with blatant signals. Don't fold your arms or 'protect' your chest with hands, clipboard, briefcase or anything else during the interview. You can, however, keep a notebook and pen on your lap. It makes you look organized and gives you something to do with your hands. Holding a pad and pen and keeping your arms on the arms of the chair will also help you to avoid slouching. Remember to show one or both of your palms occasionally as you make points, but do not overuse this gesture.

Feet

Some foot signals can have negative connotations. Women and men wearing slip-on shoes should beware of dangling the loose shoe from the toes; this can be distracting, and, as it is a gesture often used to signal physical attraction, it has no place in a job interview. Likewise, avoid compulsive jabbing of floor, desk or chair with your foot; this can be perceived as a hostile and angry motion, and is likely to annoy the interviewer.

Some people (your author included) have an annoying habit of jiggling one leg up and down on the ball of the foot. Those of us who do this know it is a tic that says we are totally engaged and excited about some topic (and sometimes even the one under discussion), but those forced to endure it find it distracting and can interpret it as impatience. If you are a dreaded jiggler, you must get this under control for your job interviews!

Walking

Many interviews will require that you walk from one place to the next – on a guided tour or from one office to another. How long these walks last is not as important as how you use them to reinforce positive professional behaviours and impressions.

Posture is your main concern: keep your shoulders back and maintain an erect posture. Smile and make eye contact as appropriate. Avoid fidgeting with your feet as you move, rubbing one shoe against the other or kicking absentmindedly at the ground if you stop to talk; these signals will lead others to believe that you are anxious or insecure. Crossing your arms or legs while standing carries the same negative connotations as it does when you are sitting. Hands-in-pockets, hands-on-hips or thumbs-in-belt postures are all to be avoided. These send messages that you are aggressive and dominating.

Putting it all together

Now you have the big picture, and you can begin to be more aware of the signals your body can unwittingly send. Let's reduce all this information into a handful of simple recommendations. Positive signals reinforce one another; employing them in combination yields an overwhelmingly positive message that is truly greater than the sum of its parts.

So far you have focused primarily on the pitfalls to avoid; but what messages *should* be sent, and how? Here are seven general suggestions on good body language for the interview:

1 Walk slowly, and stand tall upon entering the room.

2 On greeting your interviewer, give a smile, make eye contact and respond warmly to the interviewer's greeting and handshake.

3 Sit well back in the chair; this allows the chair back to help you sit upright. Increase the impression of openness ('I have nothing to hide!') by unbuttoning your jacket as you sit down. Keep your head up. Maintain eye contact a good portion of the time, especially when the interviewer begins to speak and when you reply. Smile naturally whenever the opportunity arises.

4 Use mirroring techniques to reproduce the positive signals your interviewer sends. Say the interviewer leans forward to make a point; a few moments later, you too lean forward slightly, demonstrating that you don't want to miss a word. Perhaps the interviewer leans back and laughs; you 'laugh beneath' the interviewer's laughter, taking care not to overwhelm your partner by using an inappropriate volume level. This can seem contrived at first, but through observing

those in your own social circle, you'll notice that this is natural behaviour for good communicators.

5 Keep your head up and don't slouch in your seat.

6 Try to remain calm and do not hurry your movements; you'll look harried and are more likely to knock things over. Most people are more clumsy when they are nervous, and consciously slowing your body movements will lessen the chances of disaster and give you a more controlled persona.

7 Remember to breathe. When we are nervous we can forget to do this, which leads to oxygen deprivation and obviously affects your cognitive processes.

Open for business

The more open your body movements during the interview, the more you will be perceived as being open yourself. Understanding and directing your body language will give you added power to turn interviews into cooperative exchanges between two professionals.

Just as you interpret the body language of others, both positive and negative, your body language makes an indelible impression on those you meet. It tells them whether you like and have confidence in yourself, whether or not you are pleasant to be around and whether you are more likely to be honest or deceitful. Like it or not, your body carries these messages for the world to see.

Job interviews are reliable in one way: they bring out insecurities. All the more reason to consciously manage the impressions your body sends. You will absorb the lessons in this chapter quite quickly if you take the time to observe and interpret the body signals of friends and family. When you see and can understand body language in others, you'll be more aware of your own, and more capable of controlling it.

THE CURTAIN GOES UP ON THE JOB INTERVIEW

**First impressions are the strongest.
Here are the preparations to make before
heading out to the interview.**

Backstage in the theatre, the announcement 'Places, please' is made five minutes before the curtain goes up. It's the performers' signal to psych themselves up, complete final costume adjustments and reach the stage in time. They are getting ready to go onstage and knock 'em dead. You should go through a similar process to get thoroughly prepared for your time in the spotlight.

Winning a job offer depends not only on the things you do well but also on the mistakes you avoid. As the interview approaches, settle down with your CV and immerse yourself in your past successes and the transferable skills and professional values that made them possible. Interview nerves are to be expected; the trick is to use them to your benefit by harnessing that nervous energy to your physical and mental preparation.

Here's what you should bring with you:

- The company dossier. Always take a few copies of your CV and executive briefing that clearly defines how you match the job's requirements: one for you and the others for the interviewers you might meet. Your main interviewer will invariably have a copy of your CV, but you can't be certain of that with other people you meet. It is perfectly acceptable to have your CV in front of you at the interview; it shows you are organized, and it will remind you of essential facts. It is not unusual to hear, 'Mr Jones wasn't hired because he didn't pay attention to detail and couldn't even remember his employment dates' – just the kind of thing you are likely to forget in the nervousness of the moment.

- A decent folder with a pad of paper and writing instruments. They demonstrate your preparedness, and they give you something constructive to do with your hands during the interview. You can keep your CV in the folder.

- A list of job-related questions. Ask questions that give you practical details of the activities you will be involved with in the first few months. You might ask:
  - 'What are the most immediate challenges of the job?'
  - 'What are the most important projects of the first six months?'
  - 'What skills and behaviours are most important to success in the job?'
  - 'Why do some people succeed and others fail doing this work?'
  - 'Why is the position open?'
  - 'What is the job's relationship to other departments?'
  - 'How do the job and the department relate to the company?'

You can find more questions to ask at the end of Chapter 13, 'How to knock 'em dead'.

Note: In the early rounds of interviewing stay away from questions about where the job can lead and what the pay and benefits are. It's not that these questions aren't important to you; it is just that the timing is wrong. It won't do you any good to know what a job pays when you aren't going to get a job offer. Instead, ask the questions that will lead to a job offer being extended, then ask the questions you need to evaluate it. For questions to ask during the negotiation phase, see Chapter 21, 'Negotiating the offer'.

- Any additional information you have about the company or the job. If time permits, visit the company website, review any company literature you might have, and do an online search for news articles mentioning the company by name, and for articles that relate to your profession.

- Directions to the interview. Decide on your form of transport and finalize your time of departure, leaving enough time to accommodate travel delays. Check the route, distance and travel time. If you forget to verify date, time and place (including floor and room number), you might not even arrive at the right place, or on the right day, for your interview. Write it all down legibly and put it with the rest of your interview kit.

To arrive at an interview too early indicates overanxiousness and to arrive late is inconsiderate, so arrive at the interview on time, but at the location early. This allows you time to visit the restroom (usually your only private sanctuary at an interview) and make the necessary adjustments to your appearance, to review any notes and to put on your 'professional face'. Remember to add contact telephone numbers to your interview kit, so if you are delayed on the way to the interview, you can call and let the interviewer know.

- Dress conservatively. As you could be asked to appear for an interview at a scant couple of hours' notice, keep your best outfit freshly cleaned, your shirts or blouses wrinkle-free, and your shoes polished, and reserve them exclusively for interviews.

- Visit the hairdresser once a month, so you always look groomed, and keep your nails clean and trimmed at all times, even if you work with your hands.

- While you will naturally shower or bath prior to an interview, and the use of an unscented deodorant is advisable, you should avoid wearing aftershave or perfume; you are trying to get a job, not a date. Never drink alcohol the day before an interview. It affects eyes, skin tone and your wits.

When you get to the interview site, visit your private sanctuary to check your appearance and take a couple of minutes to do the following:

- Review the company dossier.

- Recall your commitment to the profession and the team, and the professional behaviours that help you succeed.

- Breathe deeply and slowly for a minute to dispel your natural physical tension.

- Review the questions you will need to identify first projects and initial needs.

- Turn off your mobile. If for any reason you forget and it does ring, just apologize and turn it off. Never answer a personal call during an interview.

- Smile and head for the interview – you are as ready as you are ever going to be.

Under no circumstances should you back out because you do not like the receptionist or the look of the office – that would be allowing those interview nerves to get the better of you. You are here to improve one of your most critical professional skills – turning interviews into job offers. Whatever happens, you can and must learn from this experience.

As you are shown into the office, you are on!

Do:

- Give a firm handshake – respond to the interviewer's grip and duration.

- Make eye contact and smile. Say, 'Hello, Ms Larsen. I am John Jones. I have been looking forward to meeting you.'

Do not:

- Use first names (unless asked).

- Smoke (even if invited).

- Sit down (until invited).

- Show anxiety or boredom.

- Look at your watch.

- Discuss equal rights, sex, race, national origin, religion or age.

- Show samples of your work (unless requested).

- Ask about benefits, salary or holiday.

Now you are ready for anything – except for the tough questions that are going to be thrown at you next. We'll handle those in the following pages.

PART THREE

GREAT ANSWERS TO TOUGH INTERVIEW QUESTIONS

In this part of the book you will learn why interviewers do the things they do. You'll also learn the formulas for answering tough interview questions in ways that are honest, unique to you, and which advance your application without making you sound like a con-artist. Along the way you will also learn some useful strategies to make a greater success of your career.

'Like being on trial for your life' is how many people look at a job interview. With the interviewer as judge and jury, you are at least on trial for your livelihood, so you must have winning strategies. F. Lee Bailey, one of the United States' most celebrated defence attorneys, attributes his success in the courtroom to preparation. He likens himself to a magician going into court with 50 rabbits in his hat, not knowing which one he'll really need, but ready to pull out any single one. Bailey is successful because he is ready for any eventuality and because he takes the time to analyse every situation and every possible option. He never underestimates his opposition, he is always prepared, and he usually wins.

Another famous attorney, Louis Nizer, successfully defended all of his 50-plus capital offence clients. When lauded as the greatest courtroom performer of his day, Nizer denied the accolade. He claimed for himself the distinction of being the best prepared.

You won't win your day in court just based on your skills. As competition for the best jobs increases, employers are comparing more candidates for every opening and becoming more skilled in the art of selection. To win against stiff competition, you have to be prepared for the questions that can be thrown at you, and that requires understanding what is behind them.

During an interview, employers ask you dozens of searching questions – questions that test your knowledge, skills, confidence, poise, and professional behaviours (we'll address this in some detail in a few pages). There are questions that can trick you into contradicting yourself and questions that probe your analytical skills and integrity. They are all designed so the interviewer can make decisions in these critical areas:

- Can you do the job?
- Are you motivated to take the extra step?
- Are you manageable and a team player?
- Are you professional in all your behaviours?
- Are you a problem solver?

Being able to do the job is only a small part of getting an offer. Whether you are motivated to make an extra effort, and whether you are manageable and team player, and whether you think of yourself as a problem identifier and problem solver are just as important to the interviewer. In this era of high unemployment and deep specialization, companies look more actively at the way you behave in the workplace and your professional behavioural profile. Specific desirable professional behaviours cannot be ascertained by a single question or answer, so the interviewer will seek a pattern in your replies that shows your possession of such behaviours – I discuss them in detail in Chapter 14, 'Questions of manageability and team spirit'.

You not only have to make a case for yourself in these five areas, you need to avoid these deadly traps that can damage your application:

- Failing to listen to the question.
- Answering a question that was not asked.

- Providing superfluous, inappropriate or irrelevant information.

- Being unprepared for the interview.

The effect of these blunders is cumulative, and each reduces your chance of receiving a job offer.

The number of offers you win in your search for the ideal job depends on your ability to answer a staggering array of questions in terms that have value and relevance to the employer: 'Why do you want to work here?', 'What are your greatest accomplishments?', 'How long will it take you to make a contribution?', 'Why should I employ you?', 'What can you do for us that someone else cannot do?', 'What is your greatest weakness?', 'Why aren't you earning more?' and 'What interests you about this job?'

The questions and answers in the following chapters come from across the job spectrum. Though a particular example answer might come from the mouth of an administrator, while you are a scientist or in one of the service industries, the commonality shared by all job functions in contributing to the bottom line will help you draw a parallel with your job. I'll give you the question and explain what is behind it and the types of information the employer will be looking for in your answers.

Notice that many of the example answers teach a small lesson in professional survival – something you can use both to get the job and to help you climb the ladder of success.

The answers provided in the following chapters should not be repeated word for word, exactly as they come off the page. You have to tailor them to your profession, and illustrate them with examples from your own real-world experience, and as you have your own style of speech, you'll need to put the answers into your own words.

THE FIVE SECRETS
OF SECURING
A JOB OFFER

Understanding how an interviewer thinks, and on what criteria decisions are based, is an important career management skill.

No employer wakes up in the morning saying, 'It's a wonderful day; I think I'll hire an accountant in need of a job.' Staff are only ever added to the payroll in the belief that the additional costs will be exceeded by the contribution they make to the bottom line, by earning or saving money, saving time, or otherwise increasing productivity.

An integral part of every employee's responsibility is the identification, prevention and solution of problems within their area of responsibility: problems that throw a wrench into the money-making machinery. Because these responsibilities are integral to every job, they are part of your job, too. You are hired to contribute to the bottom line in some small way, to prevent any problems within your area of expertise that get in the way of this, and, when prevention isn't an option, to solve these problems.

Whatever your job title, that job is a small but important cog in the complex moneymaking machinery of the company. Your cog has its own problem identification, prevention and solution functions and must simultaneously mesh seamlessly with other cogs, working in harmony to execute tasks beyond the scope of individual effort.

There are five criteria that intelligent managers apply to every recruitment decision to help ensure a successful outcome; for you, these are the five secrets to turning a job interview into a job offer. These secrets are based on the logical evaluations that interviewers make when recruiting for any job, at any level, and in every profession. Understanding these five secrets will revolutionize the way you perform at job interviews; and applying them every day in your work will propel your climb up the professional ladder in your next job and throughout your career.

The first secret: ability and suitability

Saying, 'Hey, I can do this job – give me a shot and I'll prove it to you' is not enough to land a job offer. You have to prove it by demonstrating a combination of all the skills that define your ability to do that job. You bring two sets of skills to a job:

1 You must demonstrate an ability to do the work: that you are in full possession of the technical skills required for execution of your responsibilities. And you have to show a clear grasp of the job and the role it plays in the department, as a small but important cog in the complex moneymaking machinery of the organization.

2 You must also establish your suitability for the job. You possess a body of professional/industry knowledge that helps you understand 'the way things get done in banking/ agribusiness/pharmaceuticals'. These ways differ from one industry to the next. It must be obvious that you speak the language and understand the protocols of your profession.

For example, a computer programmer working in a bank has technical skills. They show ability to do the job by demonstrating possession of the skills and how to apply them in writing good code. They show suitability for the job by demonstrating an understanding of how the program will be used in application and why it will be used that way. That comes from a familiarity with the operations of the financial world and the terminology used to communicate within that professional community.

Ability, suitability and career change

But wait, you say, a computer programmer doesn't have to know banking: they can pick that up fairly quickly. It's the programming skills that are important. I don't disagree, but if you were recruiting and you had to choose between two programmers with equal technical skills, who would you hire, the one who knew your business or the one who didn't?

Given the transferability of certain technical skills, suitability is one of the biggest hurdles career changers have to overcome in both their CVs and in the ensuing interviews.

If you are considering a career change, you can use understanding of this first secret as part of your preparation to make that career change. Take time to find people already doing this work in your target industry/profession who can explain the mechanics of the business and the reasons for them, the professional protocols that have been developed to deal with the realities and contingencies of that world, and the terminology professionals in the field use to discuss them, so that you can, in turn, make the connections between your credentials and the new world in which they will be applied.

The second secret: every job is about problem anticipation, identification, prevention and solution

Regardless of profession or title, at some level we are all hired to do the same job: we are all problem solvers, paid to anticipate, identify, prevent and solve problems within our areas of expertise. This applies to any job, at any level, in any organization, anywhere in the world, and being aware of this is absolutely vital to job search and career success in any field.

Once you have identified the particular problem-solving business you are in, you've gone a long way towards isolating what the interviewer will want to talk about. The TJD exercises helped you identify the problems that are the meat of your work and gave you plenty of examples of your use of analytical thinking skills in the problem resolution process. When you can tell stories of problems you've dealt with efficiently, it helps interviewers visualize you solving their problems – on their payroll, as a member of the team.

Identify and list for yourself the typical problems you tackle on a daily basis. Come up with plenty of specific examples. Then move on to the biggest, dirtiest problems you've faced. Recall specifically how you solved them.

Here's a technique used by corporate outplacement professionals to help people develop examples of their problem-solving skills and the resulting achievements (you went through a similar exercise while developing your CV):

1 State the problem. What was the situation? Was it typical of your job, or had something gone wrong? If the latter, be wary of apportioning blame.

2 Isolate relevant background information. What special knowledge or education were you armed with to tackle this dilemma?

3 List your key qualities. What professional skills and professional behaviours did you bring into play to solve the problem?

4 Recall the solution. How did things turn out in the end?

5 Determine what the solution was worth. Quantify the solution in terms of money earned, money saved, or time saved. Specify your role as a team member or as a lone player, as the facts demand.

Interviewers are impressed by candidates who ask intelligent questions about the job, because those questions demonstrate the depth of that candidate's understanding. You can definitely help your application by asking questions about the problems that lie at the heart of your job; it turns a one-sided examination of skills into a two-way conversation between professionals with a common interest. Very few candidates understand this. When you ask about the problems, challenges, projects, deadlines and pressure points that will be tackled in the early months, you demonstrate the analytical thinking skills that underlie your problem-solving abilities, which proves you will be able to hit the ground running on those first critical projects.

Show this in the way you answer questions, and in the questions you ask, and bells will ring for the interviewer; indeed, the poor old dear might drop dead and go to heaven on the spot.

The third secret: professional behaviour

Professionals are seen to be professional because they behave in a certain way. Solid possession of the transferable skills and professional values informs your judgement, opinions and conduct; it is your embodiment of them in everything you do that does most to convey quiet professional confidence. These are the skills and values that get you hired, get you noticed, land you top assignments, and lead to promotions and raises; they enable you to succeed in all your professional endeavours. Just to refresh your memory, here are those skills and values again. Keep referring back to them – they're among the most valuable things you'll take away from this book.

Transferable skills	Professional values
Technical	Motivation and energy
Critical thinking	Commitment and reliability
Communication	Determination
Multitasking	Pride and integrity
Teamwork	Productivity
Leadership	Systems and procedures
Creativity	

Showing your possession of transferable skills and professional values with the illustrative examples you give in answers to interviewers' questions, is your passport to success at any interview. They give your answers substance and a ring of truth.

Transferable skills can also help if you are undergoing a career change. There are seven transferable skills. Apart from the technical skills of the job, all these skills are transferable between all jobs in the same profession and all jobs in different professions. However, with technical skills, it is likely that only some of them will apply to jobs in different professions.

The fourth secret: motivation and intelligent enthusiasm

Motivation is one of the professional values that all employers like to see in their employees. From the employer's side of the desk, the preference for motivated, intelligently enthusiastic candidates is roughly this:

- The motivated and intelligently enthusiastic candidate will work harder and will deliver a superior product.

- Someone who really enjoys their work and is engaged in their profession will be easier to work with, and that will be a positive influence and a welcome, happy addition to the team.

- Someone who is enthusiastic and motivated by their work is likely to have a greater understanding of the job and therefore a greater commitment to taking the rough with the smooth.

In a tightly run job race, when there is really nothing to choose between two top contenders, the job offer will always go to the most intelligently enthusiastic candidate. However, interviews are stressful situations, and when you are stressed, your defences are up and you retreat behind a wall of stiff professionalism. The natural enthusiasm and motivations that are normally part of your professional persona are restrained.

So, the fourth secret is an admonishment to allow your natural enthusiasm for your work and for this job opportunity to shine through, rather than hide it because of interview nerves or a misconstrued sense of professionalism.

When it comes to a tightly run race between equally qualified candidates, remember that the offer will always go to the most intelligently enthusiastic candidate. Show enthusiasm for your work, your profession and the opportunity; it just might be the tie-breaker for your ideal job.

The fifth secret: teamwork and manageability

Teamwork concerns your ability to function productively as a member of a group focused on achieving large-scale goals. Working in a team takes patience, balance, tolerance and an ability to assert your own personality without overpowering everyone else's. You don't have to like everyone on your team, but you have to be able to work with them, and that requires emotional maturity. Your willingness to be a team player and your ability to function as an integrated member of the team is critical because many of the contributions your department must make towards the smooth running of the organization are beyond the scope of your individual contribution.

When you embrace and apply the five secrets, you will turn job interviews into job offers, and applying these secrets in your new job will steadily increase your credibility and visibility, simultaneously delivering greater job security, forward momentum and marketability.

Why you go to job interviews

You need to have the right focus going into the interview. You are not going to the interview to decide if you want the job, because you have nothing to decide until an offer is on the table. You go to any job interview for one reason only: to get a job offer. Nothing else matters. Turning interviews into job offers is a critical professional survival skill, and of all the professional skills you possess, this one is almost certainly a weakness, and needs to be strengthened. In the following chapter, I'll show you how to make it one of your most powerful tools.

Last-minute interview prep

If you read and absorb this entire section on interviewing you will be well prepared for the worst that any interviewer can throw at you. That won't stop you worrying on your way to an interview or waiting in reception. Much better that you focus on positive matters that can impact your interview performance. Here are seven meditations for before battle that will get you in fighting trim:

1 The job you are interviewing for exists to help the company make money, save money or increase productivity in some small way. When you increase productivity, you save time and money, and that makes more time to make more money. Your job fits into one or more of these categories – decide which.

2   The department you are being interviewed by is a cog in this money-making machine. Think about how it contributes to the overall company goal of achieving profitability.

3   Your target job is a smaller cog within the department's machinery that contributes to profitability. When you understand how this target job relates to the department's role, you are also able to relate your work to the company's overriding mission: making payroll and a profit.

4   You know the experience and skills for which the company is looking and the deliverables that are expected as a result. And you know that your job exists to help the company make money within your area of expertise, by your anticipation, prevention and solution of the problems that get in the way of the profit.

5   Look at each of the job's requirements in turn and determine what you do with each to anticipate, prevent and solve the problems that get in the way of profitability. You deliver all these requirements with the way you do your job – by the way you anticipate and solve the problems that are dumped on your desk every day.

6   These issues are what your job is about, and you *love* dealing with them. Knowing the issues allows you to talk intelligently about the job and simultaneously gives you intelligent questions to ask.

7   When your answers are built on this awareness, you come across as informed, thoughtful and intelligent. Tag questions about the real challenges of the job, and you turn a job interview from a one-sided examination of skills into a two-way conversation between a couple of professionals with a common interest – this is interpreted as intelligent enthusiasm.

In every tightly run job race, when there is nothing to choose between the skills of two top contenders, the job offer will *always* go to the most intelligently enthusiastic applicant because that applicant will be seen to work harder and smarter, produce better results, be a better team player and be easier to manage. That applicant is you.

WHY INTERVIEWERS DO THE THINGS THEY DO

Sitting in front of the interviewer as he looks over your CV, your mind racing with the possibilities of what could happen next, you're probably thinking, 'Why am I here? I'd rather be abducted by aliens.' What probably won't occur to you is that quite a lot of the time the interviewer feels the same way.

There is no getting around the fact that job interviews are stressful events, but you are already way ahead of many other candidates because you are seriously developing that essential skill of turning job interviews into job offers.

On the other side of the desk is not an adversary but someone who really would like to hire you. You know that the interviewer you are facing hates to interview. I guarantee that secretly they are thinking, 'Please God let this be the one, so I can get back to that pile of work on my desk.' You just have to help them make the right decision.

In this part of the book, you'll get right inside the interviewer's head to understand why interviewers do the things they do. And you'll learn the formulas for answering tough interview questions in ways that are honest, unique to you, and which further your application without making you sound like a con-artist.

There's a mistaken belief that any person, on being promoted into the ranks of management, becomes mystically endowed with all the skills of management, including the ability to interview and hire the right people. This is a fallacy; perhaps only half of all managers have been taught how to interview. Most just bumble along and pick up a certain proficiency over time. Consequently, at any job interview you are quite likely to run into one of two types of interviewer:

1 The untrained interviewer who doesn't know what they are doing and worse, doesn't know they don't know what they are doing.

2 The competent interviewer who knows exactly what they are doing and has a plan for the interview.

They both present challenges – and opportunities, when you know how to handle them.

Interview strategies

There are a number of interview strategies that interviewers can use to help gather information.

1 Behavioural.

2 Stress.

3 Situational.

I'll look at them in order.

Behavioural interview strategies

Behavioural interviewing has become an integral part of almost every job interview today. It is based on the reasonable premise that your past behaviour can predict your future performance: 'If I know how you behaved in specific situations on someone else's payroll I'll know how you will behave on mine.' To get this insight, an interviewer examines your behaviour in general work situations – 'Are you comfortable with your accounts receivable skills?' – then looks for examples: 'Tell me about a time when you had a problem with an account.'

Behavioural interviewing also looks for balance. If the interviewer is feeling impressed, he or she will try to temper a positive response with, 'Great, now tell me about a time when things didn't work out so well.' Fortunately, you prepared for this line of questioning when you completed the TJD exercises earlier.

Stress interview strategies

While every job interview is a stress interview, if the ability to function under stress is part of your job – for example, sales – then the interviewer might reasonably be expected to try to create a temporary environment that reveals how you perform under stress. He or she is most likely to do this with questions or demands; for example:

- 'Sell me this pen.'

- 'What would you say if I told you your presentation was lousy?'

- 'I'm not sure you're right for this job.'

Whenever you feel stress rising in an interview, stay calm:

- Breathe evenly and calmly. Shortness of breath will inhibit your thinking process and make you sound nervous.

- If you are offered something to drink at the beginning of the interview, always accept some water. Then if, at any time, you need a moment to collect your thoughts, you can take a sip; besides buying you time to think, swallowing helps reduce any tension you might be feeling. (There are more techniques to gain time later in this chapter.)

- Keep your body posture relaxed and open. Many people have a tendency, when under stress, to contract their bodies. This adds to the tension and sends the wrong message.

- Think through the question. Consciously remove any perceived intimidating verbal inflection. For example, depending on the tone of voice used, the question, 'I'm not sure you are right for the job. What do you think?' can be heard as, 'You just aren't right for this job.' Or you could hear it as, 'I'd like to hire you and you're one of my top candidates, but I'm not sure you're the one, so please convince me.'

The stress interview is covered in more detail in Chapter 15.

Situational interview strategies

Situational strategies give the interviewer an opportunity to see you in something close to a real work situation, with the goal of getting a better idea of how you perform your duties. The situational strategy will always relate to a frequently executed task, something at the very heart of your job, and it can happen as a formal part of the interview or very casually.

Customer service and sales jobs are prone to situational interviewing strategies more than most; if you face one of these, you'll panic a little, but the situational role play is going to recreate a task or situation that is at the core of your work, so try to relax. Ask a few questions for clarification and to get nerves under control. If it's going to take more than a few minutes, you can ask for a break first. Then, as much as you can, relax and do your job. Remember, what is being sought is confirmation that you understand the building blocks of that task: you aren't expected to deliver an Oscar-worthy performance.

The experienced interviewer

A manager's job is to get work done through others, and the first step is to employ the right people. If you cannot hire effectively, you can never manage productively, and if you can't manage productively... you lose your job. Consequently, more and more managers are learning how to interview effectively. You can also rely on just about all headhunters, recruitment agencies and HR people to run competent interviews because it's what they do every day.

Competent interviewers have a plan. They know what they are going to ask, when they are going to ask it, why they are asking it and what they hope to find. They follow a set format for the interview process to ensure objectivity in the selection process, and a set sequence of questions to ensure the facts are gathered logically and in the right areas. They have all been in many more interviews than you have. We gain three pointers from this:

- You don't need to exaggerate or fabricate. What you have to say is going to capture their full attention; besides, they can tell fact from fiction and truth from dreams.

- Interviewing can get boring if you do a lot of it. The majority of candidates make this worse. You don't need to be uptight or stiff; try to relax and become the friendly, competent, outgoing person you are on your best days.

- This is a job. It needs to be completed so they can go on to the next one. Your interviewers are hoping, praying, that you will be the one.

'OMG, here's another one'

Yes, that's the first thought in the interviewer's mind as you sit down to begin the interview. It continues, 'I hope that this is the one. All I want is someone who understands the job, can do it and wants to do it, comes to work on a regular basis, and gets on with people. I just need to hire someone and get back to the emergencies on my desk!'

Contrary to what you may think, the interviewer wants you to relax. That's because a more relaxed you is a more communicative you, and the interviewer needs information on which to base their decision. So at the beginning of an interview you'll go through some formulaic small talk and the offer of a coffee, maybe, to prepare the way for the actual questioning to begin. Always accept a drink, and ask for water. You are nervous, your throat is more prone to dryness, and water is the best remedy.

The interview gets under way with a statement from the interviewer, who will say something along the lines of, 'We're looking for a _____, and I want to find out about your experience and the strengths you can bring to our team.' They will then explain a bit about how the interview itself will go: whether you'll be talking to other people and if so, who they are. This is the time when you offer a nicely formatted version of your CV printed on decent paper, because next the interviewer is going to glance down at the CV, and say, 'So tell me a little bit about yourself.'

Going through your CV

Using your CV as a reference point, interviewers will often take you through your work history, asking you questions about different aspects of your experience. These early questions are designed to make you comfortable about talking, so they will usually be straightforward, since a good interviewer wants to limit their contributions to about 20 per cent of the interview, leaving you to talk the other 80 per cent of the time – offering plenty of time to analyse your answers. Your answers should be similarly straightforward, and you'll make an effort here to show an understanding, in general terms, of your job's role within the department, and that in essence the job is about problem anticipation, identification, prevention and solution.

Some interviews end after this journey through the CV, either because the interviewer has enough information to rule you out, or because he or she doesn't know any better. Skilled interviewers use this walk through the CV as a qualifying round. If you pass, they'll take the interview to the next level.

Your TJD work pays off

Next the interviewer, examining your CV, will want to look at your qualifications and experience in each of the critical deliverables of the job. Since you have already invested time in working back and forth between the job description, your TJD document and your CV, you will be able to connect real-world experiences to the problems anticipated, identified, prevented and solved in each area by the intelligent application of the appropriate technical and transferable skills.

If you make the time to do this, you will be able to connect any question or issue the interviewer raises to the qualifications you bring to the table and illustrate them with real-world examples, explaining:

- What you did and why you did it.
- The underlying transferable skills you used to get it done.
- The professional values that helped you make the right decisions.
- What you learned and how you grew professionally from the experience.

Any questions?

You know the interview is drawing to a close when you are asked if you have any questions. I suggest you make a list of such questions and I'll cover this in more depth later in this chapter. Bringing the list out and ticking off what hasn't been covered demonstrates the kind of intelligent enthusiasm that, again, helps set you apart from other candidates. The list you develop for your first interview can be the template for all subsequent interviews.

Next steps

The interviewer will thank you for your time and may give you some idea of next steps. If this information isn't offered, ask for it. If there is another round of interviews:

- recap your understanding of the job;
- what you bring to the table;
- that you are qualified and very interested;
- ask to arrange the next interview.

If there are no more interviews, ask when the decision will be made. Then repeat the steps above, but instead of asking for the next interview ask for the job. You have everything to gain and nothing to lose; showing motivation and intelligent enthusiasm for the job now could be the decisive factor.

Facing an interview panel

There will be situations where you will face more than one interviewer at a time. When these occur, remember the example of an interviewee who had five law partners all asking questions at the same time. As the poor interviewee got halfway through one answer, another question would be shot at her. Pausing for breath, she smiled and said, 'Hold on, ladies and gentlemen. These are all excellent questions, and, given time, I'll answer them all. Now I believe the managing partner has a question?' In so doing, she showed the interviewers exactly what they wanted to see – someone who remains calm and can function efficiently in stressful situations.

You never know when an interview can take a more stressful turn. It might appear that way because you are tense and tired (remember, it's okay to ask for a break, to recharge yourself, at any time during a day of interviews); or it can happen during what seems to be a rubber-stamp meeting with the senior executive at the end of a series of gruelling meetings. That is not surprising. While other interviewers are concerned with determining whether you are able, willing and a good fit for the job in question, the senior executive may be looking at your promotion potential. This is how competent interviewers are trained to develop structured interviews.

So much for the interviewer who knows what they are doing. Now for the hard part: dealing with the interviewer who doesn't know that they don't know what they are doing.

What is your psychological capital quotient?

Your success at work can depend on many factors: the technical skills of your profession, transferable skills and professional values, to name a few. Now new research has discovered that how you perceive your colleagues and co-workers may be just as important. It suggests that your ability to get work done is connected to how you see those around you.

Do you see your co-workers as capable, professional, decent people or incompetent idiots? Behavioural psychologists tell us that these considerations can reflect your ability to solve problems and push yourself to achieve. This is referred to as psychological capital. Psychologists have developed tests and questions designed to use an appraisal of psychological capital to identify the candidates most likely to have the ability to develop competencies fast, pursue professional knowledge, grow professionally, work well with other team members, experience greater satisfaction from involvement in groups, and experience and display less disruptive cynicism. These tests and questions essentially examine three areas:

1 Self-confidence – you believe you can achieve your goals.

2 Resilience – you believe you can overcome setbacks.

3 Optimism – you expect the future to bring good things.

For example, managers who see themselves as self-confident, resilient and optimistic are more likely to believe in and encourage success in their staff, while managers who believe their staff are incompetent and lazy will end up with a demoralized team. Apply this to yourself and you can see that how you interact with others either energizes and empowers or demoralizes them.

This awareness can be applied to how you think about yourself, the people you work with, and how you answer interview questions. Think about this: whether you choose to see your co-workers as capable, professional, decent people or as incompetent fools can influence how you come across in answering all interview questions.

The unconscious incompetent

Have you ever left an interview feeling that you could do the job but that the interviewer didn't ask you the questions that would allow you to showcase your skills? You were probably facing an 'unconscious incompetent': an interviewer who doesn't know that they don't know how to interview and who bases hiring decisions on 'experience' and 'knowing people' and 'gut feeling'.

Facing an untrained interviewer, you must understand how he or she thinks if you want to turn the situation to your advantage. Untrained interviewers reveal themselves in six distinct ways.

1 The interviewer's desk is cluttered, and they can't find the CV or application form that was handed to them a few minutes before.

   Response: Sit quietly through the bumbling and searching. Observe the surroundings. Breathe deeply and slowly to calm any lingering interview nerves. As you bring your adrenaline under control, you bring a calming tone to the interview and the interviewer.

2 The interviewer experiences constant interruptions from the telephone or people walking into the office.

   Response: Interruptions provide opportunities to review what's been happening and plan points you want to make; it's a good time to review the list of questions you want to ask. The interruptions also give you time to think through a question that has just been asked or to add new information to a point made prior to the interruption. When an interruption occurs, make a note on your pad of where you were in the conversation and remind the interviewer when conversation resumes. He or she will be impressed with your level head and good memory.

3   The interviewer starts with an explanation of why you are both sitting there, and then wanders into a lengthy lecture about the job and/or the company. This interviewer is nervous and doesn't know how to ask questions.

Response: Show interest in the company and the conversation. Sit up straight, look attentive, make appreciative murmurs, and nod at the appropriate times until there is a pause. When that occurs, comment that you appreciate the background on the company, because you can now see more clearly how the job fits into the overall scheme of things and how valuable this or that skill would be for the job. Could the interviewer please tell you some of the other job requirements?

This is now an interview that you can guide without the interviewer feeling you have taken control of the proceedings. All you have to do is ask the questions from your list. They will demonstrate a real grasp of what is at the heart of this job; this interviewer will be impressed by the grasp of the job that your questions demonstrate. Use questions like these: 'Would it be of value if I described my experience with _____?' or 'Then my experience in _____ should be a great help to you' or 'I recently completed an accounting project just like that. Would it be relevant to discuss it?'

4   The interviewer begins with, or quickly breaks into, the drawbacks of the job. The job may even be described in totally negative terms. That is often done without giving a balanced view of the duties and expectations of the position. This usually means that the interviewer has had bad experiences filling the position.

Response: Listen, then ask why some people fail in this job. The interviewer's answers tell you exactly how to sell yourself for this position. Address each of the stated negatives and ask what kind of person handles this best. Then illustrate your proficiency in that particular aspect of the job with a short example from your work history.

5 The interviewer keeps asking closed-ended questions – questions that demand no more than a yes-or-no answer and offer little opportunity to establish your skills. Now, every other candidate is facing the same problem, so if you can finesse the situation, you will really stand out.

   Response: The trick is to treat each closed-ended question as if the interviewer has added, 'Please give me a brief yet thorough answer.' Closed-ended questions are often mingled with statements followed by pauses. In those instances, agree with the statement in a way that demonstrates both a grasp of your job and the interviewer's statement. For example: 'That's an excellent point, Mr Smith. I couldn't agree more that the attention to detail you describe naturally affects cost containment. My track record in this area is...'

6 You can also run into 'situationally incompetent interviewers', usually when a manager asks colleagues or team members for evaluations without detailing the deliverables of the job clearly. This problem can be compounded when such interviewers do not know how to interview.

   Response: Always take additional copies of your CV with you to the interview to aid extra interviewers in focusing on the appropriate job functions. Be ready to hold up your end of the conversation by asking intelligent questions, the answers to which will enable you to sell yourself.

Keeping up your end of the conversation

There are a number of techniques you can use to keep up your end of the discussion:

1 You can show engagement with what the interviewer is saying by giving verbal signals. You do this with occasional short, quiet interjections that don't interrupt the employer's flow but let them know you are paying attention: 'Uh-huh', 'That's interesting', 'Okay', 'Great' and 'Yes, yes' all work. But be careful not to overdo it.

2 If you don't fully understand a question or if you need time to think, ask, 'Could you please repeat that?' The question is

not only repeated, it is usually repeated with more detail, giving additional information and time to formulate an answer.

3 If a question stumps you, and having it repeated still doesn't help, it is better to say, 'I'd like to come back to that later, I'm not used to interviews and I'm nervous and drawing a blank right now.' Odds are the interviewer will forget to ask again. If he or she remembers, at least your mind will have been working on it in the background and with the extra time will probably come up with an answer. If you have a great answer and the interviewer doesn't bring it up again, you can bring it up yourself.

Conversation etiquette

1 Speak clearly and be careful not to mumble or shout, either of which can happen when you are nervous.

2 If you find your throat gets dry, stop and take a drink of water. The interviewer will be patient.

3 If for any reason you become flustered, stop for a moment and collect your thoughts before continuing. It's better to take a few seconds to calm down than to dig a hole deeper and deeper with babbling.

4 Keep in mind that the 80/20 rule applies to you as well. It's all right to talk a lot – that's what the interviewer expects – but don't dominate the conversation to the exclusion of anyone else. If the interviewer signals that he or she wants to communicate something, let him or her do so.

5 Never interrupt. You want all information possible before engaging your mouth, and often the most important part of a statement or question comes in the latter part of the sentence. Get in the habit of listening to what is being said all the way through, rather than just waiting for your turn to talk.

Information-gathering questions

Demonstrate a good understanding of the job's deliverables and your possession of all the technical and transferable skills and professional values that help you do the job well, and you will be a top contender. If you want to turn a one-sided examination of skills into a two-way conversation between professionals with a common interest, you'll need to ask questions of your own, and the more they go to the heart of the job, the stronger the impression you will make.

Don't be afraid to ask questions. Your questions show interest, and we make our judgements of people based on both the statements they make and the questions they ask. The questions you ask show that you understand the job and take it seriously. The interviewer's answers deliver insights into the job that you wouldn't otherwise have, giving you a better focus for your responses and the points you want to make.

This is especially important when the interviewer does not give you the openings you need in order to sell yourself. Always have a few intelligent questions prepared to save the situation. The following questions will give you an excellent idea of why the position is open and exactly the kind of skilled professional the company will eventually hire:

- 'Who succeeds in this job and why?'
- 'Who fails in this job and why?'
- 'What do you consider the most important day-to-day responsibilities of this job?'
- 'What is the hardest part of the job?'
- 'What will be the first projects I tackle?'
- 'What will you want me to have achieved in the first 90 days?'
- 'What are the biggest challenges the department faces this year and what will be my role as a team member in tackling them?'
- 'Which projects will I be most involved with during the first six months?'
- 'What will you want me to have achieved in the first six months?'
- 'What skills and values do you consider critical to success in this job?'

When you get a clear understanding of an employer's needs with questions like these, you can seize the opportunity to sell yourself appropriately, using the same techniques you would use when an interviewer talks but doesn't ask questions. Using that list as a starting point, make a list of your own to take to your job interviews.

The most important questions to ask at the end of an interview are to determine whether:

- There is another interview – in which case you must ask for it, with an intelligent and enthusiastic explanation of why you are qualified and why you are interested in pursuing the opportunity.

- This is the final interview – in which case you must ask for the job with an intelligent and enthusiastic explanation of why you are qualified and why you are interested in pursuing the opportunity.

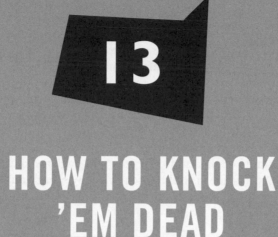

HOW TO KNOCK
'EM DEAD

One of the two bad seats at a job interview is sitting in front of the interviewer wondering what he or she is going to ask next; the other is sitting across from a candidate wondering what kind of canned platitudes you are going to be fed in response to a serious question. All any interviewer really wants is to find someone who can do the job, wants to do the job, and can get along with others. All you need to do to win the job offer is to show the interviewer you are this person.

Fortunately you have already done the lion's share of the work. You know exactly who gets hired for this job and why. Your TJD revealed how employers prioritize their requirements and how they express them. You determined the experience and skills you possess in each of the deliverable areas of the job, you developed examples of assignments that show you tackling that area's typical problems successfully, and you created a behavioural profile of the person everyone wants to work with and the person nobody wants as an employee. All this is supported by a clear understanding of how your transferable skills and professional values impact upon every aspect of your daily professional life. Showing these universally admired skills and values in action as you make passing reference to them in your answers gives those answers substance and a ring of truth.

Armed with this knowledge, you are already better prepared than the vast majority of other candidates. Apart from a healthy and perfectly natural case of pre-performance nerves, the only rational worry you have left is fear of the unknown: not knowing what questions you might be asked, what is behind them, and how to answer them. That will be my focus for the next few chapters.

I will help you understand what is behind each question – the kind of information an employer is likely to be seeking – and I'll give an example of the kind of points you might want to make in your answers. The idea is not to memorize my sample answers; they are meant to reveal the logic of the questions and to point the way towards answers that work for you.

'Tell me a little about yourself.'

This is one of the first questions you will answer, and how you answer will set the tone for the whole interview. The interviewer wants to know about your experience and qualifications for this job, and whether bringing you in for a face-to-face meeting is going to be a waste of time. Answering well will require a little careful thought. If you haven't thought the answer through, you'll ramble, and if you ramble right out of the starting gate, you'll lose the interviewer's attention and can usually kiss the job goodbye.

Plan your response

Answer the question well and you create a good first impression and set the tone for your application; you'll also immediately feel more confident when the interviewer's body language subtly signals interest and attention. Everything you say should be job focused. Your response should tell the interviewer about your professional abilities and the analytical and *communication skills* that support them.

What is your customer buying?

The first lesson we all learn on entering the world of work is 'The customer is always right.' The second lesson is 'Find out what the customers want and sell it to them'. In this context, that means think carefully about the job's requirements, and be prepared to address how your skills and experience have prepared you for this job. The work you do in preparation for this opening question will arm you with great ammunition for the rest of the interview.

Get inside the customer's head

You need to know exactly how employers prioritize, think about and express the responsibilities of the job and the deliverables that they expect to see fulfilled. You start by collecting four to six job postings for your target job and then prioritizing the needs these job postings all have in common. What you'll come up with is a list of skills and responsibilities that all employers seek when looking to hire for this position.

Every job is the same

At their core, all jobs are the same. They all exist to help the company make money, save money or increase *productivity* in some way, and they all exist to identify, prevent, and solve the problems that typically occur every day within that job.

Your job is to think through each duty and identify:

1 All the problems that regularly crop up when doing that aspect of the job.

2 The ways you execute your responsibilities every day to identify these problems and prevent them from arising.

3 How you deal with the problems when they do arise.

A cog in the machine

A company is a complex money-making machine, and each department is a cog in that machine that helps it run. In turn, your job is a still smaller cog that must mesh effectively with all the other cogs with which it comes into contact. Think about your job's role in the department and the other titles with which you have to interact effectively and harmoniously.

Putting your answer together

Take the four or five most common responsibilities and turn them into bullet points, reflecting your understanding and experience in each major area of responsibility.

This gives you a condensed professional work history that focuses on what this customer is most likely looking for. An accountant might start her answer this way: 'I have twelve years' experience with accounts payable, accounts receivable, quarterly P&Ls and compliance.'

Then add chronology: 'I spent X years at _____ and this is where I learned how to...' With this structure, you'll show the *professional development* that brought you to the point you are at today.

You might finish with something along the lines of, 'Over the years, I've developed an ever-growing frame of reference for these critical areas, and as we talk, I hope to show you that I have a real understanding of the challenges each aspect of the job presents.'

This question is often followed by another:

'What do you know about the company?'

If you don't know anything about the company, you will lose out to candidates who do. When you are asked, 'What do you know about us?' and you reply, 'Not much', you have quite likely killed your application because you've shown a lack of real interest in the job. As well, you are directly showing disrespect to the interviewer who spends the majority of his or her waking hours there.

Gather information

If a job interview is worth going to, it's worth knowing something about the company and the people who work there. Your knowledge of the company and its products is another piece of the jigsaw puzzle that helps an interviewer evaluate your enthusiasm and motivation for your work and this job. Read media coverage on the company and its key executives and look for industry commentary as well. But don't forget to check out what employees are saying at websites like glassdoor.co.uk and techcrunch.com.

You want to gather information that empowers you to talk intelligently about company activities and why they are of interest to your professional and personal goals. Your research will raise as many questions as it answers, and you can use this by adding questions of your own to the end of your answer: 'I read that _____, and wonder how this is affecting you?' 'Everyone talks about how the workplace is focused, professional and a great place to be; can you tell me...?' Such questions demonstrate engagement with your profession and with this specific opportunity.

Your research should take you beyond the ability to regurgitate facts and empower you, so that during the interview you show an understanding of the company as a group of people united for a common cause. This can help you have more meaningful discussions and encourage a sense that you are their kind of person.

As you answer, remember that by admiring the company's achievements you are, by inference, admiring the interviewer. A little flattery goes a long way. It's okay to throw in relevant personal details – perhaps that working for the company will bring you closer to your family.

Use your knowledge throughout the interview

The knowledge you gathered to answer this question, which comes at the beginning of the interview, can often be used throughout the conversation. As the meeting progresses, the interviewer will talk about the company, and your research will allow you to throw in an intelligent comment or ask a relevant question.

Likewise, when areas of common interest arise, comment on them, and agree with the interviewer when possible – people extend job offers to people like themselves.

'Talk me through your job changes. Why did you leave/want to leave this job?'

This question comes early in an interview and helps the interviewer understand the chronology and reasoning behind your career moves and gaps in employment. Don't worry about gaps; everyone has to deal with them. You must be ready to go through your CV without hesitation, making two statements about each employer:

1 What you learned from that job that applies to this one; in other words, the experience you gained from past jobs is an indicator of how you will perform in this one.

2 Why you left. You should have an acceptable reason for leaving every job you have held. The following LAMPS acronym identifies acceptable reasons for leaving a company:

– Location: the commute was unreasonably long.

– Advancement: you weren't able to grow professionally in that position, either because there were others ahead of you or there was no opportunity for growth.

- Money: you were underpaid for your skills and contribution.
- Pride or prestige: you wanted to be with a better company.
- Security: the company was not stable.

For example: 'My last company was a family-owned affair. I had gone as far as I was able to go. It just seemed time for me to join a more prestigious company and accept greater challenges.' Under no circumstances should you criticize a manager – even if he or she was a direct descendant of Attila the Hun. Doing so will only raise a red flag in the interviewer's mind: 'Will he/she be complaining about me like this in a few months?'

'Why did you leave _____ company?'

This is a 'tickbox' question: the interviewer wants to ask the question, tick the box, and move on. You get into trouble with too much information. Any answer longer than two short sentences is too long. Use a phrase from the LAMPS acronym above, keep it short and simple, and then shut up; if the interviewer wants more, he or she will ask. Use a phrase from above.

'Why have you changed jobs so frequently?'

If you have been caught in mergers and redundancies, simply explain. If you have jumped around, blame it on youth (even the interviewer was young once). Now you realize what a mistake your job hopping was, and with your added domestic responsibilities you are now much more settled. Or you may wish to impress on the interviewer that your job hopping was never as a result of poor performance and that you grew professionally as a result of each job change.

You could reply: 'My first job had a long commute. I soon realized that, but I knew it would give me good experience in a very competitive field. Subsequently, I found a job much closer to home where the commute was only half an hour each way. I was very happy at my second job. However, I got an opportunity to really broaden my experience with a new company that was just starting up. With the wisdom of hindsight, I realize that move was a mistake; it took me six months to realize I couldn't make a contribution there. I've been with my current company a reasonable length of time. So I have broad experience in different environments. I didn't just job hop; I have been following a path to gain broad experience. So you see, I have more experience than the average person of my age, and a desire to settle down and make it pay off for me and my employer.'

Or you can say: 'Now I want to settle down and make my diverse background pay off in my contributions to my new employer. I have a strong desire to contribute and I am looking for an employer who will challenge me; I think this might be the company to do that. Am I right?'

'Why do you want to come back?'

It sometimes happens that you make a move, regret it, and look back fondly at a company you were with, sometimes years ago. When you reapply to a past employer, you can expect to be asked about your reason for wanting to return.

It's a tricky question. You can't complain about a current or recent employer, but neither do you want to be seen as lacking judgment. The best advice is to talk about the *work* and *people factors* in your response.

Describe this last job positively, identifying how it has helped you develop new skills (because this adds to your desirability), and introduce personal factors as a reason for returning.

For example, my wife Angela switched to a job that would build her skills and pay more, but it wasn't working out. When asked about this in a job interview, she said: 'I really loved working here. The only reason I left was for a great opportunity to broaden my skill set and learn more about finance. In the last year and a half, I have managed accounts payable, receivable, bookkeeping, auditing, payroll, taxes, purchasing, cash management, financial reporting and grants. It has been a great experience that has helped me grow considerably. But I also learned that the people I work with are just as important as the salary and developing new skills. I still have friends here, and I have this deep feeling that I want to come back home with my new skills. I know I can make real contributions straight away.'

'Were you fired?'

If you were fired and you don't try to clean up the mess and change your ways, it can dog you for years. Firing someone is unpleasant and never a decision any manager makes lightly, so in the majority of cases the employee bears a degree of responsibility. The first and most important thing is to take responsibility for the actions or behaviour that led to your dismissal. If you do not take responsibility for your actions, you cannot change them.

However, generally speaking where industry rules do not stipulate full and comprehensive references, most employers make it their policy to limit references to the bare facts: dates of employment with that company and the position held. So what you tell the interviewer is a matter between you, your knowledge of your former employer's practice and your conscience.

'Have you ever been asked to resign?'

When someone is asked to resign, it is a gesture on the part of the employer: 'You can leave, or we can fire you, so which do you want it to be?' Because you were given the option, that employer cannot later say, 'I had to ask him to resign.' If you answer 'Yes', it's a mark against you, so answer 'No'.

'Why were you out of work so long?' 'Why does your CV have a gap?'

This question always has you scrambling for an answer; it touches a raw spot and can be humiliating, but you can turn it around by facing and using the facts of the matter. The facts are that you are a hardworking, competent professional who had always been led to believe that was enough. You'd never had a problem finding work before and no one had ever told you that job search skills were something you needed to develop – not at school, college or anywhere.

Then you got caught out by the biggest recession in 80 years and on top of this, the sudden move to internet-based recruitment (while you were working and not paying attention to such things) had changed all the rules of job search anyway.

You might try something along the lines of, 'If you look at my work history, you'll see it has been steady for _____ years. Then I lost my job. The big problem for me was my complete lack of understanding about how to find a job in the worst recession in 80 years, at a time when recruitment had moved entirely online and changed all the rules of job search.

'I'd never had a problem finding a job before, but because of the changes in how you find a job today, when I did apply for jobs, most of the time my CV got stuck in a database and was never even seen by recruiters. I didn't understand that my CV had to be written differently. The biggest reason I've been out of work is that my CV didn't work in this new environment and I just haven't been getting interviews.'

Then move the conversation forward to what's most important to the interviewer: what you can do and how long it will take you to be productive. You might finish with a question of your own, asking about the most difficult and/or urgent responsibilities of the job and why people fail in this job, 'But put me to work and I'll get straight back to doing what I do best: identifying, preventing, and solving problems. What are some of the recurring problems your people have to deal with in this job?' The interviewer's answer should give you ammunition to talk about how well suited you will be for the position.

Your answer should emphasize that while you may not have been in the workplace, neither have you been idle. Talk about how you have kept up to date with classes or part-time work, and/or what you have been doing to keep the specific technical skills of the job honed. You can also talk about how you used other transferable skills and applied professional values in whatever work you were doing, noting that these skills are fresh, current and needed in every job.

'What aspects of your work do you consider most crucial?'

All jobs exist to support profitability; you need to determine whether your job is chiefly concerned with generating revenue, protecting assets, improving productivity in some way, or is perhaps a combination of these imperatives. Once you have determined this, you have the framework for an answer. But to answer effectively, you need to grasp the core of your job, which is to identify, prevent and solve problems that occur within your area of expertise, and in the process to help your employer achieve and maintain profitability.

Your answer begins with an explanation of why the job exists and what role it plays in achieving departmental and company goals. Then itemize the most important responsibilities of the job (you prioritized these in your TJD). You then proceed to address:

- The technical skills you need to carry out these responsibilities: 'I need to be able to do _____ to execute my responsibilities.'

- 'Of course, crucial to the job is my ability to identify, prevent and solve the problems that crop up in each of these areas every day.'
  - You anticipate the ways that problems can arise in your area of responsibility and explain how you execute your work in ways that prevent many of the typical problems of your job arising in the first place. Have an example or two ready.
  - You tackle and solve problems that do occur, because they cannot be prevented, in a prompt, effective and professional manner. You'll have an illustration ready for this too.
  - You do this in a way that is courteous to customers and vendors and considerate to those co-workers who, in their jobs, must deal with the results of your work. Again, you'll have examples.

- Finally, mention one or two of the transferable skills and professional values that help you to deliver these crucial responsibilities: 'So my multitasking, communication and critical thinking skills help me to do this every day.'

'How do you manage your work deadlines?'

This examines the time management and organization abilities that enable you to multitask productively. You should address the 'prioritize, do, review' cycle: you set time at the end of every day to review that day's activities and plan tomorrow's. You prioritize all the planned activities and stick to those priorities to make sure the important work is attended to first.

'Describe to me how your job contributes to the overall goals of your department and company.'

Every company is in business to make a profit. Every company depends on individual initiative being harnessed to teamwork to achieve the complex tasks that result in profitability. Describe how your job makes an individual contribution as well as its role as an important cog in the machinery that is your department. Your cog needs to mesh with all the other cogs (your colleagues) for the gears of productivity to engage and move the department towards its goals.

Show that you are aware of the problems that crop up in your job every day and get in the way of company productivity. Identify how your job, at its core, is to anticipate and prevent problems from arising and to solve them when they do.

'What is your greatest strength?'

First, talk about a must-have technical skill. For example, a sales professional might talk about prospecting for new clients, illustrating the answer with the tactics and strategies used. Secondly, talk about one or more of the transferable skills that help you to execute this critical part of your job. For example, you could talk about the roles that communication, analytical thinking, and multitasking skills play in helping you to execute your 'greatest strength'. This way you give a complete and believable answer that also demonstrates the skills you apply in other aspects of your work.

'What is your greatest weakness?'

The greatest-strength question is often followed by asking about your greatest weakness. While this question is handled at the start of Chapter 15, 'The stress interview and illegal questions', you can start thinking about what might constitute an acceptable answer to this awful question. What parts of your job are an ongoing challenge for everyone in your profession? This can help you view weakness as a challenge shared by all conscientious people in the profession.

'What is your role as a team member?'

Think for a moment about why the job exists. It is there to contribute to the bottom line in some way. Your department, in turn, has a similar but larger role in the company's bottom line. Your ability to link your job's role to that of the department's larger responsibilities, and then to the overall success of the company, will demonstrate your sense of the importance of teamwork. The department depends on teamwork, so describe yourself as a team player.

'What kinds of decisions are most difficult for you?'

The most difficult decisions always relate to the most crucial responsibilities of your work. The employer is looking for people who can make decisions and solve problems, not those who'll dither. You want to position yourself as someone who's decisive but not rash, who considers the implications of decisions, any side effects they might have on other activities, and whether the decision conflicts with existing systems and procedures or other company priorities. Emphasize that, having analysed the situation and reached a logical conclusion, you act.

The question almost demands that you explain how you make these difficult decisions, and that you give an illustration, and if you don't give one, it might well come in a follow-up question. Your example should relate to one of the crucial responsibilities of your job, and itemize the logical steps you take in analysing the problem to help you reach the right decision.

'What bothers you most about your job?'

Think about those aspects of your work that everyone in your profession agrees are an annoying but important part of the job. Use one of these as the basis for your answer and end on a positive note about how you deal with it. You take the rough with the smooth, and take the time to do it well so you don't have to do it again. It is important that your answer shows you remain objective and don't take shortcuts.

'Tell me about a time things went wrong.'

You are being asked to talk about something that went wrong, but that doesn't mean you can't do so with an example that turned out fine. Your TJD process identified a number of such examples you can use. Choose an example and paint it black, but don't point the finger of blame.

End with how you solved the problem or contributed to its solution. Get in a subtle plug for transferable skills: '... so sticking with it and doing it by the book helped us put things right in the end'.

You can go on to explain that the next time you faced the same kind of problem you had a better frame of reference, knew what to avoid, what to do more of, and what other new approaches you could try. Finish your answer with a statement about what you learned.

How have you benefited from your disappointments/mistakes?

You learn more from failures, mistakes and errors than you do from successes, so this is an opportunity for you to demonstrate your emotional maturity (you stay calm) and analytical thinking skills (you think things through objectively).

Your answer will explain how you treat setbacks as learning experiences: you look at what happened, why it happened and how you can do things differently at each stage. Edison once explained his success as an inventor by claiming that he knew more ways *not* to do something than anyone else living; you can do worse than to quote him. In any event, sum up your answer with, 'I treat disappointments as a learning experience. I look at what happened, why it happened, and how I would do things differently in each stage should the same set of circumstances appear again. That way, I put disappointment behind me and am ready with renewed vigour and understanding to face the new day's problems.'

You don't need to be specific about your failures, but be prepared with an example in case of a follow-up question starting, 'Tell me about a time when...'

'What are you looking for in your next job?'

Ask not what your company can do for you; ask what you can do for your company. You are there to get a job offer, and you only want to address your needs when an offer is on the table and negotiation likely.

With so little real knowledge about the company – your research isn't the same as insights explained by a company representative – you need to be careful about specificity. Keep your answer general and focus on the fulfilment you experience from a job well done, with a team similarly committed, working for a company with a solid reputation. If you're lower on the success ladder, add learned and earned professional growth to this – although if your future boss is the next step up... not such a good idea. You can add that you have observed that good people seem to move forward in groups and you'd like to earn a place within this inner circle and earn the opportunity to grow as circumstances allow by making a consistent difference with your presence.

'What do you spend most of your time on, and why?'

Your answer obviously needs to show that you focus your attention on top priorities, and you can make additional points by noting that you don't ignore the important but time-consuming repetitive tasks. You can mention some small thing that has to be done frequently, because if it has to be done frequently, it is obviously critical to success. But don't do this at the expense of those top priorities, or you're likely to be pegged as someone who gets bogged down in minutiae.

Another tactic is to use an example of multitasking to emphasize how you manage the priorities of the job. For example, 'Like a lot of business people, phonecalls and meetings take up a great deal of time. What's important to me is to prioritize activities based on the deliverables of my job. I find more gets achieved in a shorter time if a meeting is scheduled, say, immediately before lunch or at the close of business. I try to allocate time in the morning and the afternoon to high-priority activities. At four o'clock, I review what I've achieved, what went right or wrong, and plan adjustments along with the priorities for tomorrow.'

'What are your qualifications for this job?'

The interviewer is interested in your experience and your possession of the technical skills to do the job, your academic qualifications and the transferable skills/professional values that enable you to do any task well. This is why you need a clear recall of which transferable skills help you to execute each aspect of your job.

When you are confident of your skills, you can learn more about the job and make points about your suitability by asking a question of your own: 'If you could tell me about specific work assignments I'll be involved with early on, I can show exactly how I can make real contributions to this job.'

'What can you do for us that someone else cannot do?'

You cannot know other candidates' capabilities, so smilingly dis-
arm your interviewer with this fact, then say, 'But what I bring is...'
Your answer will then demonstrate your grasp of the job's responsibilities, the problems that occur in each area and how you are
prepared to deal with them.

You can finish your answer with reference to the transferable
skills and professional values you also bring to the job: 'I also
bring to this job a determination to see projects through to a proper
conclusion. I listen and take direction well. I am analytical and
don't jump to conclusions. I understand we are in business to make
a profit, so I keep an eye on cost and return.' End with: 'How do
these qualifications fit your needs?' or 'What else are you looking
for?' If you haven't covered the interviewer's hot buttons, he or
she will reveal them now, and you can respond accordingly.

'How do you keep up to date?'

We live in an age of technological innovation, in which the nature
of every job is changing as quickly as you turn these pages. This
means you must look at professional education as the price of
sustained employability. In your answer, talk about the importance
of keeping abreast of changes in the profession. You can refer to:

- Courses you have taken or are planning to take.
- Books you have read or are reading.
- Membership of professional associations.
- Subscriptions to professional journals or online groups you
  belong to.

If you're not already doing some of these things, you need to start now.

'What achievements are you most proud of?'

Use an example of something that is at the core of your job and
central to its success, where you were part of a team working on
some larger project beyond the scope of individual contribution, or
where you accepted responsibility for some overlooked project that
nevertheless was important to the success of your department. Don't
exaggerate your contributions to major projects – share the success

and be seen as a team player. Be honest, and to guarantee your illustrations are relevant, take them from your TJD. For example, you might say something like, 'Although I feel my biggest achievements are still ahead of me, I am proud of my involvement with _____ I made my contribution as part of that team and learned a lot in the process.'

'Tell me about the most difficult project you've tackled.'

The interviewer wants to know:

1 If you have experience relative to current projects.

2 How you handle them.

When possible, discuss projects that parallel work you are likely to do at the new job. State the project, then identify its challenges (in some detail), your analytical thinking process used to isolate causes of the problem and possible solutions, the story of your implementation of the solution, and the value it delivered to your employer.

'Tell me about an important goal you set recently.'

Your answer should cite a goal that relates to productivity or another aspect related to the more important deliverables of your job in some way. You might use a skill-development goal, explaining why you chose it, how it helped you grow and the benefits of completion. Or you can talk about a productivity/performance goal, why you chose it and how it helped. You can add to this how you integrated achieving this goal into all your other activities, which allows you to talk about your multitasking skills.

'What have you done to become more effective in your job?'

Similarly to the prior question, behind this is an interest in your motivation to do the work being offered. The interviewer is looking for a match between your dreams and his or her reality.

All worthwhile jobs require hard work and a desire to learn. Technological changes mean your job skills must always be in development if you want to remain current and viable. The interviewer wants to know if you are committed to your profession, and is looking for at least one example. You can also talk about the mentor relationships you have formed, the books and professional commentary you've read, the professional organizations you belong to, the certifications you're earning, the courses you are studying, and the webinars you attend. If you aren't doing some of these things, wake up and start now.

'How do you feel about your progress to date?'

Your answer should illustrate a commitment to productivity and professional development. Explain how you ensure that your work is executed effectively and, if you can, cite commendations given to you by managers. You see each day as an opportunity to learn and contribute, and you see the environment at this company as conducive to your best efforts. Perhaps say something like, 'Given the parameters of my job, my progress has been excellent. I know the work, and I am just reaching that point in my career where I can make significant contributions.'

You might finish by saying that being at this interview means you've gone as far as you can with your present employer and that this environment will encourage further growth.

'Is it ever necessary to go above and beyond the call of duty in terms of effort or time to get your job done?'

If you hope to get ahead in your professional life, any job you ever hold will every now and then deliver opportunities to reschedule your personal life and otherwise mess up your weekends. But these invasions of personal time are nevertheless opportunities to show your commitment and team spirit, so you always respond when these sometimes unwelcome opportunities present themselves; doing so increases professional success... and that gives you better personal time. Answer 'Yes', and then illustrate with a story of making extra special efforts with good humour.

'Tell me about a time when an emergency meant you had to rearrange your workload/projects.'

The question examines multitasking skills and how you handle emergencies. You'll earn points when you explain how your planning and time management skills help you stay on top of your regular responsibilities even when emergency priorities throw normal scheduling off.

The story you tell should illustrate your flexibility and willingness to work extra hours when necessary. Demonstrate that your multitasking skills allow you to change course without having a nervous breakdown.

'How long will it take you to make a contribution?'

It takes time to understand systems and procedures, who the key people are and why things are done the way they are. Be sure to qualify the question: in what area does the interviewer need rapid contributions? You might ask, 'Where are your greatest areas of need right now?' You give yourself time to think while the interviewer explains priorities.

'What is the most difficult situation you have faced?'

You're really being asked two different questions: 'What do you consider difficult?' and 'How did you handle it?' This means the interviewer will be evaluating both your analytical thinking skills and your technical skills.

Don't talk about problems with co-workers. Instead, focus on a job-related problem. Throughout the book, I have talked about the importance of problem solving and the steps a professional takes to identify the most appropriate approaches and solutions; you should have numerous examples from your TJD and the CV creation process with which to illustrate your answer. Make sure to identify the benefits of your solution.

'What do you think determines progress in a good company?'

The interviewer needs to see that you understand progress is earned over time, and does not come as a result of simply showing up at work on a regular basis. Begin with each of the technical skills required to do the job, briefly citing the transferable skills that allow you to do the job well. Finish with your willingness to take the rough with the smooth that goes with every job, and the good fortune of having a manager who wants you to succeed.

'What are some of the problems you encounter in your job, and what do you do about them?'

There's a trap in this question and two areas you need to cover in your response, so your answer has three steps:

1 First the trap: note well the old saying, 'A poor workman blames his tools', and don't find problems with the job itself or the tools you have to execute that job. Next, the two areas you need to cover:

2 Whatever your title, at its heart your job is about problem identification, prevention and solution. Include details of the problems you are a specialist at preventing and solving. This part of your answer demonstrates your deep understanding of your work.

3 Your awareness that careless mistakes cost the company good money means you are always on the lookout for potential problems caused by oversight. For example: 'Some parts of my job are fairly repetitive, so it's easy to overlook problems. Lots of people do. However, I always look for them; it helps to keep me alert and motivated, so I do a better job. To give you an example, we make computer-memory disks. Each one has to be machined by hand, and, once completed, the slightest abrasion will turn one into a reject. I have a steady staff and little turnover, and everyone wears cotton gloves to handle the disks. Yet about six months ago, the reject rate suddenly went through the roof. Is that the kind of problem you mean? Well, the cause was one that could have gone unnoticed for ages. Jill, the section head who inspects all the disks, had lost a lot of weight and her diamond engagement ring was slipping around her finger, scratching the disks as she passed them and stacked them to be shipped. Our main client was giving us a big problem over it, so my looking for problems and paying attention to detail really paid off.'

'In your last job, how did you plan interviews?'

If you are a manager, getting work done through others is at the very heart of your job. Recruitment and selection are part of your job description, and you can expect this question. Your answer should give a description of how the skilled interviewer prepares, as I discussed in Chapter 12.

'If I hired you today, what would you accomplish first?'

Gear your answer to first getting settled in the job, understanding how things are done and becoming a member of the team. You would mention that of course this includes a clear priority of all your responsibilities. Then finish with a question, 'What are the most critical projects/problems you'll want me to tackle?' The response to that becomes your final answer to what you will accomplish first.

'What type of decisions do you make in your work?'

This examines the extent of your authority and how analytical thinking enters into your work. With the TJD, you will have a clear understanding of the job's deliverables and can determine the decision-making events that are integral to your job. The interviewer will certainly follow with a request for an example; your answer will address the types of decisions you make and include an example that shows how you approach making them.

'How do you handle rejection?'

This question is common if you are applying for a job in sales, including face-to-face sales, telemarketing, public relations and customer service. If you are after a job in one of these areas and you really don't like the heavy doses of rejection that are any sales-person's lot, consider a new field. The anguish you will experience will not lead to a successful career or a happy life.

With that in mind, let's look behind the question. The interviewer simply wants to know whether you take rejection as rejection of yourself or whether you simply accept it as a temporary rejection of a service or product. Here is a sample answer that you can tailor to your particular needs and background: 'I accept rejection as an integral part of the sales process. If everyone said "yes" to a product, there would be no need for the sales function. As it is, I see every rejection as bringing me closer to the customer who *will* say "yes". Sales is a profession of communication, determination and resiliency; rejection is just part of the process, it's nothing personal. I always try to leave the potential customer with a good feeling, as no sale today can well become a sale next month.'

'Tell me about a situation that frustrated you at work.'

This question is about emotional maturity. The interviewer wants to know how you channel frustration into productivity. Give an example of a difficult situation in which you remained diplomatic and objective and found a solution that benefited all concerned. Show yourself to be someone who isn't managed by emotions – you acknowledge the frustration, then put it aside in favour of achieving the goals of the job you are paid to do.

'What interests you least about this job?'

The question is potentially explosive but easily defused. Regardless of your occupation, there is at least one repetitive, mindless duty that everyone groans about but that nevertheless goes with the territory. Use that as your example: '_____ is probably the least demanding part of my job. However, I know it is important for _____, so I do it at the end of the day as part of my performance review and next-day planning.' Notice how this response also shows that you are organized and possess analytical thinking and multitasking skills; it also shows that you understand it is necessary to take the rough with the smooth.

'I'm not sure you're suitable for the job (too inexperienced).'

In a job search you quickly develop a feeling for whether a particular position is a close match, a job you've already done for so long that you might be perceived as too experienced, or a job that might be a bit of a stretch. If you can see a potential problem with an opportunity, the employer probably can too. Nevertheless, you were close enough to get the interview, so make every effort to land the offer.

This could also be used as a stress question (to see how you handle adverse situations on the job). The interviewer's 'I'm not sure' could really mean, 'I'd like to hire you, so here's a wide-open opportunity to convince me.' Either way, remain calm and accept this as another opportunity to set you apart from other candidates.

Put the ball straight back into the interviewer's court, 'Why do you say that?' You need more information and time to organize an appropriate reply, but it is also important to show that you are not intimidated.

When you might be too inexperienced, your answer itemizes all the experience and skills you bring, and offsets weaknesses with other strengths and examples of how efficiently you develop new skills. You can also talk about the motivation you bring to the job, and that you will expect to be motivated for some considerable time because of the opportunity the job offers for your professional development, while someone with all the skills is going to need a quick promotion to keep him happy. You can finish your answer with a reflexive question that encourages a 'yes' answer: 'Wouldn't you agree?'

'I'm not sure you're suitable for the job (too experienced).'

If you are told you have too much experience, respond with the positives: how your skills help you deliver immediately and why the position fits your needs; perhaps, 'I really enjoy my work, so I won't get bored, and I'm not looking for a promotion, so I'm not after anyone's job. I'll be a reliable and trustworthy person to have on your team. I have excellent skills [itemize], so I can deliver quickly and consistently. My experience makes me a steadying member of the team, and when you think I'm ready I can help to mentor.' Finish with a smile: 'And let's not forget I've already made my mistakes on somebody else's payroll.'

'Do you have any questions?'

A sign that the interview is drawing to a close. Take the opportunity to make a strong impression. Ask questions that help advance your candidacy by giving you information about the real-world experience of the job: 'Yes I do have one or two questions.' Go through the list of questions you developed after reading the interview preparation chapter and brought with you:

- Who succeeds in this job and why?
- Who fails in this job and why?
- What are the major projects of the first six months?

- What will you want me to have achieved after 90 days?
- What will you want me to have achieved after six months?
- What will my first assignment be?

For more good questions you could consider asking, take a look at Chapter 21 'Negotiating the offer'.

Most candidates ask questions about money and benefits. These are nice-to-know questions that an interviewer is not really interested in discussing at this point. As your goal at every interview is to bring the interviewer to the point of offering you the job, such questions are really irrelevant because they don't bring you closer to the job offer. It's better if you concentrate on gathering information that will help you present your skills effectively.

Ask about next steps if there are more interviews. If there are, match your skills to the needs of the job, explain your interest in the job and desire to pursue it, and ask for the next interview.

If there's not another interview, summarize your understanding of the job, how your skills match each of the deliverables, state that you want the job and want to join the team, and ask for the job.

QUESTIONS OF MANAGEABILITY AND TEAM SPIRIT

'What are you like to work with, Mr Jones?' Learn the techniques interviewers use to find out if you are manageable, if you will fit in, and most importantly, whether you are the type of person who is able to work towards common goals and with whom others like to work.

If you are offered the job and accept, you will be working with the other employees of the company, quite possibly including the interviewer, for 50 weeks of the year, so the interviewer really wants to know if you are going to reduce his or her life expectancy. Every employer wants to know whether you will fit in with the rest of the staff, whether you are a team player, and most of all, whether you are manageable. Fortunately, you have carefully thought through the behaviours of professional success and failure, and as a result, you have a clear idea of who you are and how you behave professionally. This self-awareness will help you handle the questions addressed in this chapter.

A big part of your job as that small but important cog in the moneymaking machinery of the organization is to mesh with the other cogs in your department (and beyond) to support those departmental deliverables that are beyond the scope of individual effort.

Once your ability and suitability are considered up to scratch, the final and most significant overall consideration is your willingness to take direction and work for the common good of the group. Here are the questions your interviewers will ask to assess this.

'How do you take instructions?'

The interviewer wants to know whether you are open-minded and can be a team player. Can you follow instructions, or are you a difficult employee? The employer hopes that you are a professional who is motivated to ask clarifying questions about a project before beginning and who then gets on with the job at hand, coming back with requests for direction as circumstances dictate.

This particular question can also be defined as, 'How do you accept criticism?' Your answer should cover both points: 'I take directions well and recognize that they can come in two varieties, depending on the circumstances. There are carefully explained instructions, when my boss has time to lay things out for me in detail; then there are those times when, as a result of deadlines and other pressures, the instructions might be brief and to the point. While I have seen some people get upset with that, personally I've always understood that there are probably other considerations I am not aware of. As such, I take orders and get on with the job without taking offence, so that my boss can get on with his job.'

'Would you like to have your boss's job?'

It is a rare boss who wants his livelihood taken away. On my own very first job interview, my future boss said, 'Mr Yate, it has been a pleasure to meet you. However, until you walked in my door, I wasn't out on the street looking for a new job.' You see, I had made the mistake of wanting to start at the top rather than actually work my way up.

The interviewer wants to know if you are the type of person who will be confrontational or undermining. He or she also seeks to determine how goal-orientated and motivated you are in your work life – so you may also want to comment on your sense of direction. But while ambition is admired, it is admired most by those far enough above the fray not to be threatened. Be cautiously optimistic; perhaps, 'Well, if my boss were promoted over the coming years, I would hope to have made a consistent enough contribution to warrant consideration. It's not that I am intending to take anyone's job;

rather, I am looking for a manager who will help me develop my capabilities.'

'What do you think of your current/last boss?'

Be short and sweet and shut up. People who complain about their employers are recognized as the people who cause the most disruption in a department. This question is the interviewer's way of finding out if you're going to cause trouble. 'I liked her as a person, respected her professionally, and appreciated her guidance.' The question is often followed by one that tries to validate your answer.

'Describe a situation where your work or an idea of yours was criticized.'

This is a doubly dangerous question because you are being asked to describe how you handle criticism, and to specify inadequacies. If you have the choice, describe a poor idea that was criticized, not poor work.

Put your example in the past, make it small, and show what you learned from the experience. Show that you go through the following steps to become productive:

- Listen to understand.
- Confirm the understanding.
- Ask for guidance.
- Confirm the desired outcome.
- Show a satisfactory resolution.
- Address what you learned and how the experience helped you grow.

You might end with something that captures the essence of your example: 'I listened carefully and asked a couple of questions for clarification. Then I fed back what I'd heard to make sure the facts were straight. I asked for advice, we bounced some ideas around, then I came back later and represented the idea in a more viable format. My supervisor's input was invaluable.' Those are steps you go through to become productive in these situations.

'How do you get on with different kinds of people?'

You don't have to talk about respect for others, the need for diversity, or how it took you 10 years to realize Jane was a different sex and Charley a different colour, because that is not what this question is about. If you respect others, you will demonstrate this by explaining to your interviewer that you work in a team environment (because this is, in reality, a 'team player' question) and that you invite and accept input, ideas, and viewpoints from a variety of sources. Give a quick, honest illustration of working productively with a person who is different from you in terms of personality or in terms of the demands his job places on him – and how you respond to maximize productivity and a harmonious work environment.

'Rate yourself on a scale of 1 to 10.'

This question is meant to plumb the depths of your self-esteem and self-awareness. If you answer 10, you run the risk of portraying yourself as insufferable. On the other hand, if you say less than seven, you might as well get up and leave. Your best bet is probably an eight. Say that you always give of your best, which includes ongoing personal and professional development, and how that in so doing you always increase your skills and therefore always see room for improvement.

'What kinds of things do you worry about?'

Some questions, such as this one, can seem so off-the-wall that you might start treating the interviewer as a confessor in no time flat. Your private phobias have nothing to do with your job, and revealing them can get you labelled as unbalanced. It is best to confine your answer to the sensible worries of a conscientious professional: 'I worry about deadlines, staff turnover, unpunctuality, back-up plans for when the computer crashes, or that one of my auditors will burn out or defect to the competition – just the normal stuff. It goes with the territory, so I don't let it get me down.' Whatever you identify as a worry might then be the subject of a follow-up question, so think through the worry you state and how you cope with it.

'What have you done that shows initiative?'

The question probes whether you are a doer, someone who will look for ways to increase revenue and/or productivity – the kind of person who makes a difference for good with their presence every day. Be sure, however, that your example of initiative does not show a disregard for company systems and procedures.

The story you tell shows you volunteering to do a necessary job others didn't see as important or didn't want to do. For example, 'Every quarter, I sit down with my boss and find out the dates of all his meetings for the next six months. I immediately make the hotel and flight arrangements, and attend to all the web-hosting details. I ask myself questions like, "If the agenda for the July meeting needs to reach the attendees at least six weeks before the meeting, when must it be finished by?" Then I come up with a deadline. I do that for all the major activities for all the meetings. I put the deadlines in his BlackBerry and in mine two weeks earlier to ensure everything is done on time. My boss is the best-organized, most relaxed manager in the company.'

'If you could make one constructive suggestion to management, what would it be?'

What matters here is less the specific content of your answer than the tone. Suggest what you know to be true and what your interviewer will appreciate as a breath of fresh air: most people want to do a good job. Management should create an environment where striving for excellence is encouraged and where those shirking on the job have the opportunity to change their ways or leave. Everyone would benefit.

'Why do you feel you are a better _____ than some of your co-workers?'

The trick is to answer the question without showing yourself in anything but a flattering light. 'I don't spend my time thinking about how I am better than my colleagues, because that would be detrimental to our working together as a team. I believe, however, some of the qualities that make me an outstanding _____ are...' From here, go on to itemize specific technical skills of your profession in which you are particularly strong, and a couple of the transferable skills that apply to doing these aspects of your work so well.

'What are some of the things that bother you? / What are your pet peeves? / Tell me about the last time you felt angry at work.'

It is tremendously important that you show you can remain calm. Most of us have seen a colleague lose his cool on occasion – not a pretty sight, and one that every sensible employer wants to avoid. This question comes up more and more often the higher up the corporate ladder you climb and the more frequently you are in contact with clients and the general public. To answer it, find something that angers conscientious workers. 'I enjoy my work and believe in giving value to my employer. Dealing with clock watchers and people who regularly get sick on Mondays and Fridays really bothers me, but it's not something that gets me angry.' An answer of this nature will help you much more than the kind given by one engineer who went on for some minutes about how he hated the small-mindedness of people who don't like pet rabbits in the office.

'What are some of the things about which you and your supervisor disagreed?'

You did not disagree.

'In what areas do you feel your supervisor could have done a better job?'

The same goes for this one.

You could reply, though: 'I have always had the highest respect for my supervisor. I have always been so busy learning from Mr Jones that I don't think he could have done a better job. He has really brought me to the point where I am ready for greater challenges. That's why I'm here.'

'What are some of the things your supervisor did that you disliked?'

If you and the interviewer are both nonsmokers, for example, and your boss isn't, use it. Apart from that: 'You know, I've never thought of our relationship in terms of like or dislike. I've always thought our role was to get on with each other and get the job done.'

'How well do you feel your boss rated your job performance?'

You could say: 'My supervisor always rated my job performance highly. In fact, I was always considered capable of accepting further responsibilities. The problem was there was nothing available in the company – that's why I'm here.'

You could also quote verbal appraisals of your performance from prior jobs. 'In fact, my boss recently said that I was the most organized engineer in the work group, because...'

'How do I get the best out of you/did your boss get the best out of you?'

The interviewer could be envisioning you as an employee. Encourage the thought by describing a supportive manager who outlined projects and their expected results at the start, noted deadlines, shared their greater experience and perspectives, and told you about potential problems. She always shared the benefit of experience. You agreed on a plan of attack for the work, and how and when you needed to give status updates along the way. Your boss was always available for advice and taught you to take the work seriously but encouraged a team atmosphere.

'How interested are you in sports?'

The interviewer is looking for your involvement in groups, as a signal that you know how to get on with others and pull together as a team.

'I really enjoy most team sports. I don't get a lot of time to indulge myself, but I am a regular member of _____ team.' A recently completed survey of middle- and upper-management personnel found that the executives who listed group sports/activities among their extra-curricular activities earned more per year than their sedentary colleagues.

Apart from team sports, endurance sports are seen as a sign of determination: swimming, running and cycling are all okay. Games of skill (bridge, chess and the like) demonstrate analytical skills. Despite the recent popularity of poker and recognition of it as a game of analytical, mathematical, communication and negotiation skills, I feel that mentioning it should be avoided.

'What personal characteristics are necessary for success in your field?'

You know the answer to this one: it's a brief recital of your transferable skills and professional values. You might say: 'To be successful in my field? Drive, motivation, energy, confidence, determination, good communication and analytical skills. Combined, of course, with the ability to work with others.' Your answer will be more powerful if you relate transferable skills and professional values to the prime needs of the job.

'Do you prefer working with others or alone?'

This question is usually used to determine whether you are a team player. Before answering, however, be sure you know whether the job requires you to work alone. Then answer appropriately. Perhaps: 'I'm quite happy working alone when necessary. I don't need constant reassurance. I prefer to work in a group, though – so much more gets achieved when people pull together.'

'Explain your role as a group/team member.'

You are being asked to describe yourself as either a team player or a loner. Think for a moment about why the job exists in the first place: it is there to contribute to the bottom line in some way, and as such it has a specific role in the department to contribute towards that larger goal. Your department, in turn, has a similar, but larger, role in the company's profitability. Your ability to link your small role to that of the department's larger responsibilities, and then to the overall success of the company, will demonstrate a developed professional awareness.

Most departments depend on harmonious teamwork for their success, so describe yourself as a team player: 'I perform my job in a way that helps others to do theirs in an efficient manner. Beyond the mechanics, we all have a responsibility to make the workplace a friendly and pleasant one, and that means everyone working for the common good and making the necessary personal sacrifices for it.'

'How would you define a motivational work atmosphere?'

This is a tricky question, especially because you probably have no idea what kind of work atmosphere exists in that particular office.

The longer your answer, the greater your chances of saying the wrong thing, so keep it short and sweet. 'One where the team has a genuine interest in its work and desire to turn out a good product/deliver a good service.'

'Do you make your opinions known when you disagree with the views of your supervisor?'

If you can, state that you come from an environment where input is encouraged when it helps the team's ability to get the job done efficiently. 'If opinions are sought in a meeting, I will give mine, although I am careful to be aware of others' feelings. I would never criticize a co-worker or a superior in public; besides, it is quite possible to disagree without being disagreeable. However, my last manager made it clear that she valued my opinion by asking for it. So, after a while, if there was something I felt strongly about, I would make an appointment to sit down and discuss it one-on-one.'

'What would you say about a supervisor who was unfair or difficult to work with?'

'I would make an appointment to see the supervisor and diplomatically explain that I felt uncomfortable in our relationship, that I felt he was not treating me as a professional colleague, and therefore that I might not be performing up to standard in some way – that I wanted to right matters and ask for his input as to what I must do to create a professional relationship. I would take responsibility for any communication problems that might exist and make it clear that, just as I took responsibility for the problem, I was also taking responsibility for the solution.'

'Do you consider yourself a natural leader or a born follower?'

Ouch! The way you answer depends a lot on the job offer you are chasing. If you are a recent graduate, you are expected to have high aspirations, so go for it. If you are already on the corporate ladder with some practical experience in the school of hard knocks, you might want to be a little cagier.

Assuming you are up for (and want) a leadership position, you might try something like this: 'I would be reluctant to regard anyone as a natural leader. Hiring, motivating, and disciplining other adults and at the same time moulding them into a cohesive team involves a number of delicately tuned skills that no honest person can say they were born with. Leadership requires first of all the desire; then it is a lifetime learning process. Anyone who reckons they have it all under control and has nothing more to learn isn't doing the employer any favours.'

Of course, a little humility is also in order, because just about every leader in every company reports to someone, and there is a good chance that you are talking to just such a someone right now. So you might consider including something like, 'No matter how well developed any individual's leadership qualities, an integral part of leadership ability is the ability to take direction from your immediate boss, and also to seek the input of the people being supervised. The wise leader will always follow good advice and sound business judgement, wherever it comes from. I would say that the true leader in the modern business world must embrace both.' How can anyone disagree with that kind of wisdom?

'You have a doctor's appointment arranged for noon. You've waited two weeks to get it. An urgent meeting is scheduled at the last moment, though. What do you do?'

What a stupid question, you mutter. It's not. It is even more than a question – it is what I call a question shell. The question within the shell – in this instance, 'Will you sacrifice the appointment or sacrifice your job?' – can be changed at will. This is a situational-interviewing technique, which poses an on-the-job problem to see how the prospective employee will respond. One company asks this question as part of its initial screening, and if you give the wrong answer, you never even get a face-to-face interview. So what is the right answer to this or any similar shell question?

Fortunately, once you understand the interviewing technique, it is quite easy to handle – all you have to do is turn the question around. 'If I were the manager who had to schedule a really important meeting at the last moment, and someone on my staff chose to go to the doctor instead, how would I feel?'

It is unlikely that you would be an understanding manager unless the visit was for a triple bypass. To answer, you start with an evaluation of the importance of the problem and the responsibility of everyone to make some sacrifices for the organization, and finish with: 'The first thing I would do is reschedule the appointment and save the doctor's surgery inconvenience. Then I would immediately make sure I was properly prepared for the emergency meeting.'

'How do you manage to attend interviews while still employed?'

As long as you don't explain that you faked a dentist's appointment to get to the interview you should be all right. Beware of revealing anything that might make you appear at all underhanded. Best to make the answer short and sweet, and let the interviewer move on to richer areas of inquiry. Just explain that you had some holiday due, or took a day off in lieu. 'I went to my boss and explained that I needed a couple of days off for some personal business and asked her what days would be most suitable. Although I'm planning to change jobs, I don't in any way want to hurt my current employer in the process by being absent during a busy time.'

'How have your career motivations changed over the years?'

This question only crops up when you have enough years under your belt to be regarded as a mature professional. The interviewer's agenda is to examine your emotional maturity and how realistic you are about future professional growth.

Your answer requires self-awareness. While the desire to rule the world can be seen as motivation in young professionals, it may not be interpreted so positively coming from a mature executive from whom more realism is expected.

Your answer should reflect a growing maturity as well as a desire to do a good job for its own sake and to make a contribution as part of the greater whole. Here's an example you can use as a starting point for crafting your own: 'I suppose in earlier years I was more ego-driven, with everything focused on becoming a star. Over the years I've come to realize that nothing happens with a team of one – we all have to function as part of a greater whole if we are to make meaningful contributions with our professional presence. Nowadays I take great pleasure in doing a job well, in seeing it come together as it should, and especially in seeing a group of professionals working together in their different roles to make it happen. I've discovered that the best way to stand out is to be a real team player and not worry about standing out.'

'How do you recover when things haven't gone as planned?'

At times we can all react to adversity in pretty much the same way we did as children, but that isn't always productive, and it isn't what an interviewer wants to hear. Here's a way you can deal with setbacks in your professional life and impress your interviewer in the process: 'I pause for breath and reflection for as long as the situation allows – this can be a couple of minutes or overnight. I do this to analyse what went wrong and why. I'm also careful to look for the things that went right, too. I'll examine alternative approaches and, time allowing, I'll get together with a peer or my boss and review the whole situation and my proposed new approaches.'

You can go on to explain that the next time you face the same kind of problem you'll know what to avoid, what to do more of, and what other new approaches you can try. You might consider finishing your answer with a statement about the beneficial effects of experiencing problems: 'Over the years I've learned just as much from life's problems as from its successes.'

'Have you ever had to make unpopular decisions?'

Inherent in the question is a request for an example, in which you'll demonstrate how analytical thinking and leadership skills help you to make the unpopular decisions, while teamwork and communication skills help to make them palatable. Your answer needs to show that you're not afraid to make unpopular decisions when they are in the best interests of your job or the department's goals.

Simultaneously, stress your effort to make the decision workable for all parties, and finish by explaining how everyone subsequently accepted its necessity and got on board.

'What would your co-workers tell me about your attention to detail?'

Say that you are shoddy and never pay attention to the details and you'll hear a whoosh as your job offer flies out the window.

Your answer obviously lies in the question. You pay attention to detail, your analytical approach to projects helps you to identify all the component parts of a given job, and your multitasking skills ensure that you get the job done efficiently without anything falling through the cracks.

'What do you do when there is a decision to be made and no procedure exists?'

You need to show that even though you're more than capable of taking the initiative, you're not a loose cannon. Explain that the first thing you'll do will be to discuss the situation with your boss or – if time is tight and this isn't possible – with peers. That's exactly what the interviewer wants to hear. Make it clear that in developing any new approach/procedure/idea you'll stick to the company's established systems and procedures.

'When do you expect a promotion?'

Tread warily, show you believe in yourself, and have both feet firmly planted on the ground: 'That depends on a few criteria. Of course, I cannot expect promotions without the performance that marks me out as deserving it. I also need to join a company that has the growth necessary to provide the opportunity. I hope that my manager believes in promoting from within and will help me to grow so that I will have the skills necessary to be considered for promotion when the opportunity comes along.'

If you are the only one doing a particular job in the company, or you are in management, you need to build another factor into your answer: 'As a manager, I realize that part of my job is to have done my succession planning, and that I must have someone trained and ready to step into my shoes before I can expect to move up. That way, I play my part in preserving the chain of command.' To avoid being caught off guard with queries about your having achieved that in your present job, you can finish with: 'Just as I have done in my present job, where I have a couple of people capable of taking over the reins when I leave.'

'Tell me a story.'

Wow. What on earth does the interviewer mean by that question? You don't know until you get them to elaborate. Ask, 'What would you like me to tell you a story about?' To make any other response is to risk making a fool of yourself. Sometimes the question is asked to evaluate how analytical you are. People who answer the question without qualifying it show they do not think things through carefully. The interviewer may also ask it to get a glimpse of the things you hold important. The answer you get to your request for clarification may give you direction, or it may not; but either way it demonstrates your analytical thinking skills.

You need to have a story ready that portrays you in an appropriate light. If you talk about your personal life, tell a story that shows you like people, are engaged in life and are determined. Do not discuss your love life. If the story you tell is about your professional life, make sure it shows you working productively as a member of a team on some worthwhile project that had problems but which worked out okay in the end. Alternatively, tell stories that in some way show you employing transferable skills and professional values in some subtle way.

'What have you learned from jobs you have held?'

You've learned that little gets achieved without teamwork and that there's invariably sound thinking behind systems and procedures. To get to the root of problems it's better to talk less and listen more. Most of all, you've learned that you can either sit on the sidelines watching the hours go by or you can get involved and make a difference with your presence. You do the latter because you're goal-orientated, time goes quicker when you're engaged, and besides, the relationships you build are with better people. You might finish with: 'There are two general things I have learned from past jobs. First, if you are confused, ask – it's better to ask a stupid question than make a stupid mistake. Second, it's better to promise less and produce more than to make unrealistic forecasts.'

'Define cooperation.'

The question examines manageability and asks you to explain how you see your responsibilities as a team player, both taking direction and working for the overall success of your department. Your answer will define cooperation as doing your job in a way that enables your colleagues to do theirs with a minimum of disruption. It's your desire to be part of something significant. Through hard work and good will, you help to make the team something greater than the sum of its parts.

'What difficulties do you have tolerating people with backgrounds and interests different from yours?'

Another 'team player' question with the awkward implication that you do have problems. Say, 'I don't have any.' But don't leave it there: 'I don't have any problems working with people from different backgrounds. In fact I find it energizing; with different backgrounds you get different life experiences and different ways of approaching problems. The opportunity to work with people different from oneself is golden.'

'In hindsight, what have you done that was a little harebrained?'

You are never harebrained in your business dealings, and you haven't been harebrained in your personal life since graduation, right? The only safe examples to use are ones from your deep past that ultimately turned out well. One of the best, if it applies to you, is: 'Well, I suppose the time I bought my house. I had no idea what I was letting myself in for and didn't pay enough attention to how much work the place would need. Still, there weren't any big structural problems, though I had to put a lot of work into doing it up the way I wanted. Yes, my first house – that was a real learning experience.' Not only can most people relate to this example, but it also gives you the opportunity to sell one or two of your very positive and endearing professional behaviours.

'You have been given a project that requires you to interact with different levels within the company. How do you do this? What levels are you most comfortable with?'

This is a two-part question that probes communication and self-confidence skills. The first part asks how you interact with superiors and motivate those working with and for you on the project. The second part is saying, 'Tell me whom you regard as your peer group – help me categorize you.'

To cover those bases, include the essence of this: 'There are two types of people I would interact with on a project of this nature. First, there are those I would report to, who would bear the ultimate responsibility for the project's success. With them, I would determine deadlines and a method for evaluating the success of the project. I would outline my approach, breaking the project down into component parts, getting approval on both the approach and the costs. I would keep my supervisors updated on a regular basis and seek their input whenever needed. My supervisors would expect three things from me: the facts, an analysis of potential problems, and that I will not be intimidated, as this would jeopardize the project's success. I would comfortably satisfy those expectations.

'The other people to interact with on a project like this are those who work with and for me. With those people, I would outline the project and explain how a successful outcome will benefit the company. I would assign the component parts to those best suited to each, and arrange follow-up times to assure completion by the deadline. My role here would be to facilitate, motivate, and bring the different personalities together to form a team.

'As for comfort level, I find this type of approach enables me to interact comfortably with all levels and types of people.'

'Tell me about an event that really challenged you. How did you meet the challenge? In what way was your approach different from that of others?'

This is a straightforward, two-part question. The first part probes your analytical thinking skills. The second asks you to set yourself apart from the herd. Outline the root of the problem, its significance and its negative impact on the department/company. The clearer you make the situation, the better. Having done so, explain your solution, its value to your employer and how it was different from other approaches.

'My company has offices all around the country; I am responsible for seven of them. My job is to visit each office on a regular basis and build market-penetration strategies with management, and to train and motivate the sales and customer service forces. When the recession hit, the need to service those offices was greater than ever, yet the travelling costs were getting prohibitive.

'Morale was an especially important factor: you can't let outlying offices feel defeated. I reapportioned my budget and did the following: I dramatically increased telephone contact with the offices and instituted weekly sales-technique e-mails and monthly training webinars – how to prospect for new clients, how to negotiate difficult sales, and so forth. I increased management training, again using webinars and concentrating on how to run sales meetings, early termination of low producers, and so forth.

'While my colleagues complained about the drop in sales, mine increased, albeit by a modest 6 per cent. After two quarters, the new media/coaching approach was officially adopted by the company.'

'Give me an example of a method of working you have used. How did you feel about it?'

You have a choice of giving an example of either good or bad work habits. Give a good example, one that demonstrates your understanding of corporate goals and your organizational or analytical thinking skills. If you have taken the time to develop the time management and organization skills that underlie multitasking abilities, you have a great illustrative example to use.

You could say: 'Maximum productivity requires focus and demands organization and time management. I do my paperwork at the end of each day, when I review the day's achievements; with this done, I plan for tomorrow, prioritizing all projected activities. When I come to work in the morning, I'm ready to get going without wasting time, sure that I will be spending my time and effort in the areas where it is most needed to deliver results. I try to schedule meetings just before lunch; people get to the point more quickly. I feel this is an efficient and organized method of working.'

'In working with new people, how do you go about getting an understanding of them?'

Every new employee is expected to become a viable part of the group, which means getting an understanding of the group and its individual members. Understanding that everyone likes to give advice is the key to your answer. You have found that the best way to understand and become part of a new team is to be open, friendly, ask lots of questions, and be helpful whenever you can. The answers to your questions give you insights into the ways of the job, department and company, and they help you get to know the person.

'What would your past employers say about you?'

You have nothing to lose by giving a positive answer. If you demonstrate how well you and your boss got along, the interviewer does not have to ask, 'What do you dislike about your current manager?'

Every interview is a stress interview, but sometimes interviewers will ratchet up the stress level. You need to be ready, and that's where I am headed next.

15

THE STRESS INTERVIEW AND ILLEGAL QUESTIONS

There is no greater fear than fear of the unknown, and that is exactly what you worry about going into a job interview; this worry increases your anxiety level. While interviewers categorically deny conducting stress interviews, they readily admit that if there is stress on the job, they need to know how a candidate will react to it.

Often they will try to recreate it by throwing in the occasional question to see how a candidate maintains their balance. Do they remain calm and analytical? Does their mind still process effectively when under pressure? Can they express themself effectively, and are they in control while managing stressful situations?

Any question you are unprepared for can cause stress. Interviewers can create stress unintentionally, or can consciously use stress to simulate the unexpected and sometimes tense events of everyday business life. Seeing how you handle the unexpected in a job interview gives a fair indication of how you will react to the unexpected when it crops up in real life.

The sophisticated interviewer talks very little, perhaps only 20 per cent of the time, and that time is spent asking questions. There are few comments, which means that you get no hint, verbal or otherwise, about your performance.

Interviewers are looking for the candidate who stays calm and continues to process incoming information during stressful events, and having processed it, asks questions for clarification or responds professionally with actions and/or words suitable to the situation and capable of moving it towards a desirable conclusion.

If you are ill-prepared for an interview, no one will be able to put more pressure on you than you do on yourself. The only way to combat the stress you feel from fear of the unknown is to be prepared, to know what the stress questions might be, what the interviewer is trying to discover with the question, and to prepare your strategies for these situations. Remember: a stress interview is just a regular interview with the volume turned all the way up – the music is the same, just louder.

'What is your greatest weakness?'

This is one of the toughest of all interview questions and often comes right after you have been asked, 'What is your greatest strength?' (see Chapter 13).

Every conceivable answer has already been used a hundred times, so saying you work too hard isn't going to impress anyone. The truth of the matter is that we all have weaknesses, even you and I, and this is one instance when any interviewer is going to relish an honest answer like a breath of fresh air. Your goal is to be honest and forthright without torpedoing your chances.

We all share a weakness: keeping up with rapid changes in technology. Changes in technology give everyone an ongoing challenge: getting up to speed with the new skills demanded if you are to do your job well. Your answer can address this very issue and in the process still show that you are someone capable of staying on top of things in a rapidly changing workplace.

First talk about these constantly evolving challenges, then follow with examples that show how you *are* keeping up with the technologies that affect your productivity. 'I'm currently reading about...', 'I just attended a weekend workshop...', or 'I'm signed up for classes in...'

With this type of answer you identify your weakness as something that is only of concern to the most dedicated and forward-looking professionals in your field.

You could also talk about the general difficulties of keeping up with all the deliverables of the job and use it to talk about what you are doing to develop your multitasking skills. You can also consider the following as effective alternatives or as additional illustrations if they are demanded:

- If there is a minor part of the target job where you lack knowledge – but knowledge you will pick up quickly and can prove that you will pick it up quickly – use that.

- Identify a weakness that has no possible relation to the needs of this job. Although if you do this, you might be asked for another example, which will bring you back to the first two options.

'How do you go about solving problems in your work?'

Every position, from CEO to fast-food server, has its problems and challenges. This question examines your grasp of analytical thinking, and asks you to explain your approach to problem solving. There is an established approach to problem solving that everyone who gets ahead in his or her professional life learns. When confronted with a problem, you take these steps:

- Define the problem.
- Identify why it's a problem and for whom it's a problem.
- Identify what's causing the problem.
- Seek input from everyone affected by the problem.
- Identify possible solutions.
- Identify the time, cost and resources it will take to implement each option.
- Evaluate the consequences of each solution.
- Decide upon the best solution.
- Identify and execute the steps necessary to solve the problem.

Your answer should cover these steps. If asked for a real-world example, you'll have plenty in mind from your TJD exercises. Remember to recall the results and benefits of your solution and the transferable skills that came into play.

'With hindsight, how could you have improved your progress?'

This is a question that asks you to discuss your commitment to success. As professional success affects so many other parts of your life, take time to think through the mistakes you have made and commit to getting better control of your career for the future. Whatever you choose to say, when it comes to questions asking for information detrimental to your chances, always put your answer in the past: you woke up, took responsibility and corrected the situation. Show that, having learned from the experience, you are now committed to ongoing professional development.

'What kinds of decisions are most difficult for you?'

You are human – admit it, but be careful what you admit. The employer is looking for people who can make decisions and solve problems, not those who'll dither. You want to come over as someone who's decisive but not precipitate, who considers the implications of actions on outcomes, any side effects those actions might have on other activities, and whether they conflict with existing systems and procedures or other company priorities.

If you have ever had to fire someone, you are in luck, because no one likes to do that. Emphasize that, having reached a logical conclusion, you act. If you are not in management, tie your answer to transferable skills and professional values: 'It's not that I have difficulty making decisions – some just require more consideration than others. A small example might be holiday leave. Now, everyone is entitled to it, but I don't believe you should leave your boss in a bind. I think very carefully at the beginning of the year when I'd like to take my holiday, and then think of some alternative dates as well. I go to my supervisor, tell him what I hope to do, and see whether there is any conflict. I wouldn't want to be out of the office for the two weeks prior to a project deadline, for instance. So by carefully considering things far enough in advance, I make sure my plans fit in with my boss and the department for the year.'

Here you take a trick question and use it to demonstrate your consideration, analytical abilities and concern for the department – and for the company's bottom line.

'Tell me about the problems you have living within your means.'

If you have experienced severe financial difficulties, you'll need to address them and how they have been handled. The answer needs to be carefully thought-out and short, emphasizing that you are in control of the situation. Otherwise, say that you continually strive to improve your skills and your living standard: 'I know few people who are satisfied with their current earnings. As a professional, I am continually striving to improve my skills and my living standard. But my problems are no different from those of this or any other company – making sure all the bills get paid on time and recognizing that every month and year there are some things that are prudent to do and others that are best deferred.'

'What area of your skills/professional development do you want to improve at this time?'

Another 'tell me all your weaknesses' question. Don't damage your image with careless admissions of weakness. Choose a skill where you are competent but that everyone, including the interviewer, knows demands constant personal attention. Technology skills as they apply to your job could be a good example of a 'weakness' that every committed professional shares. Cite the importance and challenge of keeping up in this area and finish by saying, '_____ is so important, I don't think I will ever stop paying attention to this area.' Be prepared to explain how you are working on this skill development right now. 'In fact, I'm reading a book on this now', or 'I'm taking another course next...' There are plenty of books and online courses on every topic under the sun, so if you are engaged with your career, you should be able to give some details.

One effective answer to this is to say, 'Well, from what you told me about the job, I seem to have all the necessary skills and background. What I would really find exciting is the opportunity to work in a job where...' At this point, you replay the skill-development area you cited. This approach allows you to emphasize what you find exciting about the job and that you have all the required technical skills and are proactively committed to professional skill development. It works admirably.

You can finish by saying, 'These areas are so important that I don't think anyone can be too good or should ever stop trying to polish their skills.'

'Your application shows you have been with one company a long time without any appreciable increase in rank or salary. Tell me about this.'

Analyse why this state of affairs exists. It may be that you like your professional life exactly as it is. You take pride in your work and haven't pushed for promotions. If so, tell it like it is, because most people are eager for a promotion – someone who isn't could make a good employee; it could be your ace.

Here are some tactics you can use. First of all, try to avoid putting your salary history on application forms. No one is going to deny you an interview for lack of a salary history if your skills match those the job requires. And of course, you should never put such unnecessary information on your CV.

Now, we'll address the delicate matter of, 'Hey, wait a minute; why no promotions?' The interviewer has posed a truly negative inquiry. The more time either of you spend on it, the more time the interviewer gets to devote to concentrating on negative aspects of your career. Make your answer short and sweet, then shut up. For instance, 'My current employer is a stable company with a good working environment, but there's minimal growth there in my area – in fact, there hasn't been any promotion in my department since _____. Your question is the reason why I am here today; I have the skills and ability to take on more responsibility, and I'm looking for a place to do that.'

'In your current job, what should you spend more time on and why?'

Without a little self-control you could easily blurt out what you consider to be your greatest weaknesses. Tricky question, but with a little forethought your answer will shine.

Enlightened self-interest dictates that your ongoing career management strategies identify and develop the skills demanded in a constantly changing work environment that make you desirable to employers, and that each of your job changes should occur within the context of an overall career management strategy.

So your answer might address the fact that existing skills always need to be improved and new skills acquired, citing an example of some skill development initiative you are working on now. Unless you are in sales/marketing, you could add that with networking seen as so important by everyone today, you should probably be investing more time in that; in sales and marketing, of course, this is your very lifeblood.

Your answer might include, 'With the fast pace of change in our profession, existing skills always need to be improved and new skills learned. For instance, in this job I think the organizational software now available can have a major impact on personal productivity. If I stayed with my current employer this would be a priority, just as it will be when I make the move to my next job; it's in my own best interests to have good skills.'

With an answer along these lines you show foresight instead of a weakness. You can then end with:

- Courses you have taken and are planning to take.
- Books you have read or book clubs to which you belong.
- Memberships of professional associations.
- Subscriptions to professional journals.

Such an answer will identify you as an aware, connected and dedicated professional.

'Are you willing to take calculated risks when necessary?'

Confirm your understanding of the question by qualifying it: 'How do you define calculated risks? Can you give me an example?' This will give you more information as well as more time to think while the interviewer repeats the question in more detail. You can use this 'qualifying the question' technique with tough questions when you want a little recovery time.

Once you understand the question, you'll probably answer 'Yes' if you want the job offer. Be prepared with an example for the possible follow-up question showing how your calculations and preparation minimize potential risk. Whatever your answer, the risk taken must be within the normal bounds of the execution of your duties and in no way jeopardize colleagues or company.

'See this pen I'm holding? Sell it to me.'

This question often comes up for sales professionals, but every employee needs to know how to communicate effectively and sell appropriately – sometimes products, but more often ideas, approaches and concepts. This is what the interviewer is getting at with this apparently out-of-the-blue request.

As such, you are being examined on your understanding of constitutive/needs-based features and benefits sales, how quickly you think on your feet, and how effectively you use verbal communication. For example, say the interviewer holds up a yellow highlighter. First you will want to establish the customer's needs with a few questions like, 'What sort of pens do you currently use? Do you use a highlighter? Do you read reports and need to recall important points? Is comfort important to you?' Then you will proceed calmly, 'Let me tell you about the special features of this pen and show you how it will satisfy your needs. First of all, it is tailor-made for highlighting reports, and that will save you time when recalling the most important points. The case is wide for comfort and the base is flat so it will stand up and be visible on a cluttered work area. It's disposable – and affordable enough to have a handful for desk, briefcase, car and home. And the bright yellow means you'll never lose it.' Then close with a smile and a question of your own that will bring a smile to the interviewer's face: 'How many boxes shall we deliver?'

'How will you be able to cope with a change in environment after _____ years with your current company?'

Another chance to take an implied negative and turn it into a positive: 'That's one of the reasons I want to make a change. After five years with my current employer, I felt I was about to get stale. I have exemplary skills in _____, _____ and _____. It's time for me to take these skills to a new and more challenging environment and experience some new thinking and approaches. Hopefully, I'll have the chance to contribute from my experience.'

'Why aren't you earning more at your age?'

Accept this as a compliment of your skills and accomplishments. 'I have always felt that solid experience would stand me in good stead in the long run and that earnings would come in due course. Also, I am not the type of person to change jobs just for the money. At this point, I have a set of desirable skills [itemize them as they relate to the job's priorities] and the time has come for me to join a team that needs and values these skills. How much should I be earning now?' The figure could be your offer.

'What is the worst thing you have heard about our company?'

This question can come as something of a shock. As with all stress questions, your poise under stress is vital. If you can carry off a halfway decent answer as well, you are a winner. The best response to this question is simple. Just say with a smile and a laugh, 'You are a tough company to get an interview with, and you demand a lot of your employees. But I actually like that about you, because I'm looking to gain the sort of expertise that will help my professional growth.' This way you compliment the company and pass off the negative judgement as a misperception by all those other idiots who think that hard work is a bad thing.

'Why should I hire an outsider when I could fill the job with someone inside the company?'

The question isn't as stupid as it sounds. Obviously, the interviewer has examined existing employees with an eye towards their promotion or reassignment. Just as obviously, the job cannot be filled from within the company. If it could be, it would be, and for two very good reasons: it is cheaper for the company to promote from within, and it is better for employee morale.

Hiding behind this intimidating question is a pleasant invitation: 'Tell me why I should hire you.' Your answer should include two steps. The first is a recitation of your technical and transferable skills, tailored to the job's needs.

For the second step, understand that whenever a manager is filling a position, he or she is looking not only for someone who can do the job, but also for someone who can benefit the department in a larger sense. No department is as good as it could be – each has weaknesses that need strengthening. So in the second part of your answer, include a question of your own: 'Those are my general attributes. However, if no one is promotable from inside the company, you must be looking to add strength to your team in a special way. How do you hope the final candidate will be able to benefit your department?' The answer to this is your cue to sell your applicable qualities.

'Have you ever had any financial difficulties?'

A common question, especially if you deal with money. Tell the truth because your answers can be checked. If you are asked, and you've had problems, give the circumstances, the facts of your difficulties and where you stand today in resolving those issues. Do not bring up financial problems until this question is asked or an offer is on the table and references are to be checked.

If you have had to file for bankruptcy be honest, professional and as brief as possible. Don't give any information about the circumstances: it isn't necessary and no one wants to know. What employers do want to hear is that you have turned the corner and everything is under control now. They also want to know, very briefly, what you learned and have done to rebuild your credit and get back on your feet.

Financial difficulties aren't the deal-breaker they used to be, unless they affect the employer's insurance obligations, and in light of the corporate and personal financial crises of recent years, many organizations are re-evaluating and taking a more realistic stance on these matters.

'How should I handle a motoring offence?'

Will the job require you to drive a company vehicle and will the offence affect the company's insurance? If the application form asks, answer honestly and leave it be; if not, don't offer this information unless asked for it.

'How should I handle a criminal record?'

Briefly, it depends on the length and type of sentence you incurred and the job you are applying for. Some convictions are considered 'spent' after a certain time or in certain circumstances. It can be complicated, and if you are in any doubt about what applies in your own situation, check on the NACRO website or contact Citizens Advice. Learn what you have to disclose to an employer and don't disclose more than you have to. Briefly, tell the employer what you've learned and that it is behind you.

There's no need to discuss issues that didn't result in conviction or anything that has been 'spent'.

'Tell me about a time things didn't work out well.'

There are two techniques that every skilled interviewer will use, especially if you are giving good answers. In this question, the interviewer looks for negative balance; in the follow-up, the interviewer might look for negative confirmation. Here, you are required to give an example of an inadequacy. The trick is to pull something from the past, not the present, and to finish with what you learned from the experience.

For example: 'That's easy. When I first joined the workforce, I didn't really understand the importance of systems and procedures. There was a sales visit report everyone had to fill out after visiting a customer. I always put a lot of effort into it until I realized it was never read; it just went in a file. So I stopped doing it for a few days to see if it made any difference. I thought I was gaining time to make more sales for the company. I was so proud of my extra sales calls, I told the boss at the end of the week. My boss explained that the records were for the long term, so that should my job change, the next salesperson would have the benefit of a full client history. It was a long time ago, but I have never forgotten the lesson: There's always a reason for systems and procedures. I've had the best-kept records in the company ever since.'

To look for negative confirmation, the interviewer may then say something like, 'Thank you. Now can you give me another example?' He or she is trying to confirm a weakness. If you help, you could cost yourself the job. Here's your reaction: you sit deep in thought for a good 10 seconds, then look up and say firmly, 'No, that's the only occasion when anything like that happened.' Shut up and refuse to be enticed further.

'Tell me about a time when you put your foot in your mouth.'

Answer this question with caution. The interviewer is examining your ability and willingness to interact pleasantly with others. The question is tricky because it asks you to show yourself in a poor light. Downplay the negative impact of your action and end with positive information about your professionalism. The best thing to do is to start with an example outside the workplace and show how the experience improved your performance at work.

'About five years ago, I let the cat out of the bag about a surprise birthday party for a friend, a terrific faux pas. It was a mortifying experience, and I promised myself not to let anything like that happen again.' Then, after this fairly innocuous statement, you can talk about communications in the workplace: 'As far as work is concerned, I always regard employer–employee communications on any matter as confidential unless expressly stated otherwise. So, putting my foot in my mouth doesn't happen to me at work.'

'What was there about your last company that you didn't particularly like or agree with?'

Be careful not to criticize a manager, or you might be seen as a potential management problem. It is safest to say that you didn't have any of these problems. If there was an unhappy work environment and this opinion was shared by many, you can mention it, but remain nonspecific, although you might mention that some people didn't seem to care about anything they did, and you found this difficult.

Another option: 'I didn't like the way some people gave lip service to the "customer comes first" mantra, but really didn't go out of their way to keep the customer satisfied. I don't think it was a fault of management, just a general malaise that seemed to affect a lot of people.'

'What do you feel is a satisfactory attendance record?'

There are two answers to this question – one if you are in management, and one if you are not. As a manager: 'I believe attendance is a matter of management, motivation and psychology. Letting the employees know you expect their best efforts and won't accept half-baked excuses is one thing. The other is to keep your employees motivated by a congenial work environment and the challenge to stretch themselves. Giving people pride in their work and letting them know you respect them as individuals have a lot to do with it, too.'

If you are not in management, the answer is even easier: 'I've never really considered it. I work for a living, I enjoy my job, and I'm rarely sick.'

'What is your general impression of your last company?'

Always answer positively. There is a strong belief in management ranks that people who complain about past employers will cause problems for their new ones. Your answer is, 'A good department and company to work for.' Then smile and wait for the next question. If pressed for more, add, 'I had gone as far as I could and could see no opportunities opening up, so I decided it was time to make a strategic career move.'

'What are some of the things you find difficult to do? Why do you feel that way?'

This is a variation on a couple of earlier questions. Remember, anything that goes against the best interests of your employer is difficult to do. Your answer should share a difficulty common to the job and everyone who does that job, and at the same time advance your cause; difficult, but not impossible.

'That's a tough question. There are so many things that are difficult to keep up with, considering the pace of business today and the pace of change technology brings to our profession. One of my problems has been staying on top of the customer base in a productive and responsible fashion. I built my territory and had 140 clients to sell to every month, and I was so busy touching base with all of them that I never got a chance to sell to any of them. So I graded them into three groups. I called on the top 20 per cent of my clients every three weeks. The balance of my clients I called on once a month, but with a difference – each month, I marked 10 of them to spend time with and really get to know. I still have difficulty reaching all my clients in a month, but with time management, prioritization and organization, my sales have tripled and are still climbing.'

'Jobs have pluses and minuses. What were some of the minuses of your last job?'

A variation on the question, 'What interests you least about this job?' which was handled earlier. Potentially explosive but easily defused. Regardless of your occupation, there is at least one repetitive, mindless duty that everyone groans about but which has to be done. You just need to show that you recognize its importance despite the boredom factor and take care of business responsibly. For example, 'Client visit reports are probably the least exciting part of my job. However, I know they are important for reference and continuity, so I do them at the end of the day as part of my daily performance review and next-day planning.' This response answers the question without shooting yourself in the foot, and shows that you possess analytical thinking and multitasking skills. You can finish with a nod towards your professional values and teamwork skills: 'Besides, if I don't do the paperwork, that holds up other people in the company.'

Or perhaps, 'In accounts receivable, it's my job to get the money. Half the time, the goods are shipped before I get the paperwork because Sales says, "It's a rush order." That's a real minus for me. It was so bad at my last company that we tried a new approach. We had a meeting with Sales and explained our problem. The result was that incremental commissions were based on cash in, not on invoice date. They saw the connection, and things are much better now.'

'What kind of people do you like to work with?'

This is the easy part of what can be a tricky three-part question. Obviously, you like to work with people who are fully engaged with their work and who come to work with a smile and who make a difference with their presence. People who are there to get results, not just mark time until the end of the day. You like to work with people who have pride, honesty, integrity and commitment to their work.

'What kind of people do you find it difficult to work with?'

This question can stand alone or can be the second part of a three-part question. Your answer comes from understanding why your job exists. It's a small cog in the complex machinery of making a company profitable, so you might say, 'People who don't care about their work and don't care about being part of something larger than themselves, people who have the time to find fault but not to find solutions.' End by noting that while they aren't the best co-workers, you don't let them interfere with your motivation.

Or, 'People who don't follow procedures, or slackers – the occasional rotten apples who don't really care about the quality of their work. They have plenty of complaints, but few solutions.'

'How have you worked with this difficult type of person successfully?'

Sometimes this question stands alone; other times it's the third part of a three-part question. First, you don't let such people affect your motivation or quality of work. Secondly, you don't sustain their negativism by encouraging them. You are polite and professional but prefer to ally yourself with the people who come to work to make a difference. You maintain cordial relations but don't go out of your way to seek close acquaintance. Life is too short to be demotivated by people who think their cup is half empty and it's someone else's fault.

Or you might reply with something like: 'I stick to my guns, stay enthusiastic, and hope some of it will rub off. I had a big problem with one person – all he did was complain, and always in my area. Eventually, I told him how I felt. I said if I was a millionaire, I'd clearly have all the answers and wouldn't have to work, but as it was, I wasn't, and had to work for a living. I told him that I really enjoyed his company but I didn't want to hear it anymore. Every time I saw him after that, I presented him with a work problem and asked his advice. In other words I challenged him to come up with positives, not negatives.'

You might even end by noting that sometimes you've noticed that such people simply lack enthusiasm and confidence, and that energetic and cheerful co-workers can often change that.

'How did you get your last job?'

The interviewer is looking for initiative. Show that you went about your search with planning, organization and intelligence, the same way you'd approach a work project. At least show determination. For example: 'I was turned down for my last job for having too little experience. I asked the manager to give me a trial for the afternoon, then and there. I was given a list of companies they'd never sold to. I picked up the phone and didn't get close to a sale all afternoon, but she could see I had guts.'

'How would you evaluate me as an interviewer?'

The question is dangerous, maybe more so than the one asking you to criticize your boss. If you think the interviewer is a congenital imbecile whom you wouldn't work for on a bet, don't tell the truth, because behind this question is a desire to see your verbal and diplomacy skills in action. This is an instance when honesty is not the best policy: remember, you are there to get a job offer.

It is best to say, 'This is one of the toughest interviews I have ever been through, and I don't relish the prospect of going through another. I have great professional skills, but interviewing is not one of them; it's not something I have had much experience doing. Yet I do realize that you are just trying to determine if I have the skills you need.' Then go on to explain how your skills match the job. You may choose to finish the answer with a question of your own: 'I think I can do this job, and I think I would like it. What do you think?'

'Wouldn't you feel better off in another company?'

Relax, things aren't as bad as you might assume. This question is usually asked if you are really doing quite well or if the job involves a certain amount of stress. A lawyer, for example, might well be expected to face this one. The trick is not to be intimidated. Your first step is to qualify the question. Relax, take a breath, sit back, smile, and say, 'You surprise me. Why do you say that?' The interviewer must then talk, giving you precious time to collect your wits and come back with a rebuttal.

Then answer 'No', and explain why. All the interviewer wants to see is how much you know about the company and how determined you are to join its ranks. Overcome the objection with an example showing how you will contribute to the company. You could reply, 'Not at all. My whole experience has been with small companies. I am good at my job and in time could become a big fish in a little pond. But that is not what I want. This organization is a leader in its business. You have a strong reputation for encouraging skills development in your employees. This is the type of environment I want to work in. Coming from a small company, I have done a little bit of everything. That means that no matter what you throw at me, I will learn it quickly.'

Then end with a question of your own. In this instance, the question has a twofold purpose: first, to identify a critical area to sell yourself, and secondly, to encourage the interviewer to imagine you working at the company; for example, 'What would be the first project you'd need me to tackle?'

You end with a question of your own that gets the interviewer focusing on those immediate problems. You can then move the conversation forward with an explanation of how your background and experience can help.

'What would you say if I told you your presentation this afternoon was terrible?'

This question is asked to help a manager understand how emotionally mature you are. When it is a manager's duty to criticize performance, he or she needs to know that you will respond in a professional and emotionally mature way.

'If' is the key word here. The question tests your poise, analytical thinking, and communication skills. Don't assume you are being criticized. An appropriate response would be: 'First of all, I would ask which aspects of my presentation were bad. I would need to find out where you felt the problem was. If there was a miscommunication, I'd clear it up. If the problem was elsewhere, I would seek your advice, confirm that I understood it, and be sure that the problem did not recur.'

Building stress into a sequence of questions

Sometimes an interviewer will build stress into a sequence of questions. Starting off innocently enough, the questions are layered and sequenced to dig deeper and deeper, but these stress question sequences will hold few surprises for you. Let's take the simple example of 'Can you work under pressure?'

This example will use a reporter's technique of asking who, what, where, when, why and how. The technique can be applied to any question you are asked and is frequently used to probe those success stories that sound too good to be true. You'll find them suddenly tagged on to the simple closed-ended questions as well as to the open-ended ones. They can often start with phrases like, 'Tell me about a time when...', or 'I'm interested in finding out about...', followed by a request for specific examples from your work history.

'Can you work under pressure?'

A simple, closed-ended question that requires just a yes-or-no answer, but you won't get off so easy.

'I'd be interested to hear about a time when you experienced pressure in your job.'

An open-ended request to tell a story about a pressure situation. After this, you will be subjected to the layering technique – six layers in the following instance.

'Why do you think this situation arose?'

It's best if the situation you describe is not a peer's or manager's fault. Remember, you must be seen as a team player.

'How do you feel others involved could have acted more responsibly?'

An open invitation to criticize peers and superiors, which you should diplomatically decline.

'Who holds the responsibility for the situation?'

Another invitation to point the finger of blame, which should be avoided.

'Where in the chain of command could steps be taken to avoid that sort of thing happening again?'

This question probes your analytical skills and asks whether you are the type of person who takes the time to revisit the scene of the crime to learn for the next time.

After you've survived that barrage, a friendly tone may conceal another zinger: 'What did you learn from the experience?' This question is designed to probe your judgement and emotional maturity. Your answer should emphasize whichever of the key professional behaviours your story was illustrating.

When an interviewer feels you were on the edge of revealing something unusual in an answer, you may well encounter 'mirror statements'. Here, the last key phrase of your answer will be repeated or paraphrased, and followed by a steady gaze and silence. For example, 'So, you learned that organization is the key to management.' The idea is that the silence and an expectant look will work together to keep you talking. It can be disconcerting to find yourself rambling on without quite knowing why. The trick is knowing when to stop. When the interviewer gives you an expectant look in this context, expand your answer (you have to), but by no more than a couple of sentences. Otherwise, you will get that creepy feeling that you're digging yourself into a hole.

The illegal question

Of course, one of the most stressful – and negative – questions is the illegal one, a question that delves into your private life or personal background. Such a question will make you uncomfortable if it is blatant and could also make you angry.

Your aim, however, is to overcome your discomfort and avoid getting angry. You want to be offered the job, and any self-righteousness or defensive reaction on your part will ensure that you *don't* get it. You may feel angry enough to get up and walk out or say things like, 'These are unfair practices; you'll hear from my solicitor in the morning.' However, the result will be that you won't get the job and, therefore, won't have the leverage you need. Remember, no one is saying you can't refuse the job once it's offered to you.

So, what is an illegal question? The Equality Act of 2010 forbid employers from discriminating against any person on the basis of sex, age, race, marital status, disability, national origin or religion:

- An interviewer may not ask about your religion, church, synagogue or parish, the religious holidays you observe or your political beliefs or affiliations. He or she may not ask, for instance, 'Does your religion allow you to work on Saturdays?' but may ask something like, 'This job requires work on Saturdays. Is that a problem?' Similarly, the interviewer may enquire if the usual number of hours a week required will be acceptable.

- An interviewer may not ask about your ancestry, national origin or parentage. In addition, you cannot be asked about the naturalization status of your parents, spouse or children. The interviewer cannot ask about your birthplace, *but* may ask (and probably will, considering the current immigration laws) whether you are a citizen or resident with the right to work in this country.

- An interviewer may not ask about your native language, the language you speak at home or how you acquired the ability to read, write or speak a foreign language. *However,* he or she may ask about the languages in which you are fluent, if knowledge of those languages is pertinent to the job.

- An interviewer may not ask about your age, date of birth or the ages of your children. *However,* he or she may ask you if you are over 18 years old.

- An interviewer may not ask about maiden names or if you have changed your name, your marital status, number of children or dependants or your spouse's occupation or, if you are a woman, whether you wish to be addressed as Miss, Mrs or Ms. *However,* the interviewer may ask about how you like to be addressed (a common courtesy) and if you have ever worked for the company before under a different name. If you have, you may want to mention that, especially as your prospective manager may check your references and additional background information.

As you consider a question that seems to verge on illegality, you should take into account that the interviewer may be asking it innocently and may be unaware of the laws on the matter. Even more likely is that the interviewer likes you and is interested in you as a person. When we meet someone new, the first questions will often be, 'Where are you from?' 'Are you married?' 'Do you have children?' Bear this in mind so that you don't overreact.

Your best bet is to be polite and straightforward, as you would in any other social situation. You also want to move the conversation on to an examination of your skills and abilities, and away from personal issues. Here are some common illegal questions and possible responses. Remember, your objective is to get job offers; if you later decide that this company is not for you, you are under no obligation to accept the position.

'What religion do you practise?'

If you do practise, you can say, 'I attend my church/synagogue/ mosque regularly, but I make it my practice not to involve my personal beliefs in my work. My work for the company and my career are too important for that.'

If you do not practise a religion, you may want to say something like, 'I have a set of personal beliefs that are important to me, but I do not attend any organized services. And I do not mix those beliefs with my work, if that's what you mean.'

'Are you married?

If you are, the company is concerned with the impact your family duties and future plans will have on your time there. Your answer could be, 'Yes, I am. Of course, I make a separation between my work life and my family life that allows me to give my all to a job. I have no problem with travel or late hours – those things are part of this line of work. I'm sure my references will confirm this for you.'

'Do you plan to have children?'

This isn't any of the interviewer's business, but he or she wants to know whether or not you will leave the company early to raise a family. You can answer 'No' of course. If you answer 'Yes' you might add, 'But those plans are for the future and they depend on the success of my career. Certainly, I want to do the best, most complete job for this company I can. I consider that my skills are right for the job and that I can make a long-term contribution. I certainly have no plans to leave the company just as I begin to make meaningful contributions.' However, unless this question is also asked of male applicants, it could be considered as discriminating against women. The skilful interviewer can usually elicit such information without asking a direct question.

If the questions become too pointed, you may want to ask, innocently, 'Could you explain the relevance of that issue to this position?' That response, however, can seem confrontational, so you should only use it if you are extremely uncomfortable or are quite certain you can get away with it. Sometimes, the interviewer will drop the line of questioning.

Illegal questions tend to arise not out of brazen insensitivity but, rather, out of an interest in you. The employer is familiar with your skills and background, feels you can do the job and wants to get to know you as a person. Outright discrimination these days is really quite rare. With illegal questions, your response must be positive – that's the only way you're going to be offered the job and winning that creates a platform for getting other jobs. You don't have to work for a discriminatory company, but you can certainly use the firm to get to something better.

How to fight age discrimination in your job search

It is illegal to discriminate against an applicant on grounds of age; however, the appearance of age can give rise to some valid unspoken concerns from the other side of the desk: that you could be a management problem, that perhaps you won't fit in, that you aren't technologically up-to-date and that you aren't there for the long haul.

The older you get, the greater the chance that your interviewer will be younger and quite possibly intimidated about the management threats you could pose.

Since lots of reasons for this discrimination have nothing to do with your ability to do the job, the smart course is to fight back with some of the hard-won street smarts that come with age, experience and understanding.

Age discrimination at job interviews comes in two flavours, spoken and unspoken. Learning to address both types can make the difference between job offers and rejection.

Spoken age discrimination

Questions about age at an interview can usually be considered illegal. However, that doesn't stop them being asked, so the question is how to handle them.

Since it won't be to your advantage to take offence, just tell yourself that the interviewer is showing interest in you as a person, as we've discussed previously, and look for ways that you can answer that make a contribution towards your candidacy at the same time.

In answer to a direct question about your age, you could simply reply: 'I'm 49.' That's okay as far as it goes, but it doesn't do anything to advance your application, so let's examine an alternative, where you answer the question and show that your age is a plus: 'It's interesting that you should ask. I just turned 49. That gives me _____ years in the profession, and _____ years doing exactly the job you're trying to fill. In those years, I've gained experience in all kind of situations and environments, made my share of mistakes on someone else's payroll, and learned from them. [Smile.] I suppose the great benefit of my experience and energy level is...'

Then finish with a benefit statement about what you bring to the job.

Unspoken age discrimination

Even if questions about age remain unspoken, you know they are still being asked – it's only human. In my coaching practice, I tell clients that, if age-related questions are not asked, they have two options:

1 Say nothing and hope age isn't an issue.

2 Face the fact that age discrimination exists and find ways to make your age a benefit to this manager.

You should own your age and seize appropriate opportunities to share how it can be a benefit to the department and to the manager personally. I suggest you personalize an answer along the lines of: 'Jack, if I sat in your chair looking at me, a seasoned professional, I'd have age-related questions that I couldn't ask. I'd be considering issues like energy, drive, manageability, how well you'd get on with a team where everyone looks _____ years younger, and I'd be thinking about your ability to keep up professionally.'

If you don't have a chance earlier in the interview, raise this point when asked, 'Do you have any questions?' You can then proceed, as in the previous example, with the benefits of your experience and maturity as they relate to the job under consideration. You can add comments about the following issues too, as they relate to your circumstances:

Emergencies

- 'My experience means that I have already lived through panics, emergencies and times when everything goes wrong. When crises occur, as they do in even the best-run operations, I know how to handle them calmly. I've been there and lived through them and learned from the experience.'

- 'Because I've been through panics and emergencies before, you'll find me a steadying influence who won't get flustered about a little extra effort and who will do my part in bringing the team together to tackle the issue.'

Loyalty

- 'The average professional stays in a job four years, and the younger your workforce, the faster the turnover; the older the worker, the slower the turnover. High turnover is disruptive to meeting the deliverables of this department and it affects your job and your reputation.'

- 'Hire another young Turk and you know that she will constantly be haggling for promotions and possibly your job, and on top of this, she will be gone in four years.'

- 'I don't want your job, I want this job, and I'm not intending to change again in four years. I just want to find a first-class team, settle down and, over time, earn my place as a trusted member of your workforce – as someone you can count on.'

Your right hand

- 'I'm competent, experienced, conscientious, calm, and motivated.'

- 'You'll come to see me as someone you can rely on to get the job done and who is a positive influence.'

- 'You'll see me as someone who can be trusted, and most of all, someone who will support you in all things.'

- 'At your request I could mentor less-experienced team members.'

You can indeed bring all these benefits to an employer and a department. Take the time to think about each of these points and personalize them to your profession and work experience. The result will be an increased awareness of your unique selling points, and this will increase your self-confidence.

Make statements such as the previous ones, as they apply to you and your profession, and you will do more than answer the unspoken questions. You will make a series of compelling arguments in favour of your candidacy. You will show yourself to be unusually perceptive, balanced, focused on the issues, and to the point, and you will doubtless score some other points in your favour.

ANSWERING UNANSWERABLE QUESTIONS

Job interviews are scary. You are being judged professionally, and it's easy to *feel* you're being judged as a person, too. Almost everyone feels invalidated when things don't pan out. And then every year you read something about the 'stupid questions' employers ask, questions like:

- 'How many children are born every day?'
- 'If you were asked to unload a 747 full of jelly beans, what would you do?'
- 'Why are manholes round?'
- 'What kind of tree would you like to be and why?'

How do you answer questions like these? How do such questions help employers make decisions? Actually, *most* of these questions aren't as daft as they might sound, and yes, they do all have answers.

Engage with your profession, the world and your life

We live in a post-industrial era alternatively known as 'the Knowledge Era', 'the Digital Age', 'the Information Age', and other names. What they all convey is that our jobs increasingly demand the analysis, manipulation, and movement of information. This makes our analytical and processing abilities increasingly important to potential employers. Some of us have these skills naturally, and some of us don't; however, we can all increase our analytical and processing skills.

Successful professionals consistently engage with professional journals, podcasts and blogs that address issues relating to their profession. Reading, watching, listening and engaging in professional discussion with your peers will keep you informed about all the critical issues of your professional arena, and the world in which it operates. It will make you a more competent professional with a far wider frame of reference, and together these will hone your analytical skills. It will also make you a more interesting colleague for others who share the same commitment.

If you are thoroughly engaged with your profession and take an interest in the world around you, answering the following mind-boggling questions will become much easier as you become a better-informed and smarter person.

The point is that these seemingly absurd questions are invariably conceived with a purpose: to evaluate intelligence, analytical and processing skills as they relate to individual and team performance. We'll start with the easy ones.

What kind of tree would you like to be?'

I've never heard it asked and never communicated with anyone who has been asked it, so this one may well be apocryphal. But people claim that it is asked, so what would you say? Remember:

- to think with your professional hat on;
- the values and behaviours most valued by employers;
- as a manager, what makes a good team member.

With these thoughts in mind, imagine yourself to be an employer asking this question. What are you be thinking? You're wondering about all the obvious issues surrounding skills and the deliverables of the job, and you're wondering about a candidate's values and how she sees herself. With this in mind it isn't really very hard to come up with a reasonable answer.

Remember that interviews are focused on evaluating the *professional you*. It is easy to see that asking, 'How do you see yourself?' is likely to generate a rehearsed answer. But by asking the question in an unusual way you throw the applicant off-guard, and you are likely to get a more revealing answer. This is the thinking that leads interviewers to ask many of the very unsettling questions discussed in this chapter.

In developing ideas for what your answer might be, focus on the behaviours and values that are relevant to your profession and that (in our example) might be applied to a tree – I know this sounds strange but just bear with me and it will all start to make sense.

Determine a tree onto which you can apply *professional values and transferable skills*; something like this: 'I would like to be an oak. It is strong with a deep root system that keeps it steady and it survives no matter what the weather. It doesn't matter what you throw at it (even lightning bolts); the oak can and does take it. Living more than 200 years, it is reliable and provides support and sustenance to many different plants and animals, and its permanence supplies shade and shelter to anyone who needs it. It is strong, substantial, deep, reliable and is always a good landmark.'

Even a crazy question like this can be answered if you know what is important to your work and to being a productive *team player*. In fact, all these seemingly crazy questions have roots in these considerations, because that is what is important to a manager: find someone who can do the job, play well with others and not give me headaches.

'Why are manhole covers round?'

This question examines logic and analytical skills. Asked in the context of a job that deals with design, building or manufacturing, it also examines spatial intelligence and your understanding of basic design principles. Manhole covers are round because:

- rectangular manhole covers can fall into the hole;
- round manhole covers cannot fall into the manhole;

- rectangular manhole covers have to be aligned to fit back into the manhole once work is completed;

- round manhole covers don't need to be aligned;

- manhole covers are made of cast iron and are incredibly heavy. If you have to move a heavy object you can either lift it or roll it. Rectangular covers have to be lifted to be moved; round covers don't have to be lifted and can be rolled.

By making these points in an answer you demonstrate analytical skills that nail the problems, causes and solutions. If you ever face this question, answer it with pleasure in your voice over the elegant simplicity of the design and the very real problem it solves. Your answer will be correct, and your tone of voice will show that you appreciate such thinking.

'Name three previous Nobel Prize winners'

Who can answer this question and how they answer it holds the solution to how you should approach it.

The only people who can readily answer this question are people who love absorbing information for its own sake; people who are attuned to what is going on in their profession and with an interest in the activities and figures who help make the world a better place – exactly what we have been talking about previously.

Why you give the answer you do is just as important as your answer itself.

There are 573 Nobel prize winners in six categories (physics, chemistry, medicine, literature, peace, economic sciences). Consequently, I don't think the interviewer will necessarily know if you actually named three Nobel prize winners.

Now, if you just give names, you will probably be asked for your reasoning, so this is one of those questions where you want to forestall further questions and get onto the next topic as soon as possible. I'd recommend a response and a reason; for example: 'Alfred Nobel – he invented dynamite and then left his fortune to making amends via the Nobel Prize. Nelson Mandela, because of all he did to achieve racial equality and peaceful resolution of conflict. Marie Curie, for her discovery of radium and all the implications of that for our modern society.'

Are these all Nobel Prize winners? I honestly don't know. But the answer shows wide knowledge covering divergent fields and indicates desirable behaviours and values: getting along with people, finding peaceful resolutions to conflict, making a change for good.

'What if' questions

We now come to questions that everyone asks about what you would do in different situations. The key to answering them all is showing that when presented with a challenge, you automatically examine it from different perspectives (evaluating the upside and downside of each) before offering a solution.

'If I came to your house for dinner, what would you serve?'

This is about how you decide what to serve. So you'd ask about food allergies, preferences, dietary restrictions, favourite and least favourite foods. Then you'd devise a menu and run it by the manager's administrative assistant to double-check the choices before you started implementation. You'd even go a little further and ask about environmental allergies – so you have time to put your cats outside and vacuum your home.

'If you had a choice between two superpowers (being invisible or able to fly) which would you choose?'

This one sometimes gets asked by product managers for high-tech companies, as well as in interviews for sales and marketing positions. Again, it is not so much the answer as your reasoning. You might say, 'If I were invisible no one would see what I am doing, which would be a negative, and I could also be perceived as deceptive. On the other hand, flying? That's going to get anyone's attention, plus you can get much more done.'

A variation of this question is, 'If you could be a superhero, who would you be?' Your answer can be the same – just give a name to the one that can fly, and no, it's not Mighty Mouse.

'Who would win in a fight between Spiderman and Batman?'

There is no right answer. I checked this out online and found hundreds of pages of people arguing this issue. Mark Hughes, the film critic at *Forbes*, has been quoted as saying, 'It's impossible to answer a question about comic book characters.' So I'd quote Mark Hughes in response to this question.

'Who is your favourite Disney princess?'

Cinderella, Esmeralda, Rapunzel... there have to be a hundred of them. Who knows and who even cares? All that matters is that you have a name and a reason. Fortunately, princesses are usually sickeningly perfect, so pick a name, any name, and align her behaviours and values with behaviours and values we talk about elsewhere in the book. The important thing is to show you think about the answer and that the answer you give reveals something about the *professional you*.

'Describe the colour yellow to somebody who is blind.'

This one is about listening and analytical skills. So you turn the challenge into questions: 'I would ask whether or not you can experience colours; what colours do you 'see'? I'd ask how you experience each of these colours. With this information, I can identify how you cognitively experience colour and also understand the vocabulary you use to express your understanding. This would give me the base data to evaluate and turn into metaphors that you're most likely to interpret accurately.'

'If you were shrunk to the size of a pencil and put in a blender, how would you get out?'

Any eight-year-old can answer this, but we adults have forgotten what the undersides of chairs and tables look like. With that change of viewpoint as we got older, we lost the fantasy and invention that went with being short (remember underneath that table, when it was a cave, a fort, a tepee?). We also lose our sense of wonder and creativity.

The question poses a fantasy situation. Once you work your way into it, the question becomes an exercise in basic logic: 'A pencil is about seven inches long, and a blender is six to twelve inches tall on the inside and rarely more than five inches across at the mouth. If I were shrunk small enough to fit in a blender it would mean that my legs would still be long enough to reach out and brace against the sides; I could gradually work my way up a few inches until I could reach the lip and pull myself out.'

'Why are there ridges around a coin?'

Unless you are a numismatist you won't know this one, which is perhaps why the only known occurrences of this question occur in financial houses. This is a question that enquires into a candidate's involvement with the arcane details of coins and money.

The ridges around the outside of some coins are called *milled edges*, and they are there to:

- Make counterfeiting that much more difficult.

- Prevent theft and fraud. Look at any old gold or silver coins without milled edges and you will see that many of them have tiny slivers of the gold or silver shaved off. The precious metal was stolen and the coin then fraudulently passed on at its face value.

Milled edges were invented to prevent this theft and fraud when our coinage was gold and silver based.

'What would you do if you were the one survivor of a plane crash?'

Always look for what is behind the question. A plane crash is a disaster and by applying the question to the workplace you can translate it this way: things go wrong in the best-run departments, and the interviewer wants to know about your reactions to stress. Your answer, then, should be about remaining calm and taking considered actions that exhibit leadership, creativity, practicality and logic.

First of all you display common sense. For safety, you get yourself away from the wreckage and regroup. What do you need? Water, shelter, communication and heat, so you return to the wreckage and search for water, food, clothing or other coverings, lighters and matches.

Most problematic is going to be finding matches or lighters because of security regulations, so you look for emergency supplies that exist in every cabin and look for the carry-on baggage of the flight crew. As you do these things you look for signs of life.

Next you withdraw and decide on where you will establish a base of operations: somewhere that offers defence against the elements and predators. In short, you stay calm enough to make sensible decisions that can help resolve a bad situation.

'If you were asked to unload a Boeing 767 full of jelly beans, what would you do?'

It's about how well you listen to the question, which is not how you would do it but what you would do. This means the short answer is, 'I'd do it.' But the smart applicant would answer, 'I'd do it of course, but I'd want to do the best job possible as efficiently as possible so I'd want to know where the jelly beans are to be moved to, how they are packed now, if I need to be concerned about repackaging and the time by which the task needs to be completed. Next, I'd want to get on site and evaluate the problem first hand and discover what resources are available to help execute the task – equipment, people and money.' You'd finish with something along the lines of, 'Then I'd devise a plan of attack that would deliver the desired outcome in the time available. From there I would roll up my sleeves and start work, constantly evaluating and revising as I went along.'

'How many children are born every day?'

We started the chapter with discussion of taking an interest in the world around you, and that answering these mind-boggling questions will become much easier if you do.

You might not know the answer but you can think of global associations involved with the wellbeing of children and say that you would consult these resources. Incidentally, UNICEF estimates 353,000 children are born a day. That's 245 a minute or 4.1 babies every second.

'Design a spice rack for the blind.'

This reveals your ability to think like your customer so that you can deliver what that customer needs. It also requires you to think of the cost of solutions from the company perspective.

There are a number of common-sense approaches to this question. You want to suggest some options and a means of evaluating them. Since it all begins with the customer, you would want to know what suggestions blind people have. You could create a focus group to generate some starter ideas and ask participants to enrich their suggestions.

Perhaps the most utilitarian approach is already in use:

- Most often used.
- Less frequent but necessary.
- Hot and spicy.

Blind people can read and write so three broad categories based on usage that incorporates an alphabetical system coupled with peel-off braille stickers would certainly be a front-runner. Finally, you'd need to construct a cabinet to hold the spices and their labels, one without any sharp edges or fittings that could cut or snag.

Questions to determine high analytical skills

Behavioural questions ('Tell me about a time when...') examine past performance to predict future behaviours while situational questions ('What is the problem with this invoice?') strive to confront candidates with typical on-the-job challenges.

There are a limitless number of questions that examine analytical skills. You could face these types of questions in any job interview, but you are far more likely to face them if you work in professions that demand high analytical skills: technology, science, research, finance, auditing and accounting. These and other statistics- and research-orientated occupations that demand superior analytical skills are the most likely to present you with seemingly odd questions.

Additionally, these questions are intended to examine your love of problem solving and the approaches to analytical examination that you have mastered.

Many of these questions, by their very nature ('How many windows are there in Glasgow?') have no definitively 'correct' answer. How you explain your approach to answering the question or solving the proffered problem is just as important as any final answer you might offer. The interviewer is just as interested in how you define the problem and break it down into problems small enough that there are business, common-sense and analytical tools available to process them.

These questions all require that you define the problem from different perspectives; in other words, stepping back from the challenge, examining what has to be achieved by whom, for whom, in what time frame, and the potholes to be avoided along the way.

'How many piano tuners are there in Liverpool?'

No one knows. This question and others like it (some to follow) have become known as Fermi equations or estimates. A Fermi estimate seeks to quantify problems that would be extremely difficult, if not impossible, to actually measure.

Enrico Fermi was a physicist, who was known for his ability to make good approximate calculations with little or no actual data. Fermi problems typically involve making logical guesstimates about the upper and lower ranges of likely quantities.

This type of estimate involves careful analysis of the problem to break it down into challenges that can be defined and therefore are more likely to be fairly accurately measured. In this instance, we would need to know the number of households owning pianos, the number of public buildings housing pianos, the frequency with which pianos are typically tuned (usually on an annual basis) and how long a tuning takes (1–2 hours). We should also know how many pianos a single piano tuner could expect to tune in an average working week.

Such a series of rough estimates are then multiplied together to deliver an answer that is within the bounds of reason, without any claim to precise numerical accuracy.

Other Fermi questions might include, 'How many footballs can you fit in this room?', which poses the challenges of evaluating spheres fitting into rectangles. Or, 'If you had a machine that produced £100 a week for life, what would you be willing to pay for it today?' This would require estimates of life expectancy, expected standard of living, inflation and cost of living based on locale. 'How many cows are there in the UK?' How do we break this down? How many counties? How many farms per county? How many cows per farm, etc. Your answer would begin, 'Let's say there are...'

There is an endless supply of Fermi-style questions. Your initial challenge is to break it down into component challenges that are small and defined enough to be evaluated, then depending on your mathematical abilities to go as deep into creating and solving the equations as your professional skills will allow.

17

WELCOME TO THE REAL WORLD

As a recent graduate, probably entering the professional world for the first time, you can expect questions designed to determine your potential.

Companies liken the gamble of hiring recent graduates to laying down wines for the future: some will develop into full-bodied, excellent vintages, but others will be disappointments. When hiring professionals with work experience, there is a track record to evaluate; with recent graduates, there is little or nothing. Often, the only solid things an interviewer has to go on are the degree itself and the odd holiday job. That's not much on which to base a decision.

Of all the steps a recent graduate will take up the ladder of success over the years, none is more important or more difficult than getting a foot on that first rung. You have no idea how the professional game is played and you are up against thousands of other graduates with pretty much the same to offer. Differentiating yourself by demonstrating your understanding of the professional world and your motivation and potential will be important tools in helping get your career off to a good start.

Interviewers will look at what you have done to show initiative, and how willing you are to learn, grow and get the job done.

Your goal is to stand out from all the other entry-level candidates as someone altogether different. You are more engaged in the success of your professional life, more knowledgeable about the job and the world in which it functions, and more prepared to listen, learn, and do whatever it takes to earn your place on a professional team. Don't be like thousands of others who, in answer to questions about their greatest strength, reply lamely, 'I'm good with people', or 'I like working with others.' Answers like this brand you as average. To stand out, a recent graduate must recount a past situation that illustrates how they are good with people, or one that demonstrates an ability to be a team player.

Fortunately, the transferable skills and professional values discussed throughout the book are just as helpful for getting your foot on the ladder as they are for increasing your employability and aiding your climb to the top.

It isn't necessary to have snap answers ready for every question, and you never will. It is more important for you to pause after a question and collect your thoughts before answering: that pause shows that you think before you speak, an admired trait in the professional world. Remember that analytical thinking is one of the transferable skills.

Asking for a question to be repeated is useful to gain time and is quite acceptable, as long as you don't do it with every question. And if a question stumps you, as sometimes happens, do not stutter incoherently. It is sometimes best to say, 'I don't know', or 'I'd like to come back to that later.' Odds are the interviewer will forget to ask again; if he or she does come back to it, at least your mind, processing it in the background, has had some time to come up with an answer.

The following questions are commonly asked of entry-level professionals, but these are not the only questions you will be asked, so you will still need to study the other chapters on turning interviews into offers. For example, the first two questions you are likely to face at most of the job interviews you go to over your entire career are likely to be, 'Tell me a little about yourself' and 'What do you know about our company?' The questions in this chapter are just those aimed exclusively at entry-level professionals.

'How did you get your summer jobs?'

Employers look favourably on recent graduates who have any work experience, no matter what it is. In fact internships are the new entry-level jobs; it is getting increasingly hard to get full-time professional work straight out of university without having had an internship. Employers always say, 'If they have had internship experience, they manage their time better, are more realistic, and more mature. Any work experience gives us much more in common.' So, as you think about some of those lowly jobs you held, take the time to consider, in hindsight, what you actually learned about the professional world from that experience.

It's not the job that defines you, it's what you bring to the job that defines you; countless successful people in all professions trace their big breaks back to going beyond the call of duty in menial jobs. In any job you can learn that business is about making a profit, that making a profit means taking care of the little things... and that when you are starting out, your job is just dealing with the little things. You also learned about doing things more efficiently, working together as a team, solving problems, adhering to systems and procedures (which are always there for good reason), and putting in whatever effort it took to get the job done. In short, you treated your summer jobs, no matter how humble, as a launch pad for greater things.

In this particular question, the interviewer may also be looking for initiative, creativity and flexibility. Here's an example: 'Where I live, summer jobs were hard to come by, but I applied to local restaurants for a position waiting on tables. I called the manager at each one to arrange an interview, and finally landed a job at one of the most prestigious. I was assigned to the afternoon shift, but because of my efficiency and ability to keep customers happy, they soon moved me to the evening shift. I worked there for three summers, and by the time I left, I was responsible for the training and management of new waiting staff and the evening's final closing and accounting. All in all, my experience showed me the mechanics of a small business and of business in general.'

'Which of the jobs you have held have you liked least?'

It is probable that your work experience has contained a certain amount of repetition and drudgery, as all starter jobs do. So beware of saying that you hated a particular job 'because it was boring'. Regardless of your occupation, there is at least one repetitive, mindless duty that everyone groans about, but which nevertheless goes with the territory. The job you liked least or what you liked least about a job, and how you express it, demonstrates your willingness to take the ups and the downs that go with every job. Put your answer in the past; perhaps, 'Working in a burger bar, I always stank of chips.' Then show that you learned something, too: 'When you get involved, there's always something to learn. I learned that _____.' End by moving the conversation forward. 'Every job I've held has given me new insights. All of my jobs had their good and bad points, but I've always found that if you want to learn, there's plenty to pick up every day. Each experience was valuable.' Notice how this response also shows that you are organized and possess analytical thinking and multitasking skills. You should be prepared with examples of things you have learned from those jobs, and if examples don't jump to your mind as you read this, refer back to the transferable skills and professional values.

If the question is, 'What interests you least about this job?' it's because interviewers want to gauge your understanding of the work, and when you don't have any real-world experience this also evaluates your motivation in researching the job and the profession.

One way to prepare for this question is to make it part of your social networking research: 'What's the least interesting part of the job, and how do you make yourself pay attention to the boring but necessary details?'

'What are your future vocational plans?'

The mistake all entry-level professionals make is to say, 'In management', because they think that shows drive and ambition. But it has become such a trite answer that it immediately generates a string of questions most recent graduates can't answer, questions like, 'A manager in what area?' and 'What is a manager's job?' Your safest answer identifies you with the profession you are trying to break into and shows you have your feet on the ground: 'I want to get ahead in _____, but without real experience it is difficult to see where the opportunities will be and how my skills will develop to meet them. I intend to develop a clear understanding of how to deal with the problems and challenges that lie within my area of responsibility. I know that I want to make a career in this profession and channel my skills into my profession's areas of growth, and with the support of a good manager, I think these plans will unfold in a logical manner. Right now I need the opportunity to roll up my sleeves and start earning that expertise.'

'What college/university did you attend, and why did you choose it?'

The college you attended isn't as important as your reasons for choosing it – the question examines your reasoning process. Emphasize that it was your choice, and that you didn't go there because that was the only option available to you. Focus on the practical: 'I went to _____; it was a choice based on practicality. I wanted somewhere that would not only offer the course I wanted but would prepare me for the real world.

_____ has a good record for turning out students fully prepared to take on responsibilities in the real world. It is [or isn't] a big university, and [or but] it has certainly taught me some big lessons about the value of [transferable skills and professional values] in the real world of business.'

'Are you looking for a permanent or temporary job?'

This question is often asked of young candidates. The interviewer wants reassurance that you are genuinely interested in the position and won't disappear in a few months. Go beyond saying, 'Permanent.' Explain why you want the job: 'Of course, I am looking for a permanent job. I intend to make my career in this field, and I want the opportunity to learn the business, face new challenges, and learn from experienced professionals like you.'

You will also want to qualify the question with one of your own: 'Is this a permanent or a temporary position you are trying to fill?' Don't be scared to ask. The occasional unscrupulous employer will hire someone fresh out of school for a short period of time – say, for one particular project – then lay them off.

'How did you pay for university?'

Avoid saying, 'Oh, Daddy handled all that.' Your parents may have helped you out, but if you can, emphasize that you worked part-time and took out loans – as most of us have to during university. People who contribute to their own education costs gain more points with employers because it shows motivation and the experience always delivers a better grasp of the professional world.

'How do you rank among your peers?'

The question examines your self-esteem. Look at yourself and your peers in different ways until you can come up with a viewpoint that gives you an edge. In some cases it may be possible for you to quantify this: 'I was the only person in my year to achieve a commendation with my diploma.' If you can't say something like this, or perhaps came from a background where such a start was never on the cards, you might talk about being the first person in your family to go to university, or about how you've been working since you were 10. Your goal is to differentiate yourself from your peers, and in this example to show that you are professionally grounded with a life experience that gives you greater professional maturity than many of your peers.

'I'd be interested to hear about some things you learned at school that could be used in the job.'

The interviewer wants to hear about real-world skills, so explain what the experience of school or university taught you about the world of work, rather than specific courses. Use internships or any work experience to differentiate yourself.

You can find examples in every school or university activity that gave you the opportunity to develop transferable skills and professional values. Your answer might say, in part, 'In academic and other activities, I always looked for the opportunity to apply and develop some of the practical skills demanded in the professional world, such as _____.'

'Do you like routine tasks/regular hours?'

The interviewer knows from bitter experience that most recent graduates hate routine and are hopeless as employees until they come to an acceptance of such facts of life. Explain that routine is the efficient cycle of procedures that delivers services and products to the company's customer base, you appreciate that the routine and the repetitive have a role in even the most creative of jobs, and you understand that it is only by paying attention to the repetitive details that the work gets done. If regular hours are required, respond, 'A company expects to make a profit, so the doors have to be open for business on a regular basis.'

'What have you done that shows initiative and willingness to work?'

You can tell a story about how you landed or created a job for yourself, or got involved in some volunteer work. Your answer should show that you both handled unexpected problems calmly and anticipated others. Your motivation is demonstrated by the ways you overcame obstacles. For example: 'I was working in a warehouse and found out an extra shipment was due. I knew that room had to be made, so I worked out how much room was needed, cleaned up the mess in the loading bay, and made room in the warehouse. When the shipment arrived, the lorry just backed in.'

After your illustration, recap with something similar to, 'I stick with my commitments. I am serious about doing good work and commit whatever time and effort is necessary to finish tasks properly, because I know other people's productivity depends on all aspects of my work being done properly.'

After an effort above and beyond the call of duty, a manager might congratulate you; if so, you can conclude your answer with: 'The manager came along just as I was finishing the job and said she wished she had more people who took such pride in their work.'

'How do you take instructions?'

Can you take directions and criticism not only when it is carefully and considerately given, but more importantly when it isn't? Can you follow directions and accept constructive criticism, or are you a difficult young know-it-all?

If you take offence easily or bristle when your mistakes are pointed out, you won't last long with any employer. Competition is fierce at the entry level, so take this as another chance to set yourself apart: 'Yes, I can take instruction – and more important, I can take constructive criticism without feeling hurt. Even with the best intent, I will still make mistakes, and at times someone will have to put me back on the right track. I know that if I'm ever to rise in the company, I must be open to that.'

'Have you ever had difficulties getting on with others?'

This question examines your people skills and, by extension, your manageability. Are you a team player, or are you going to be a cog that doesn't mesh, and so disrupts the department's functioning and makes the manager's life miserable?

You can give a yes-or-no answer and shut up, but if you think through what you are going to say, your answer can also emphasize your transferable skills and professional values. In this case, you say that there are two types in every department: the type who is engaged and committed to peak performance every day, and the type who does his or her job but without the same level of commitment. You can and do get on with everyone, but tend to bond more with the people who take a genuine pride in becoming their best.

'What type of position are you interested in?'

Another entry-level question that tempts you to mention management. Tell the interviewer you are interested in an entry-level job, which is what you will be offered anyway. 'I am interested in an entry-level position that will enable me to learn this business from the ground up and will give me the opportunity to grow professionally as and when I prove myself.'

'What qualifications do you have that will make you successful in this field?'

There is more to answering this question than reeling off your academic qualifications. You will also want to explain that your skills match the job's responsibilities, and talk about the transferable skills and professional values that will help you do the job well. Include any relevant work experience to support your argument; even a little experience is a better argument than none. It's a wide-open question that says, 'We're looking for an excuse to hire you. Give us some help.'

'Why do you think you would like this type of work?'

Answering requires you to have researched job functions. One thing you can do is prepare by networking with people already doing this job. Ask what the job is like and what that person does day-to-day, what are the challenges related to each major responsibility of the job, and how that person executes his or her work in ways that anticipate and prevent these problems from arising. Armed with these insights into the realities of the job, you can show that you understand what you are getting into. 'I think the big challenges with this job are _____, and helping people solve their problems is just the kind of work I enjoy.'

'What's your idea of how this industry works?'

The interviewer does not want a dissertation, just the reassurance that you don't think this company and the business world in general work along the same lines as a registered charity. Your understanding should be something like this: 'The role of any company is to make as much money as possible, as quickly and efficiently as possible, and in a manner that will encourage repeat business from the existing client base and new business from word of mouth and reputation.' Finish with the observation that it is every employee's role as a team member to help achieve those goals: 'I am a small but important cog within this moneymaking machinery. I need to mesh well with the other cogs in my department so that we can collectively deliver the department's responsibilities. On an individual basis my job is to enhance productivity and profitability by the prompt identification, anticipation, prevention, and solution of the problems that arise within my areas of professional expertise.'

'Why do you think this industry will sustain your interest over the long haul?'

You can expect interviewers to ask questions that gauge your level of interest. You need to know what is going on in whatever profession and industry you intend to enter, because you will be asked.

Your answer should address both your pragmatism and your motivation. 'I have always been interested in [your new profession/industry]. I believe it offers stability and the potential for professional growth over the years [explain why]. Also, I'll be using skills [itemize strong skill sets that are relevant to the job] that are areas of strength from which I derive great personal satisfaction.'

'What do you think determines progress in a good company?'

These pages have given you a clear blueprint for professional advancement. Your answer will reference the deliverables of the job as defined in your TJD and the transferable skills that help you execute every aspect of your job effectively, thereby becoming a productive member of the team.

Finish by referring to the professional values of integrity, commitment, and a willingness to play by the rules (systems and procedures).

'Do you think exam results should be considered by first employers?'

If your results were good, the answer is obviously 'Yes'. If they weren't, your answer needs a little more thought: 'Of course, an employer should take everything into consideration. Along with results there should be an evaluation of real motivation and manageability, the applicant's understanding of how business works, and actual work experience. Plus, the best academics don't always make the most productive professionals: Einstein and Edison, two of the most intellectually and economically productive minds of modern times, had terrible academic records.'

Many candidates are called for entry-level interviews, but only those who prepare themselves with an understanding of their target jobs will be chosen. Preparation takes time, so don't leave preparing for them until the last minute. You are taking a new product to market. Accordingly, you've got to analyse what it can do, who is likely to be interested, and how you are going to sell it to them. Start now and hone your skills to get a head start on your peers; you'll get more interviews, and the more interviews you have, the better you'll get at them.

THE GRACEFUL EXIT

To paraphrase Shakespeare, all the working world's a stage. Curtains rise and fall, and your powerful performance must be capped with a professional and memorable exit. To ensure that you leave the right impression, this chapter will review the dos and don'ts of leaving an interview.

A signal that the interview is drawing to a close comes when you are asked whether you have any questions. Ask questions, and by doing so, highlight your strengths and show your enthusiasm. Remember, your goal at the interview is to generate a job offer. Make sure your exit is as graceful as your entrance.

Dos

1 Ask appropriate job-related questions. When the opportunity comes to ask any final questions, review your notes. Bring up any relevant strengths that haven't been addressed.

2 Show decisiveness. If you are offered the job, react with enthusiasm. Then sleep on it. If it's possible to do so without making a formal acceptance, secure the job for now and put yourself in control; you can always change your mind later.

Before making any commitment with regard to compensation, see Chapter 21, 'Negotiating the offer'.

3 When more than one person interviews you, be sure you have the correct spellings of their names. 'I enjoyed meeting your colleagues, Ms Smith. Could you give me the correct spellings of their names, please?' This question will give you the names you forgot in the heat of battle and will demonstrate your consideration.

4 Review the job's requirements with the interviewer. Match them point by point with your skills and attributes.

5 Find out whether this is the only interview. If so, you must ask for the job in a positive and enthusiastic manner. Find out the time frame for a decision and finish with, 'I am very enthusiastic about the job and the contributions I can make. If your decision will be made by the fifteenth, what must I do in the meantime to ensure I get the job?'

6 Ask for the next interview. When there are subsequent interviews in the procedure, ask for the next interview in the same honest and forthright manner.

7 Keep yourself in the game. A good leading question to ask is, 'Until I hear from you again, what particular aspects of the job and this interview should I be considering?'

8 Always depart in the same polite and assured manner in which you entered. Look the interviewer in the eye, put on a smile (there's no need to grin), give a firm handshake, and say, 'This has been an exciting meeting for me. This is a job I can do, and I feel I can contribute to your goals, because the atmosphere here seems conducive to doing my very best work. When can we speak again?'

Don'ts

1 Don't discuss salary, holidays, or benefits. It is not that the questions are invalid, just that the timing is wrong. Bringing up such topics before you have an offer is asking what the company can do for you – instead, you should be saying what you can do for the company. Those topics are part of

the negotiation (handled in Chapter 21, 'Negotiating the offer'); remember, without an offer you have nothing to negotiate.

2 Don't press for an early decision. Of course, you should ask, 'When will I know your decision?' But don't press it. Don't try to use the 'other opportunities I have to consider' gambit as leverage when no such offers exist – that annoys the interviewer, makes you look foolish, and may even force you to negotiate from a position of weakness. Timing is everything; the issue of how to handle other opportunities as leverage is explored in detail later.

3 Don't show discouragement. Sometimes a job offer can occur on the spot. Usually it does not. So don't show discouragement if you are not offered the job at the interview, because discouragement shows a lack of self-esteem and determination. Avoiding a bad impression is the foundation of leaving a good one, and the right image to leave is one of enthusiasm, integrity, and openness – just the professional behaviours you have been projecting throughout the interview.

4 Don't ask for an evaluation of your interview performance. That forces the issue and puts the interviewer in an awkward position. You can say that you want the job, and ask what you have to do to get it.

PART FOUR

FINISHING TOUCHES

The successful completion of every interview is a big stride towards getting job offers, yet it is not the end of your job hunt.

Once the interview is over, you move on to the next step in the process of securing job offers. You are never the only qualified applicant for a job and the better the job, the stiffer the competition is likely to be.

A company rarely takes on the first competent person they see. A hiring manager will sometimes interview as many as 15 people for a particular job, but the strain and pace of conducting interviews naturally dim the memory of each applicant. The impression you make will fade and if you are not remembered, you will not be offered the job. You must develop a strategy to keep your name and skills constantly in the forefront of the interviewer's mind. These finishing touches often make all the difference.

Some of the suggestions here may seem just sensible demonstrations of your manners, enthusiasm and determination, but remember that all employers are looking for people with that extra little something. You can be certain of creating a positive impression by following these guidelines.

19

OUT OF SIGHT, OUT OF MIND?

You leave your interviewer with a strong, positive image and don't want that memory to slip with the passage of time and a busy schedule. But out of sight means out of mind and out of mind means out of the job-offer stakes! The longer the decision-making period, the less distinct applicants become from each other in the employer's memory. Following up after your interview shows that you pay attention to detail and are enthusiastic about the job.

The first thing you do on leaving the interview is breathe a sigh of relief. The second is to make sure that 'out of sight, out of mind' will not apply to you. You do this by starting a follow-up procedure immediately after the interview.

Sitting in your car, on the bus, train or plane, do a written recap of the interview while it is still fresh in your mind. This information will help you to follow up, and reviewing all your notes after two or three interviews may also alert you to a weakness you hadn't noticed. Make notes on these categories:

- Who did you meet?

- What were their titles and e-mail addresses?

- What did you find out about the job?

- What are the first projects, the biggest challenges?

- What did the interviewer say about the job, company, competition, industry or profession that might give you more information were you to follow it up on the internet?

- Why can you do the job? What are the problems?

- What aspects of the interview went well? Why?

- What aspects of the interview went poorly? Why?

- What did the interviewer say was the next step?

- What was said during the last few minutes of the interview?

- Are there other applicants under consideration?

- What stage has the employment process reached? When will a decision be made?

Probably the most difficult – and most important – thing to do is analyse which aspects of the interview went poorly. A person is not offered a job based solely on strength. On the contrary, many people get new jobs based on their relative lack of negatives compared to the other applicants. So, look for and recognize any negatives from your performance. That is the only way you will have an opportunity to overcome them in your follow-up procedure and during subsequent interviews.

After your analysis of the interview, your next step is to send the follow-up e-mail or letter to the interviewer. This shows that you are organized, enthusiastic and motivated by the opportunity. In a tightly run job race, when there is nothing to choose between the ability and suitability of two candidates, the job offer always goes to the most enthusiastic. It's common sense when you think about it from the employer's viewpoint: the enthusiastic person is going to put more effort into the job.

A follow-up letter should make four points clear to the interviewer:

- you understand the job and can do it;

- you paid attention to what was being said;

- you are excited about the job, and want it;

- you have the experience to contribute to those first major projects.

Use the right words and phrases in your letter

Here are some you might want to include:

- Appreciation – as a courtesy and mark of professional manners, express appreciation for the time the interviewer took out of his or her busy schedule: 'I enjoyed meeting you to discuss...' Remember to identify the date and time of the meeting and the job you interviewed for.

- If interview nerves caused you to forget something, you can introduce it with 'On reflection', or 'Having thought about our meeting I should have mentioned that...'

- Recognition – 'I recognize the importance of...'

- Observation – 'Listening to the points you made...'

- Enthusiasm – talk about your enthusiasm, as it is very effective, especially when your letter arrives while other applicants are nervously sweating their way through the interview. Let the interviewer know you were impressed with the people/product/service/facility/market/position, but do not overdo it: 'I was impressed with...'

- Confidence – draw attention to one of the topics that was of special interest; there is a job to be done and a challenge to be met, so let the interviewer know you are confident about doing both well: 'I feel confident I can handle the challenge of...' Show that you feel you would be challenged to do your best work in this environment.

- Motivation – if you want the job (or next interview), say so, as at this stage the company is buying and you are selling – ask for the job in a positive and enthusiastic manner. Let the interviewer see that you are motivated by the opportunity the job offers.

Mention the names of the people you met at the interview

Do this whenever it is possible and appropriate to do so. Draw attention to one of the topics that was of general interest to the interviewers.

Address the follow-up letter to the main interviewer

Address the follow-up e-mail/letter to the main interviewer. You can send separate e-mails/letters to others in the selection cycle. Each makes a positive impression and shows extra effort and attention to detail.

Don't write too much

Keep it short – less than one page – and don't make any wild claims that might not withstand close scrutiny.

Send the letter or e-mail within 24 hours of the interview

If the decision is going to be made in the next couple of days, e-mail the letter or hand-deliver it. The follow-up letter will help to set you apart from other applicants and will return your image to the mind of the interviewer just when it would normally be starting to dim.

Perhaps call the interviewer

If a decision is to be made imminently, follow up with an e-mail then a telephone call within 24/48 hours as time constraints dictate; your follow-up is dictated by the time constraints of the employer. 'Mr Massie? Martin Yate. We met for an interview on Wednesday afternoon. I know you are making a decision by close of business tomorrow and I wanted to catch up with you personally to say:

- Thanks for your time;
- I can do the job and this is why;
- I am excited about the job and this is why;
- I will make a good employee and this is why.'

If you are in an extended series of interviews, you will need to pace yourself a little differently. If you do not hear anything after five days (which is quite normal), make a telephone call to the interviewer; I have always thought it a good idea to make sure that the interviewer is reminded of your application just before the weekend begins. Cover the same points as addressed in the last item, asking either for the job or the next interview in the cycle, whichever is appropriate.

Sometimes interviews can stretch into weeks and occasionally months, so a couple of considerations here. You can't e-mail and call every week, but you can touch base every couple of weeks. Google has a nice feature that allows you to track news on any topic you choose. Taking advantage of this allows you to keep up to speed on your profession and factors affecting it, and this knowledge gathering can be put to additional good use.

Reposted jobs

Sometimes jobs might stay open for long periods or be put on hold because of budgetary constraints after you have interviewed and then relisted under a different job title. Here's what you do:

1 Match the needs of the new job description with your CV and what was addressed at the interviews. Refocus a customized copy of the CV using as many keywords from the job posting as you reasonably can.

2 If you are out of touch with the decision makers, apply again in the requested manner.

3 If in touch with decision makers, approach them again with the newly customized CV, reiterating your continued interest and qualifications.

4 Make a follow-up call to the company.

5 After a couple of follow-up letters to decision makers, you need to change the tone and maybe try the article from the professional media approach mentioned earlier; something that is of relevance to your profession and therefore by extension your target decision makers.

Not sure this will work? As I was writing these updates I heard from Michael: 'I have been tracking jobs since last spring that are now reappearing and I'm wondering what to do.'

Not long after I sent him the above ideas I heard from him again: 'Thanks, Martin. I spoke to the company a couple of times, then last Thursday called the manager directly. We spoke for almost 10 minutes, so it was a well-received call. *She admired my courage in calling her directly because she had recently been out of work herself, and hated making those calls.'* (My italics.) It is this kind of extra effort that pays off in job offers.

Now, while you will enthusiastically follow up all your interviews, you should recognize a difficult fact of life: the longer an interview cycle drags on, the less likely it is to result in an offer. Consequently, you will not place your professional future on that ever diminishing chance. Instead, stick to your plan, making new contacts, reaching out by e-mail, mail and telephone and focusing on the generation of new interviews every day, remembering that the job offer that cannot fail invariably will.

This is simply the sensible approach. Just as every job is not right for you, you will not be right for every job. Once in a while though, you might come in second on a job you really want. In the next chapter I'll show you ways to snatch victory from the jaws of defeat.

20

SNATCHING VICTORY FROM THE JAWS OF DEFEAT

Rejection? Impossible! Then again, you won't be right for every job. Here are some techniques that help you to create opportunity even in the face of rejection.

During the interviewing process, there are bound to be interviewers who erroneously come to the conclusion that you are not the right person for the job they need to fill. When that happens, you will be turned down. Such an absurd travesty of justice can occur in different ways:

- at the interview;
- in a letter of rejection;
- during your follow-up telephone call.

While you may be responsible in part for the initial rejection, you still have the power to correct the situation and get the job in the end.

Almost every job is obtainable once you understand the process from the interviewer's side of the desk. Your initial – and temporary – rejection is attributable to one of these reasons:

- the interviewer does not feel you can do the job;

- the interviewer feels you lack a successful profile;

- the interviewer does not feel your personality would contribute to the smooth functioning of the department – perhaps you didn't portray yourself as either a team player or as someone willing to take the extra step.

With belief in yourself, you can still succeed. Repeat to yourself constantly through the interview cycle, 'I will get this job because no one else can give as much to this company as I can!' Do that and implement the following plan immediately when you hear of rejection, whether in person, via mail or over the telephone.

Step 1

Thank the interviewer for his or her time and consideration. Then ask politely, 'To help my future job search, why wasn't I chosen for the position?' Assure the interviewer that you would truly appreciate an honest, objective analysis. Listen to the reply and do not interrupt regardless of the comments. Use your time constructively and take notes. When the interviewer finishes speaking, show you understood the comments. (Remember, understanding and agreeing are different animals.)

'Thank you, Mr Smith – now I can understand the way you feel. Because I don't get interviewed that often, I'm afraid my nerves got in the way. I'm very interested in working for your company [use an enthusiastic tone] and am determined to get the job. Let me meet you once again. This time, when I'm not so nervous, I am confident you will see I really do have the skills you require' [then provide an example of a skill you have in the questionable area]. 'You name the time and the place and I will be there. What's best for you, Mr Smith?'

End with a question of course, and note that you are asking *when* you can meet again not *if*. An enthusiastic request like that is very difficult to refuse and will usually get you another interview. An interview, of course, at which you must shine.

Step 2

Check your notes and accept the interviewer's concerns. Their validity is irrelevant; the important point is that the negative points represent the problem areas in the interviewer's perception of you. List the negative perceptions and, using the techniques and exercises discussed throughout the book, develop different ways to overcome or compensate for every negative perception.

Step 3

Reread Part Three of this book.

Step 4

Practise aloud the statements and responses you will use at the interview. If you can practise with someone who plays the part of the interviewer, so much the better. That will create a real interview atmosphere and be helpful to your success. Lacking a role-play partner, you can create that live answer by putting the anticipated objections and questions on a tape and responding to them.

Step 5

Study all available information on the company.

Step 6

Congratulate yourself continually for getting another interview after initial rejection. This is proof of your self-worth, ability and tenacity. You have nothing to lose and everything to gain, having already risen phoenix-like from the ashes of temporary defeat.

Step 7

During the interview, ask for the job in a positive and enthusiastic manner. Your drive and staying power will impress the interviewer. All you must do to win the job is overcome the perceived negatives and you have been given the time and information to prepare. Go for it.

Step 8

Even when all has failed at the subsequent interview, do not leave without a final request for the job. Play your trump card: 'Mr Smith, I respect the fact that you allowed me the opportunity to prove myself here today. I am convinced I am the best person for the job. I want you to give me a trial and I will prove on the job that I am the best decision you have made this year. Will you give us both the opportunity?'

Even if the answer is still no, you can keep your application in the interviewer's mind. First of all, send a thank-you note to the interviewer, acknowledging your understanding of the state of affairs and reaffirming your desire to work for the company. Conclude with a polite request that he or she bear you in mind for the future.

Then, keep an eye out for any news item about the company in the press. Whenever you see something, cut it out and post it to the interviewer with a very brief note that says something like, 'I came across this in the *Financial Times* and thought you might find it interesting. I am still determined to be your next account manager, so please keep me in mind when the next opening occurs.'

You can also call the interviewer once every couple of months, just to check in. Remember, of course, to keep the phone call brief and polite – you simply want to keep your name at the top of the interviewer's mind.

Maybe something will come of it. Ultimately, however, your only choice is to move on.

21

NEGOTIATING THE OFFER

The job offers finally begin to arrive and in this chapter you will learn the essentials of good salary and benefits negotiation, how to handle good job offers and poor job offers, negotiating future salary, and how to evaluate the salary and the offer. After all, you're never going to have this much leverage with this employer ever again.

The crucial period after you have received a formal offer and before you accept it is probably the one point in your relationship with an employer at which you can say that you have the upper hand. The advantage, for now, is yours. They want you but don't have you and their wanting something they don't have gives you a negotiating edge. An employer is also more inclined to respect and honour a person who has a clear understanding of his or her worth in the marketplace.

You don't have to accept or reject the first offer, whatever it is. In most instances you can improve the initial offer in a number of ways, but you have to know something about the existing market conditions. If you are female, bear in mind that simply settling for a few points above your current rate of pay is bad advice for anyone and downright crazy for you.

Statistics tell us that even if a woman's responsibilities, background and accomplishments are exactly the same as those of her male colleague, she is statistically unlikely to take home a payslip equal to his. According to statistics, male engineers make 14.3 per cent more than their female counterparts. Male mathematicians make 16.3 per cent more. Male advertising and public relations professionals make 28 per cent more. Male lawyers and judges make 28 per cent more. And male editors and reporters make a whopping 43 per cent more than women performing the same or comparable work. My belief is that much of the gap can be attributed to a simple lack of knowledge of professional negotiating skills, and that women in the workplace are picking these skills up fast.

Man or woman, there is no guarantee that you are being paid what you are worth. But if you don't get it while they want you and don't have you, you can't count on getting it once they do have you. Remember, too, that if you start at a reduced figure, every subsequent pay rise will come from a proportionately lower base, so the real amount of money lost over an entire career could be substantial.

Take the time to understand what you have achieved, what you have to offer and what you are worth to the employer.

Everything in this book has been written with the aim of maximizing your professional worth and salary negotiation is certainly no exception. The ideas presented in this chapter will be helpful to you if they represent the culmination of your successful campaign to set yourself apart from the competition, but you cannot negotiate a terrific salary package if an employer is not convinced that you are in the top tier of applicants.

Follow this three-step procedure when planning your salary discussions with employers.

Step 1

Before getting into negotiations, work out your minimum cash requirements for any job – what it is going to take to keep a roof over your head and bread on the table. It's necessary to know this figure, but you need never discuss it with anyone – knowing it is the foundation of getting what you need, what you are worth and what you want.

Step 2

Get a grip on what your skills are worth in the current market. There are several ways to do that. Consider the resources and methods outlined below:

- You can find salary surveys at online employment sites.

- You may be able to find out the salary range for the level above you and the level beneath you at the company in question.

- Ask headhunters – they know better than anyone what the market will bear and you should, as a matter of career prudence, establish an ongoing relationship with a reputable headhunter because you never know when his or her services will come in handy.

- Many professional journals publish annual salary surveys that you can consult and look at recent job ads and compare salaries offered to people with your skills.

Step 3

This is the fun part. Come up with the figure that would make you smile, drop dead and go to heaven on the spot.

You now have three figures: a minimum, a realistic middle-of-the-road desired salary and a dream salary.

Your minimum is, you will recall, what you need to cover personal consumption – never discuss it with anyone. Put it aside and what do you have left? A salary range, just like the one every employer has for every interview you attend. Yours extends from your midpoint to your dream salary. Yes, that range represents the 'top half' of what you want, but there's a reason for that. You will find that it is far easier to negotiate down than it is to negotiate up and you must find a starting point that gives you every possible advantage.

When to bring up salary

Although questions of salary are usually brought up after you are under serious consideration, you must be careful to avoid painting yourself into a corner when you fill out the initial company application form that requests your required salary. Usually you can get away with 'open' as a response; sometimes the form will instruct you not to write 'open', in which case you can write 'negotiable' or 'competitive'.

So much for basic considerations. Let's move on to the money questions that are likely to come up during interview.

The salary/job negotiations begin in earnest in two ways. The interviewer can bring up the topic with statements like the following:

- 'How do you think you would like working here?'

- 'People with your background always fit in well with us.'

- 'You could make a real contribution here.'

- 'Well, you certainly seem to have what it takes.'

Alternatively, if it is clearly appropriate to do so, you can bring on the negotiating stage and ask questions which make the interviewer face the fact that you certainly are able to do the job and that the time has come to talk frankly:

- 'How do you think I would fit in with the group?'

- 'I feel my background and experience would definitely complement the work group, don't you?'

- 'I think I could make a real contribution here. What do you think?'

- 'I know I have what it takes to do this job. What questions are lingering in your mind?'

Now then. What do you do when the question of money is brought up before you have enough details about the job to negotiate from a position of knowledge and strength? Postpone money talk until you have the facts at hand. Ask something like, 'I still have one or two questions about my responsibilities and it will be easier for me to talk about money when I have cleared them up. Could I first ask you a few questions about...?'

Then proceed to clarify duties and responsibilities, being careful to weigh the relative importance of the position and the individual duties to the success of the department you may join.

The employer is duty-bound to get your services as reasonably as possible, while you have an equal responsibility to do the best you can for yourself. The rest of this chapter is going to address the many questions that might be asked or that you might ask to bring matters to a successful conclusion.

'What is an adequate reward for your efforts?'

A glaring manageability question and money probe all in one. The interviewer probably already has a typist on staff who expects a Nobel Prize each time he or she gets out a faultless letter. Your answer should be honest and cover all angles. 'My primary satisfaction and reward comes from a job well done and completed on time. The occasional good word from my boss is always welcome. Last but not least, I think everyone looks forward to a salary review.'

'What is your salary history?' or 'How did your salary progress in your last job?'

The interviewer is looking for a couple of things here. First, for the frequency, percentage and monetary value of your pay rises, which, in turn, tell him or her about your performance and the relative value of the offer that is about to be made. What you want to avoid is tying the potential offer to your salary history – the offer you negotiate should be based solely on the value of the job in hand. Again, this is even more important if you are a woman.

Your answer needs to be specifically vague. Perhaps, 'My salary history has followed a steady upwards path and I have never failed to receive merit increases. I would be glad to give you the specific numbers if needed, but I shall have to sit down and give it some thought with a pencil and paper.' The odds are that the interviewer will not ask you to do that; if he or she does, nod in agreement and say that you'll get right to it when you get home. Don't begin the task until you are requested a second time, which is unlikely.

If for any reason you find yourself with your back against the wall with this one, be sure to include in the specifics of your answer that, 'One of the reasons I am leaving my current job is that pay rises were standard for all levels of employees, so, despite my superior contributions, I got the same percentage rise as the poor employee. I want to work in an environment where I will be recognized and rewarded for my contributions.' Then end with a question: 'Is this the sort of company where I can expect that?'

'What were you earning at your last job?'

A similar but different question. It could also be phrased, 'What are you earning now?' or 'What is your current salary?'

While I have said that your current earnings should bear no relation to your starting salary on the new job, it can be difficult to make that statement clear to the interviewer without appearing objectionable. A short answer might include: 'I am earning £X, although I do want you to know that a major reason for making a job change right now is to significantly increase my remuneration, as I am currently underpaid for my skills and experience.'

It is important to understand the areas of allowable fudge. For instance, if you are considerably underpaid, you may want to include the monetary value of such perks as medical and other health plans, pay in lieu of holidays, profit-sharing and pension plans, bonuses, stock options and other incentives. For many people, these can add between 20 and 35 per cent to their basic salary, so you might honestly be able to mention a higher figure than you at first thought possible. Also, if you are due for a pay rise imminently, you are justified in adding it in.

It isn't common for current or previous salaries to be verified by employers, although certain industries, because of legal requirements, check more than others do. Before your 'current salary' figure disappears through the roof, however, it is safest to remain within credible bounds. After all, once you have been given the job and are starting work at the company, you will have to hand over your P45 and your present salary could be extrapolated from that.

'Have you ever been refused a salary increase?'

This implies that you asked. An example of your justifiable request might parallel the following true story. An accountant for a tyre distributorship made changes to an accounting system that saved thousands of pounds a year, plus 30 staff hours a week. Six months after the methods were obviously working smoothly, he requested a salary review, was refused, but was told he would receive a year-end bonus. He did: £75. If you can tell a story like that, by all means tell how you were turned down for a pay rise. If not, it is best to play it safe and explain that your work and salary history showed a steady and marked continual improvement over the years.

'How much do you need to earn to support your family?'

This question is sometimes asked of people who will be working in a sales job, where remuneration is based on a draw against forthcoming commissions. If this scenario describes your income patterns, be sure you have a firm handle on your basic needs before you accept the position.

For salaried positions, this question is of little relevance. It implies the employer will try to get you at a subsistence salary, which is not why you are there. In this instance, give a range from your desired high-end salary down to your desired midpoint salary.

'How much will it take to get you?' 'How much are you looking for?' 'What are your salary expectations?' 'What are your salary requirements?'

You are being asked to name a figure here. Give the wrong answer and you can find you're eliminated. It is always tempting to ask for the moon, knowing you can come down later, but there are better approaches. It is wise to confirm your understanding of the job and its importance before you start throwing numbers around, because you will have to live with the consequences. You need to ensure the best possible offer without pricing yourself out of the market, so it's time to dance with one of the following responses.

'Well, let's see if I understand the responsibilities fully...' You then proceed to itemize exactly what you will be doing on a daily basis and the parameters of your responsibilities and authority. Once that is done you will seek agreement: 'Is this the job as you see it or have I missed anything?' Remember to describe the job in its most flattering and challenging light, paying special attention to the way you see it fitting into the overall picture and contributing to the success of the department, work group and company. You can then finish your response with a question of your own: 'What figure did you have in mind for someone with my track record?' or 'What range has been authorized for this position?' Your answer will include, in part, something along the lines of, 'I believe my skills and experience will warrant a starting salary between _____ and _____.'

You also could ask, 'What would be the salary range for someone with my experience and skills?' or 'I naturally want to make as much as my background and skills will allow. If I am right for the job, and I think my credentials demonstrate that I am, I am sure you will make me a fair offer. What figure do you have in mind?'

Another good response is, 'I would expect a salary appropriate to my experience and ability to do the job successfully. What range do you have in mind?'

Such questions will get the interviewer to reveal the salary range and concentrate his or her attention on the challenges of the job and your ability to accept and work with those challenges.

When you are given a range, you can adjust your money require-ments appropriately, latching on to the upper part of the range. For example, if the range is £30,000–£35,000 a year, you can come back with a range of £34,000–£37,000.

Consequently, your response will include: 'That certainly means we have something to talk about. While your range is £30,000–£35,000, I am looking for a minimum of £34,000 with an ideal of £37,000. Tell me, what flexibility is there at the top of your salary range?' You need to know this to put yourself in the strongest nego-tiating position and this is the perfect time and opportunity to gain the information and the advantage.

All this fencing is aimed at getting the interviewer to show his or her hand first. Ask for too much and it's, 'Oh dear, I'm afraid you're overqualified', to which you can reply, 'So, overpay me.' (Actually, that works when you can carry it off with an ingratiating smile.)

When you have tried to get the interviewer to name a range and failed, you must come up with a specific figure. The key is to under-stand that all jobs have salary ranges attached to them. Consequently, the last thing you will ever do is come back with a specific figure – that traps you. Instead, you will mention your own range, which will not be from your minimum to your maximum, but, rather, from your midpoint to your maximum. Remember, as before, you can always negotiate down, but rarely negotiate up.

'What do you hope to be earning two to five years from now?'

A difficult question. The interviewer is probing your desired career and earning path and is trying to see if you have your sights set high enough – or too high. Perhaps a jocular tone doesn't hurt here: 'I'd like to be earning just about as much as my boss and I can work out!' Then, throw the ball back with your own question: 'How much is it possible to make here?'

If you give a specific figure, the interviewer is going to want justification. If you come up with a salary range, you are advised to have a justified career path to go along with it.

You could also say, 'In two years, I will have finished my exams, so with that plus my additional experience, industry norms say I should be earning between £X and £Y. I would hope to be earning at least within that range, but hopefully, with a proven track record of contributions, I would be making above the norm.' The trick is to use industry statistics as the backbone of your argument, express confidence in doing better than the norm and, whenever possible, stay away from specific job titles unless pressed.

'Do you think people in your occupation should be paid more?'

This one can be used prior to serious salary negotiation to probe your awareness of how your job really contributes to the bottom line. Otherwise, it can occur in the middle of salary negotiations to throw you off-balance. The safe and correct answer is to straddle the fence: 'Most jobs have salary ranges that reflect the job's relative importance and contribution to a company. Those salary ranges reflect the norm for the great majority of people within that profession. That does not mean, however, that the extraordinary people in such a group are not recognized for their extra performance and skills. There are always exceptions to the rule.'

Good offers, poor offers

After a period of bantering back and forth like this, the interviewer names a figure, hopefully meant as a legitimate offer. If you aren't sure, qualify it: 'Let me see if I understand you correctly: are you formally offering me the position at £X a year?'

The formal offer can fall into one of two categories.

It sounds fair and equitable

In that case, you still want to negotiate for a little more – employers almost expect it of you, so don't disappoint them. Mention a salary range again, the low end of which comes at about the level of their offer and the high end somewhat above it. You can say, 'Well, it certainly seems that we are close. I was hoping for something more in the range of £X to £Y. How much room do we have for negotiation here?'

No one will withdraw an offer because you say you feel you are worth more. After all, the interviewer thinks you are the best person for the job and has extended a formal offer – the last thing he or she needs now is to start from square one again. The employer has a vested interest in bringing the negotiation to a satisfactory conclusion. In a worst-case scenario, the interviewer can stick to the original offer.

It isn't quite what you expected

Even if the offer isn't what you thought it would be, you still have options other than accepting or rejecting it as it stands. Your strategy for now is to run the money topic as far as you can in a calm and businesslike way. Once you have gone that far, you can back off and examine the other potential benefits of the job. That way you will leave yourself with an opening, if you need it, to hit the money topic once more at the close of negotiations.

If you feel the salary could do with a boost, say so: 'I like the job and I know I have what it takes to be successful in it. I would also be prepared to give you a start date of 1 March, to show my sincerity, but, quite honestly, I couldn't justify it with your initial salary offer. I hope that we have some room for negotiation here.'

Alternatively, you can say, 'I could start on 1 March and I do feel I could make a contribution here and become an integral part of the team. The only thing standing in the way is my inability to make ends meet based on your initial offer. I am sincerely interested in the opportunity and flattered by your interest in me. If we could just solve this money problem, I'm sure we could come to terms. What do you think can be done about it?'

The interviewer will probably come back with a question asking how much you want: 'What is the minimum you would be prepared to work for?' he or she might ask. You can reply, 'I'd really like to make at least (now respond with your mid-point). Is something in this range going to be a stumbling block?' Depending on the interviewer's response, this is the time to be non-committal but encouraged and move on to the benefits included with the position:

'Well, yes, that is a little better. Perhaps we should talk about the benefits.'

Alternatively, the interviewer may come back with another question: 'That's beyond our salary range for this job title. How far can you reduce your salary needs to fit our range?'

That question shows good faith and a desire to close the deal, but don't give in too easily – the interviewer is never going to want you as much as he or she does now. Your first response might be: 'I appreciate that, but if it is the job title and its accompanying range that is causing the problem, couldn't we upgrade the title, thereby putting me near the bottom of the next range?' Try it – it often works. If it doesn't, it is probably time to move to other negotiable aspects of the job offer, but not before one last try. You can take that final stab by asking, 'Is that the best you can do?' With this question, you must look the interviewer directly in the eye, ask the question and maintain eye contact. It works surprisingly well. Remember that the *tone* in which such a question is delivered is critically important: with the wrong intonation this can be interpreted as a statement of contempt.

Negotiating your future salary

At this point, you have probably ridden present salary as hard as you reasonably can (for a while, anyway), so the time has come to shift the conversation to future remuneration: 'Even though the offer isn't quite what I'd hoped for to start the job, I am still interested. Can we talk about the future for a while?'

Then you move the conversation to an on-the-job focus. Here are a few arrangements corporate headhunters frequently negotiate for their recruits.

A single lump sum signing bonus

Known as a 'golden hello', it is nice to have, though it is money that is here today and gone tomorrow. Don't make the mistake of adding it on to the basic salary figure. If you get a £2,500 signing bonus, that money won't be included when it comes to your year-end review – your pay rise will be based on your actual salary – so the bonus is a little less meaningful than it appears.

A performance review with pay rise attached

You can frequently negotiate a minimum percentage increase here, if you have confidence in your abilities.

Promotion

You might be able to negotiate a review after a certain period of time.

An end-of-year bonus

When you hear talk about an end-of-year bonus, don't rely on 'what it's going to be this year' or 'what it was last year', because the actual bonus will never bear any resemblance to either figure. Base any bonus expectations on a five-year performance history.

Things other than cash

Also in the realm of real disposable income are things like a company car, petrol, maintenance and insurance. They represent hard cash you would not have to spend. It's not unusual to hear of employers paying car or insurance allowances, picking up servicing bills for your personal vehicle or paying petrol up to a certain amount each month. But if you don't ask, you can never expect an employer to offer. What have you got to lose? Remember to get any of those unusual goodies in writing – even respectable managers in respected companies can suffer amnesia.

Influencing and evaluating the offer

No two negotiations are going to be alike, so there is no absolute model you can follow. Nevertheless, when you have addressed present and future remuneration, this might be the time to get some more information about the company and the job itself.

Even if you haven't agreed on money, you are probably beginning to get a feeling as to whether or not you can put the deal together – you know the employer wants to. Many of the following questions will be appropriate here.

Full knowledge of all the relevant facts is critical to your successful final negotiation of money and benefits.

The questions come in these categories:

- nuts-and-bolts job clarification;

- job and department growth;

- corporate culture;

- company growth and direction.

The following section is also worth reading between first and second interviews.

Evaluating non-salary factors

Money is important, but your career trajectory is more so. If you have career aspirations, you want to land a job in a company that believes in promoting from within. To find out, ask a few of these questions: 'How long has the job been open?' 'Why is it open?' 'Who held the job last?' 'What is he/she doing now?' 'Promoted, fired, quit?' 'How long was he/she in that job?' 'How many people have held this job in the last three years?' 'Where are they now?' 'How often have people been promoted from this position and to where?'

You could also ask, 'What is the timetable for filling the position?' The longer the job has been open and the tighter the time frame for filling it, the better your leverage. That can also be determined by asking, 'When do you need me to start? Why on that date particularly?'

Here are some more good questions:

- 'What are the first projects to be addressed?' or 'What are the major problems to be tackled and conquered?'

- 'What do you consider the five most important day-to-day responsibilities of this job? Why?'

- 'What personality traits do you consider critical to success in this job?'

- 'How do you see me complementing the existing group?'

- 'Will I be working with a team or on my own? What will be my responsibilities as a team member? What will be my leadership responsibilities?'

- 'How much overtime is involved?'

- 'How much travel is involved?' and 'How much overnight travel?' With overnight travel you need to find out the number of days per week and month and, more importantly, whether or not you will be paid for weekend days or given time off in lieu. I have known companies that expect you to get home from a long weekend trip at 1.00 am and be at work at 8.30 am on Monday – all without extra pay or time off.

- 'How frequent are performance and salary reviews? What are they based on – standard pay rises for all or are they weighted towards merit and performance?'

- 'How does the performance appraisal and reward system work? Exactly how are outstanding employees recognized, judged and rewarded?'

- 'What is the complete financial package for someone at my level?'

Job and department growth

Gauging the potential for professional growth in a job is very important for some; for others, it comes slightly lower down the list. Even if you aren't striving to head up the company in the next few years, you will still want to know what the promotional and growth expectations are:

- 'To what extent are the functions of the department recognized as important and worthy of review by upper management?' If upper management takes an interest in the doings of your work group, rest assured you are in a visible position for recognition and reward.

- 'Where and how does my department fit into the company pecking order?'

- 'What does the department hope to achieve in the next two to three years? How will that help the company? How will it be recognized by the company?'

- 'What do you see as the strengths of the department? What do you see as weaknesses that you are looking to turn into strengths?'

- 'What role would you hope I would play in these goals?'

- 'What informal/formal benchmarks will you use to measure my effectiveness and contributions?'

- 'Based on my effectiveness, how long would you anticipate me holding this position? When my position and responsibilities change, what are the possible titles and responsibilities I might grow into?'

- 'What is the official corporate policy on internal promotion? How many people in this department have been promoted from their original positions since joining the company?'

- 'How do you determine when a person is ready for promotion?'

- 'What training and professional development assistance is available to help me grow professionally?'

- 'Does the company encourage outside professional development training? Does the company sponsor all or part of any costs?'

- 'What are my potential career paths within the company?'

- 'To what jobs have people with my title risen in the company?'

- 'Who in the company was in this position the shortest length of time? Why? Who has remained in this position the longest? Why?'

Corporate culture

All companies have their own way of doing things – that's corporate culture. Not every corporate culture is for you.

- 'What is the company's mission? What are the company's goals?'

- 'What approach does this company take to its marketplace?'

- 'What is unique about the way this company operates?'

- 'What is the best thing you know about this company? What is the worst thing you know about this company?'

- 'How does the reporting structure work? What are the accepted channels of communication and how do they work?'

- 'What kinds of checks and balances, reports or other work-measurement tools are used in the department and company?'

- 'What advice would you give me about fitting into the corporate culture – about understanding the way of doing things round here?'

- 'Will I be encouraged or discouraged from learning about the company beyond my own department?'

Company growth and direction

For those concerned about career growth, a healthy company is mandatory; for those concerned about stability of employment, the same applies. See how things are by asking the following questions:

- 'What expansion is planned for this department, division or organization?'

- 'What markets does the company anticipate developing?'

- 'Does the company have plans for mergers or acquisitions?'

- 'Currently, what new endeavours is the company actively pursuing?'

- 'How do market trends affect company growth and progress? What is being done about them?'

- 'What production and employee redundancies and cutbacks have you experienced in the last three years?'

- 'What production and employee redundancies and cutbacks do you anticipate? How are they likely to affect this department, division or organization?'

- 'When was the last corporate reorganization? How did it affect this department? When will the next corporate reorganization occur? How will it affect this department?'

- 'Is this department a profit centre? How does that affect pay?'

The package

Take-home pay is, naturally, the most important part of your package. That means you must carefully negotiate any possible benefits accruing to the job that have a monetary value, but are non-tax deductible and/or add to your physical and mental happiness. The list is almost endless, but below you will find those most commonly available. Although many of these benefits are available to all employees at some companies, you should know that, as a rule of thumb, the higher up the ladder you climb, the more benefits you can expect. Because the corporate world and its concepts of creating a motivated and committed workforce are constantly in flux, never assume that a particular benefit will not be available to you.

The basic rule is to ask – if you don't ask, there is no way you will get. A few years ago, it would have been unthinkable for anyone but an executive to expect something as glamorous as a health club membership in a benefits package. Today, however, more companies have a membership as a standard benefit; an increasing number are even building their own health club facilities. What's this benefit worth in your area? Call a club and find out.

Benefits to your package may include some of the following:

- investment opportunities;
- insurance plans;
- car allowance;
- car insurance or an allowance;
- car servicing and petrol or an allowance;
- car;
- time off in lieu – as recompense for unpaid overtime/business travel time;

- country club or health club membership;
- accidental death insurance;
- deferred compensation;
- dental insurance – note deductibles and the percentage that is employer-paid;
- employment contract and/or termination contract;
- expense account;
- financial planning help and tax assistance;
- life assurance;
- medical insurance – note deductibles and the percentage that is employer-paid;
- pension plans;
- personal days off;
- profit sharing;
- short- or long-term disability compensation plans;
- shares;
- more holidays.

Evaluating the offer

Once the offer has been negotiated to the best of your ability, you need to evaluate it. Some of your requests and questions will take time to be answered and, very often, the final parts of negotiation – 'Yes, Mr Jones, we can give you the extra £2,000 and six weeks holiday you requested' – will take place over the telephone. Regardless of where the final negotiations are completed, never accept or reject the offer on the spot.

Be positive, say how excited you are about the prospect and that you would like a little time (overnight, a day, two days) to think it over, discuss it with your spouse, whatever.

Use the time to speak to mentors or advisers but, be sure you know exactly where that advice is coming from – you need clear-headed objectivity at this time.

Once the advice is in, weigh it up along with your own observations – no one knows your needs and aspirations better than you do. While there are many ways of doing that, a simple line down the middle of a sheet of paper, with the reasons to take the job written on one side and the reasons to turn it down on the other, is as straightforward and objective as you can get.

Weigh salary, future earnings and career prospects, benefits, journey time, lifestyle and stability of the company, along with all those intangibles that are summed up in that technical term 'gut feelings'. Make sure you answer these next questions for yourself:

- Do you like the work?
- Can you be trained in a reasonable period of time, thus having a realistic chance of success on the job?
- Are the title and responsibilities likely to provide you with a challenge?
- Is the opportunity for growth in the job compatible with your needs and desires?
- Are the company's location, stability and reputation in line with your needs?
- Is the atmosphere/culture of the company conducive to your enjoying working at the company?
- Can you get along with your new manager and immediate work group?
- Is the money offer and total compensation package the best you can get?

Notice that money is but one aspect of the evaluation process. Even a high-paying job can be less advantageous than you think and you should be careful not to be foxed by the gross figure. It really is important that you get a firm handle on that actual, spendable, after-tax money – the money that pays the rent or mortgage, puts food on the table, and all those other necessities.

Accepting new jobs, resigning from others

Once your decision has been made, you should accept the job verbally. Spell out exactly what you are accepting: 'Mr Smith, I'd like to accept the position of engineer at a starting salary of £X. I will be able to start work on 1 March. I understand my package will include life, health and dental insurance, and a company car.' Then, you finish with: 'I will be glad to start on the above date pending a written offer received in time to give my present employer adequate notice of my departure. I hope that's acceptable to you.'

Notify your current employer in the same fashion. Resigning is difficult for almost everyone, so you can write a pleasant letter, walk into your boss's office, hand it to him or her, then discuss things calmly and pleasantly once he or she has read it.

Notify any other companies who have been in negotiation with you that you are no longer on the market, but that you were most impressed with meeting them and would like to keep communications open for the future. (See the next chapter for details on how to handle – and encourage – multiple job offers.)

It bears repeating that your resignation is not the time to air your grievances; you have simply been presented with a great opportunity and are thankful for the skills this job gave you. This same person may be checked for a reference down the line, and you want the recollections to be positive.

MULTIPLE INTERVIEWS, MULTIPLE OFFERS

Relying on one interview at a time can only lead to anxiety, so you must create and foster an ever-growing network of interviews and, consequently, job offers.

False optimism leads many job hunters to be content with only one interview in process at any given time. That severely reduces the odds of landing the best job within your chosen time frame. Complacency guarantees that you will continue to operate in a buyer's market.

The recommended approach is to generate as many interviews as possible in a two- to three-week period. Interviewing skills are learned and consequently improve with practice. With improved skills comes a greater confidence and those natural interview nerves disperse. Your confidence shows through and you are perceived in a positive light. Because other companies are interested in you, everyone will move more quickly to secure your services. That is especially important if you are unfortunate enough to be unemployed.

Being out of work is when you need money the most but is the time when the salary you can command on the open market is substantially reduced. The interview activity you generate will help offset this.

By generating multiple interviews, you bring the time of the first job offer closer. That one job offer can be multiplied into a number of others. With a single job offer, your unemployed status has, to all intents and purposes, passed.

Immediately, you can call every company with whom you've interviewed and explain the situation. 'Mr Johnson, I'm calling because, while still under consideration by your company, I have received a job offer from one of your competitors. I would hate to make a decision without the chance of speaking to you again. I was very impressed by my meeting with you. Can we get together in the next couple of days?' End, of course, with a question that carries the conversation forward.

If you were in the running at all, your call will usually generate another interview – Mr Johnson does not want to miss out on a suddenly prized commodity. Remember, it is human nature to want the very things one is about to lose. So, you see, your simple offer can be multiplied almost by the number of interviews you have in process at the time.

A single job offer can also be used to generate interviews with new firms. It is as simple as making your usual telephone networking presentation, but you end it differently. You would be very interested in meeting them because of your knowledge of the company/product/service, but also because you have just received a job offer – would it be possible to get together in the next couple of days?

Relying on one interview at a time can only lead to prolonged anxiety, disappointment and, possibly, unemployment.

Self-esteem, on the other hand, is vital to your success and happiness. With it you will begin to awake each day with a vitality previously unknown. Vigour will increase, your enthusiasm will rise and desire to achieve will burn within. The more you do today, the better you will feel tomorrow.

Even when you follow this plan to the letter, not every interview will result in an offer. However, with many irons in the fire, an occasional firm 'No' should not affect your morale. It won't be the first or last time you face rejection. Be persistent and, above all, close your mind to all negative and discouraging influences. The success you experience from implementing this plan will increase your store of willpower and determination, affect the successful outcome of your job hunt and enrich your whole life. Start today.

The key to your success is preparation.

In conclusion

Having read this book, you're ready to win.

Your attitude is positive and active – dream jobs don't come to those who sit and wait – and you realize that success depends on getting out and generating interviews for yourself. At those interviews, you will maintain the interviewer's interest and attention by carrying your half of the conversation. What you ask will show your interest, demonstrate your analytical abilities and carry the conversation forward. If in doubt about the meaning of a question, you will ask one of your own to clarify it.

The corporate body recognizes that its most valuable resource is those employees who understand and contribute towards its goals. These people have something in common: they all recognize their differing jobs as a series of challenges and problems, each to be anticipated, met and solved. It's that attitude that lands jobs and enhances careers.

People with such an attitude advance their careers faster than others because they possess a critical awareness of universally admired business practices and value systems. They then advance their careers by projecting the personality traits that most closely complement those practices and values.

As I said at the beginning of this book, your job search can be seen as a ritualized dance. Now that you know the steps, you are ready to whirl away with the glittering prizes. There is no more to say except go to your next interview and knock 'em dead.

INDEX
OF QUESTIONS

INDEX

Also available from Martin John Yate

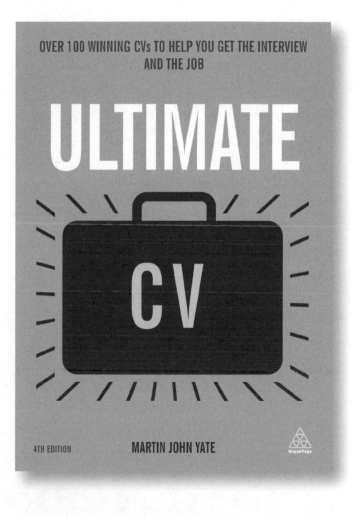

OVER 100 WINNING CVs TO HELP YOU GET THE INTERVIEW AND THE JOB

ULTIMATE

CV

4TH EDITION   MARTIN JOHN YATE

Also available from
Martin John Yate

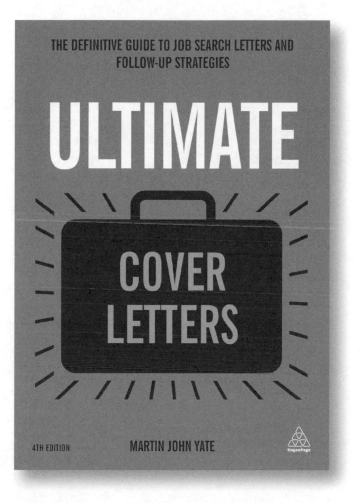